# CRITICAL INSIGHTS

## Adventures of Huckleberry Finn

HUCKLEBERRY FINN.

FROM THE BUST BY KARL GERHARDT.

Frontispiece pages that faced each other in the original edition of
*Huckleberry Finn* (see page 131).

# CRITICAL INSIGHTS

# Adventures of Huckleberry Finn

Editor

**R. Kent Rasmussen**

Editor of *Critical Insights: Mark Twain*

SALEM PRESS

A Division of EBSCO Information Services, Inc.

Ipswich, Massachusetts

**GREY HOUSE PUBLISHING**

Publisher's Cataloging-In-Publication Data
(Prepared by The Donohue Group, Inc.)

Names: Rasmussen, R. Kent, editor.
Title: Adventures of Huckleberry Finn / editor, R. Kent Rasmussen, editor of
    Critical Insights: Mark Twain.
Other Titles: Critical insights.
Description: [First edition]. | Ipswich, Massachusetts : Salem Press, a division
    of EBSCO Information Services, Inc. ; Amenia, NY : Grey
    House Publishing, [2016] | Includes bibliographical references
    and index.
Identifiers: ISBN 978-1-68217-122-6 (hardcover)
Subjects: LCSH: Twain, Mark, 1835-1910.Adventures of Huckleberry Finn.
    | Twain, Mark, 1835-1910--Criticism and interpretation. | Finn,
    Huckleberry (Fictitious character) | Slavery in literature. | Humor in
    literature.
Classification: LCC PS1305 .R37 2016 | DDC 813/.4--dc23

First Printing

# Contents

## Resources

# About This Volume

R. Kent Rasmussen

If one measure of the greatness of a literary work is the variety and breadth of new scholarship it inspires, then *Adventures of Huckleberry Finn* is inarguably great. Despite the fact that Mark Twain's novel has been examined and re-examined in scores of books and hundreds, if not thousands, of articles for more than a century, its ability to continue raising new questions and suggesting new perspectives is demonstrated yet again by the fresh ideas in the thirteen new essays in the present volume. In selecting topics for these essays, one of the editor's primary goals was to encourage innovative ways of looking at *Huckleberry Finn*. It is gratifying to report that goal has been exceeded. Within this volume, readers will encounter many perspectives they have never before seen articulated in print. They will, of course, revisit some familiar questions about such issues as slavery and racism in the novel, Jim's degradation in the so-called "evasion" chapters, and Huck's narrative voice and Mark Twain's use of dialects. However, they will also find these and other issues examined from fresh and wholly original perspectives.

The first section of the volume, "The Book and Author," contains the editor's views on Mark Twain and what makes *Huckleberry Finn* worthy of study.

Essays in the next section, "Critical Contexts," examine *Huckleberry Finn* in its broadest cultural and historical contexts. The section opens with a penetrating exploration of how the novel traveled from Mark Twain's pen to the printed page in "'Bessie' or 'Becky': Should We Care about Text?" Its author, Victor Fischer, is a veteran editor of the Mark Twain Papers and Project at the University of California in Berkeley, which prepares the most authoritative editions of Mark Twain's works ever published. Few people—if any—in the world know more about *Huckleberry Finn*'s tortuous publishing history than Fischer, who was deeply involved in editing two critical editions of *Huckleberry Finn*. After beginning his essay with a fascinating discussion of how the name "Bessie Thatcher" accidentally found its way into the first edition of the novel—where it mistakenly remained in almost every subsequent edition ever since—he goes on to give examples of things that have gone wrong in editions over the years. Then, drawing on his unique expertise, he explains the painstaking work that has gone into restoring the text of the novel to what Mark Twain himself originally intended. The essay is the fullest explanation of the process of preparing a critical edition of *Huckleberry Finn* yet published, outside the Mark Twain Project's own editions of *Huckleberry Finn*. Readers who carefully follow Fischer's fascinating step-by-step explanations should come away not only with an appreciation of what goes into producing "critical editions" but also with an enhanced understanding of how Mark Twain himself crafted his fiction. Equally important, they should better appreciate *why* editions do matter. Teachers assigning *Huckleberry Finn* to classes should pay special attention to this essay.

*Huckleberry Finn* is now almost universally regarded as one of the greatest works in American literature—perhaps even the greatest. Such has not always been the case, however. Indeed, one of the most interesting things about the novel is the surprisingly rocky history of its reception by critics, other professional writers, and ordinary readers. In "Huck's Reception during Three Centuries," Kevin Mac Donnell surveys that history, citing numerous specific examples of what critics and readers have said about the book. This is a subject that has been examined before, but Mac Donnell is able to bring a broader perspective to it. One way is by drawing on recently published letters to Mark Twain from his contemporary readers. Of particular interest are the opinions of twelve-year-old Gertrude Swain, who in 1902 told Mark Twain she had read his novel about fifty times. Even more interesting, perhaps, is Mark Twain's reply to Gertrude. Meanwhile, because Mac Donnell is known to be one of the most original and prolific researchers in the field of Mark Twain studies, he also throws in a few surprises—including radical revisions of what Louisa May Alcott and Ernest Hemingway really said—or did *not* say—about *Huckleberry Finn*.

A racially offensive word frequently repeated in *Huckleberry Finn* has made the book the target of calls for removal from classrooms and libraries throughout the United States for many years. In 2011, Alabama's NewSouth Books published editions of *Tom Sawyer* and *Huckleberry Finn* from which that offending word was removed in order to make reading the novel more acceptable to students, especially African Americans. Not surprisingly, those editions became the focus of a heated national controversy about "censorship" that settled hard on the scholar behind them—Professor Alan Gribben of Auburn University at Montgomery. In the next essay, "Huck Finn and Tom Sawyer Expelled: Censorship and the Classroom," Professor Gribben himself recounts, for the first time at length in print, the full story of the NewSouth editions. He also discusses the impact those editions are now having in schools and raises compelling questions about what really constitutes censorship. It is an essay that may change the opinions of many readers.

The social issue with which *Huckleberry Finn* is most closely associated is doubtless slavery, as one of the novel's central themes is Jim's flight from bondage down the Mississippi River on the raft he shares with Huck Finn. Another nineteenth-century novel even more closely associated with slavery is Harriet Beecher Stowe's *Uncle Tom's Cabin* (1852). Stowe's story of the oppression of enslaved African Americans so riled northerners during the 1850s, it is generally credited with playing a role in starting the Civil War that would lead to the abolishment of the "peculiar institution." In 1996, novelist Jane Smiley published an influential essay in *Harper's Magazine* comparing Mark Twain's and Stowe's treatments of slavery. She concluded that not only is *Uncle Tom's Cabin* vastly superior but also that *Huckleberry Finn* is essentially a failure as an antislavery novel. In "*Huckleberry Finn* vs. *Uncle Tom's Cabin* as Antislavery Novels," Jocelyn A. Chadwick takes issue with Smiley's conclusions. Drawing on her three-decade career as an educator who has visited schools and teachers' groups across the country and tirelessly promoted Mark Twain's novel as a powerful antiracist work, she makes a persuasive argument for why *Huckleberry Finn* is, in fact, the superior book, while also arguing that schools should continue teaching both novels.

The next section in this volume, "Critical Readings," contains ten essays exploring more specialized topics that provide additional fresh insights into *Huckleberry Finn*. The first, "Animating the Unsaid: Between the Lines in *Huckleberry Finn*" by novelist Jon Clinch, offers a truly unique perspective into Mark Twain's novel. Since the 1930s, many writers have used characters from Mark Twain's works in new novels of their own. Some have simply tried to pick up where Mark Twain's stories left off. Others have retold all or parts of his stories, typically recasting his characters and story lines. In 2007, Clinch published a novel, *Finn*, which does neither. A backstory about Huck's cruel father, Pap Finn, his book scrupulously adheres to the characters, events, and details of *Huckleberry Finn*, while fleshing out Huck's father as a character and providing explanations for unanswered questions that Mark Twain's novel raises. His essay for the present volume is an ingenious analysis of how he constructed his own novel to mesh with Mark Twain's. It will open readers' eyes to aspects of *Huckleberry Finn* they have probably never before considered and will also help readers to appreciate how a work of fiction, such as *Finn*, can be as valuable a tool as a work of traditional scholarship in understanding classic literature.

If there is one aspect of *Huckleberry Finn* on which virtually everyone agrees, it is probably the book's humor. The novel is undeniably a funny book. One would almost have to be one of the old and dry mummies in Mark Twain's *The Innocents Abroad* (1869) to read *Huckleberry Finn* without laughing at least occasionally. How humor works in the novel is the subject of Tracy Wuster's essay, "'How a body can see and don't see at the same time': Reading Humor in *Huckleberry Finn*." A recognized authority on American humor and the author of a recent stout book on Mark Twain's humor, Wuster explores what makes *Huckleberry Finn* funny and how its humor works to increase readers' awareness of the novel's important cultural issues. Wuster concludes that reading the book *as* humor can make it both clearer and more fun.

Wuster's essay notes that *Huckleberry Finn*'s readers "must interpret the puzzling link between Mark Twain as an author of books and Huck Finn as an ostensibly 'real' person who was the subject of one of those books (*Tom Sawyer*) and who is now framed as the creator of the book they are reading." What he is talking about, of course, is *metafiction*—which happens to be the subject of the next essay. John H. Davis's "The Reluctant Author: Huck Finn's Metafictional Partnership with Mark Twain" is a stunning roller-coaster ride through the truly puzzling links between Mark Twain's and Huck Finn's interconnected roles as joint authors of *Huckleberry Finn*. Davis is the kind of relentlessly thorough scholar who not only leaves no stones unturned but in the process squeezes every drop of blood from those same stones. Metafiction is a slippery kind of concept that at times seems to be built on circular arguments and ideas too nebulous to get a firm grip on. Davis drills deeply into the subject, building arguments that may make some readers feel they are in a hall of mirrors. However, careful readings of his essay will prove richly rewarding and leave readers with a fuller appreciation of the complexity of Mark Twain's masterpiece.

In "Is *Huckleberry Finn* a Picaresque Novel?," Robert C. Evans undertakes an exhaustive analysis of another complex aspect of *Huckleberry Finn*. As he explains, Mark Twain's novel has long been regarded by some as America's only true picaresque novel. To answer the question of whether that view may be true, he begins by defining "picaresque" and examining how the definitions have been applied to classic works of fiction, including Miguel de Cervantes' famous seventeenth-century masterpiece, *Don Quixote*. When he goes on to show why *Don Quixote* not only might be dismissed as a true picaresque but also may be regarded as the "opposite" of a picaresque, it is clear that *Huckleberry Finn* is in for a rough ride. Drawing heavily on the work of Ulrich Wicks, a leading authority on picaresque writing, Evans then offers a point-by-point analysis of Mark Twain's novel that builds toward a persuasive and satisfying conclusion.

In "Identity Switching in *Huckleberry Finn*," Linda A. Morris turns toward a subject that readers will find both easy to grasp and a great deal of fun. A frequent effect of reading an essay that makes a strong argument about an aspect of Mark Twain's novel is that it may leave one thinking its subject is the single most important theme of the novel. Such is the impression that Morris's fascinating essay may make on readers. Anyone familiar with the novel knows that Huck goes through multiple identity switches, adopting such alternative names as "Sarah (Mary) Williams," "George Peters," "Charles William Allbright," "George Jackson," "Adolphus," and even "Tom Sawyer." Morris's essay discusses all these and Huck's other identity changes, while also making us fully aware of all the other characters undergoing identity switching—and there are many of them. All this is fun, to be sure, but Morris also makes a serious point about what the identity switching says about the characters—especially Huck—themselves.

If the next essay is not at least as much fun as the identity-switching essay, it may well be regarded as the most provocative in this volume. In "'Pow-wows of Cussing': Profanity and Euphemistic Variants in *Huckleberry Finn*," Sarah Fredericks (no relation to Sarah Williams) examines Mark Twain's use of profanity—which she describes as one of his favorite vices—in the broader context of his life and all his writings. She carefully categorizes "foul language" as it was defined during his time and looks for patterns in his usage of it throughout his writing career, all the while paying particular attention to the language of *Huckleberry Finn*. Along the way, she also examines numerous specific examples of Mark Twain's saltiest language and discusses some of struggles he went through to find a balance between his personal inclinations to cuss and what his reading public would accept.

Huck's concluding words in *Huckleberry Finn*, expressing his fear of being "sivilized" by Aunt Sally Phelps, are among the novel's best-known lines. In "Why Huck Finn Can't Stand Being Sivilized," Philip Bader offers one of the most thorough examinations yet published of what "civilization" means to Huck. Not surprisingly, much of what Huck sees in it is violence, cruelty, and hypocrisy. Indeed, Bader's essay makes such a strong case for rejecting civilization that readers may find themselves reconsidering their own views on the subject. Given the sheer power of *Huckleberry Finn*'s indictment of civilization—as Mark Twain himself saw it— one of the most extraordinary things about Huck, as Bader notes, is the boy's steadfast refusal to respond to the cruelty and violence of others with cruelty and violence of his own. Readers are thus apt to come away from this essay with an even greater respect for what a remarkable character Huck Finn is.

Another dominant theme in *Huckleberry Finn*, and one that has received far less attention than it merits, is the role of family and parenting. Incomplete and dysfunctional families pervade Mark Twain's fiction, and Huck Finn has one of the most incomplete and dysfunctional families of all. His father, Pap, is a brutal drunk who appears to have been absent throughout much of Huck's childhood, and we know nothing about his unnamed mother, except that she was illiterate and died sometime in the past. Pap Finn dies early in *Huckleberry Finn*, making Huck a full orphan, but Huck does not know his father is dead until the conclusion of the novel. Meanwhile, he lives in a series of temporary homes—including the raft he shares with Jim—that provide surrogate families. In "'Huck Finn, He Hain't Got No Family': Home, Family, and Parenting in *Huckleberry Finn*," John Bird builds a persuasive case that a central and neglected theme of the novel is Huck's constant quest for a permanent home and family. As Philip Bader's essay points out, the novel ends with Huck expressing his fear of being civilized by Sally Phelps and his wish to flee. Bird's essay, however, offers a different interpretation of the novel's ending that is certain to surprise most readers.

Hugh H. Davis, a high school teacher with considerable experience in interesting young people in literature, addresses an original subject likely to appeal especially to the young in this volume's last essay, "'It's Tom Sawyer!' (No it ain't . . . it's Huck Finn!)." Adapted from a remark made by Aunt Sally Phelps when she mistakes Huck for her nephew Tom in chapter 32 of *Huckleberry Finn*, the essay's title is an allusion to how Tom and Huck are often confused in readers' eyes, thanks largely to popular culture. Davis's densely rich essay explores how preconceptions of Tom and Huck as characters are molded by stage, film, and television adaptations as well as by advertisements, toys, memorabilia, and illustrations. In addition to making a powerful case for Tom and Huck as popular cultural icons, the essay should impress readers with the sheer volume of its consistently fascinating evidence.

The final section of the book, "Resources," contains a substantial bibliography and a detailed chronology of Mark Twain's life that emphasizes dates relevant to *Huckleberry Finn*. There are also notes on the volume's editor and contributors as well as a detailed index.

# Note on Names and Terms Used in This Book

R. Kent Rasmussen

In contrast to the title of *The Adventures of Tom Sawyer*, Mark Twain titled that novel's sequel simply *Adventures of Huckleberry Finn*. That is the title appearing on the spine, front cover, and title page of the book's first American edition. More importantly, that is the title Mark Twain himself composed and instructed his publisher to use. Nevertheless, as Victor Fischer explains in the first essay in the present volume, almost every later edition has added "The" to the novel's title (see pages 40-41). That form of the title is correct in references to those other editions, but is not Mark Twain's title.

Mark Twain's name can also get confusing. He was born **Samuel Langhorne Clemens** and used that name throughout his life. He adopted "**Mark Twain**" as his pen name while writing for a Nevada newspaper in 1863 and thereafter signed that name to everything he published. At the same time, he continued to use his real name and never hid the fact that "Mark Twain" and "Sam Clemens" were the same person. Writing about the man is thus tricky, as one is not always sure what to call him. Some scholars use "Clemens," others prefer "Mark Twain," and still others like to use "Twain." I have not attempted to impose uniformity in this book, confident that whichever name is used, readers will know who is being discussed.

The **date** of the book's first edition is also a little confusing. Mark Twain sent his novel to his American publisher first, in 1884. Due to a complication, the American edition was delayed until early 1885. Meanwhile, the British edition came out in late 1884 after taking its text from proof pages prepared for the American edition. Although the British edition was dated 1884, the 1885 date of the first American edition is generally recognized as the book's original publication date, and that is the date used in the present volume.

Questions about when certain words appearing in the novel should or should not be capitalized have long bedeviled scholars and copyeditors alike, as *Adventures of Huckleberry Finn* poses some unusually tricky capping questions. For example, Mark Twain did not capitalize "**duke**," "**king**," or even "**pap**" in his novel, but most scholars writing about the book have done so because those terms are the closest things to proper names that the characters known by them have. Well, just because E. E. Cummings did not capitalize his own name does not mean we cannot. Likewise, there is no reason not to capitalize "Duke," "King," and "Pap"—so long as we are not quoting Mark Twain directly.

Technically, "pap" is a description, not the name of Huck Finn's father, which is why Mark Twain did not cap it. "**Pap Finn**," however, is a phrase we would certainly expect to be capitalized according to modern English conventions, but that phrase actually never appears in Mark Twain's writings. The parallel constructions, "**Aunt Polly**" and "**Aunt Sally**," do, however, appear frequently. In virtually all instances in the first edition of *Huckleberry Finn*, "Aunt" is capitalized before the women's names. That, however, is not how Mark Twain rendered the names in his original manuscript, but because their capping conforms to modern English usage, it is the style followed in the present book—again, when not quoting Mark Twain directly.

Note that because readers are likely to use many different editions of *Huckleberry Finn*, references to the novel provide chapter numbers, not page numbers.

# THE BOOK
# AND
# AUTHOR

# On Mark Twain and *Adventures of Huckleberry Finn*

R. Kent Rasmussen

*Adventures of Huckleberry Finn* is a book that can be read and enjoyed on many levels and for many different reasons. To achieve a full appreciation of the novel, however, one should approach it with some understanding of its author's background. *Huckleberry Finn* is not merely a story that Mark Twain created out of whole cloth, a fantasy novel crafted by an imaginative writer. Almost everything in the novel—its settings, characters, and themes—has an intimate, indeed, almost an organic connection with its author. It is almost certainly a novel that Mark Twain alone could have written, as he alone lived the life from which it sprang.

Samuel Langhorne Clemens—the man who would become famous as "Mark Twain"—was born in the obscure northeastern Missouri village of Florida on November 30, 1835. He was thus in his fiftieth year in February 1885, when *Huckleberry Finn* first appeared in the United States. Between those two events, a great deal happened in his life that would lift him from poverty and anonymity to great wealth and fame. One of the first questions that readers of *Huckleberry Finn* might bring to the novel, therefore, is how the circumstances of its author's life influence the way he wrote his book.

The sixth of seven children of parents who had migrated to rural Missouri from eastern Tennessee shortly before he was born, Sam Clemens grew up in a home so strongly affected by his father's business failings that he would spend the rest of his life obsessed with avoiding his father's financial mistakes. As things turned out, he would himself experience massive business failures a decade after publishing *Huckleberry Finn*. He would, however, also recover financially, pay off all his debts in full, and go on to great public acclaim for that very reason. Meanwhile, he would also outlive all his siblings, his wife, and three of four children and die in his last home in Redding, Connecticut, on April 21, 1910—just under five months after turning seventy-four. To place his life in historical perspective, it may help to note that the American short story writer O. Henry and the great Russian novelist Leo Tolstoy would also die later that same year.

The village in which Sam Clemens (a name he always used even after adopting "Mark Twain" as his pen name in 1863) was born, incidentally, still exists. However, its twenty-first century population has shrunk to almost zero, and virtually the only thing keeping its name on maps is the fact that "Mark Twain" was born there. Nearby, his name is preserved in Mark Twain State Park, whose Mark Twain Birthplace Museum looks over the waters of the artificially made Mark Twain Lake.

The first American edition of the *Huckleberry Finn* that was published in 1885 was issued by the newly created firm of Charles L. Webster & Co. of New York. The fact that Mark Twain himself owned that firm says a great deal about how far he had come since his humble birth. Given his fame and prosperity at the time, it may seem ironic that his most famous novel is about a boy at the other end of the social and economic scale. Huck Finn had actually made his first appearance nine years earlier in *The Adventures of Tom Sawyer*, which described him as "the juvenile pariah of the village . . . son of the town drunkard" who "was cordially hated and dreaded by all the mothers of the town, because he was idle, and lawless, and vulgar and bad" (chapter 6). Before concluding that such a contrast between a prosperous author and his apparently destitute creation is ironic, however, it should be noted that the Huck Finn of *Huckleberry Finn* does not exactly fit *Tom Sawyer*'s description of him. At the end of that earlier novel, Huck and Tom find a genuine pirate treasure that leaves each of them in possession of six thousand dollars in gold—an amount equivalent to far more than $100,000 in today's money. No longer a penniless waif when *Huckleberry Finn* opens, Huck is instead one of the wealthiest people in the village of St. Petersburg—no thanks, of course, to his drunken and dissolute father. Huck's wealth thus sets up a fascinating contrast between his story and that of his creator. Whereas Sam Clemens grew up determined to make up for his father's economic failings, Huck's actions are driven by his father's efforts to take his wealth away from him. Pap Finn returns to St. Petersburg in chapter 4 for the sole purpose of claiming Huck's six thousand dollars for himself. Huck tries to head off Pap's effort by "selling" his fortune to Judge Thatcher, only to have his father come after him anyway. His wealth, then, is the driving force behind everything that follows in *Huckleberry Finn*. Without it, Huck Finn would have no adventures to tell about. As Mark Twain grew older, he turned increasingly to writing maxims, one of which turned around a famous adage to read, "The lack of money is the root of all evil" (Johnson 10). Perhaps he was thinking of Pap when he wrote that.

## Mark Twain's Youth in Missouri

After Sam Clemens's parents abandoned their hopes of prospering in Florida, Missouri, in 1839, they moved about thirty-five miles northeast to the Mississippi River port town of Hannibal, where Sam spent most of his formative years. Sam would later give that town a form of literary immortality by making it the fictional "St. Petersburg" in his writings about Tom Sawyer and Huck Finn. Those works would eventually include two published novels, two published novellas—*Tom Sawyer Abroad* (1894) and *Tom Sawyer, Detective* (1896)—and three unfinished stories that would eventually be published posthumously. It is generally believed Mark Twain chose the name "St. Petersburg" for his fictional town to symbolize its being a "heavenly" place for children—especially boys. Whether or not he saw Hannibal as a heavenly place during his boyhood, it is clear that many of the activities in which characters engage in his stories are things he and his boyhood friends had done in Hannibal. For example, he based the famous episode in *Tom Sawyer* in which Tom and his sweetheart Becky Thatcher get lost in a labyrinthine cave on an incident that really happened to him.

Young Sam Clemens did nothing during his youth that could have given anyone any reason to imagine the incredible life that lay ahead for Mark Twain, but one of the hallmarks of his best writing would be his skill at converting the grist from his own life into poignant fiction. The grist he milled from his youth in Hannibal was extraordinarily bountiful. His life there and in the even smaller inland village of Florida, where he spent many of his summers while growing up—would provide the primary settings not only for *Tom Sawyer* and the opening chapters of *Huckleberry Finn* but also for parts of *The Gilded Age* (1874), which he coauthored with Charles Dudley Warner, and *Pudd'nhead Wilson* (1894). The latter novel transforms Hannibal into "Dawson's Landing," which is located *south* of St. Louis, unlike St. Petersburg, which—like the real Hannibal—is well north of that major river port. However, while its name and location may differ from those of St. Petersburg, it is essentially the same place.

St. Petersburg's heavenly imagery has not been lost on modern Hannibal, which has built a healthy tourist industry around its ties to Mark Twain and used those ties to advertise itself as "America's Home Town." While the town has long emphasized its connections with *Tom Sawyer*, it has had much less to say about *Huckleberry Finn*. Some reasons should be obvious. The earlier novel is set entirely within or near Hannibal's fictional clone of St. Petersburg, while *Huckleberry Finn* merely begins there and soon moves down the river. *Tom Sawyer* also has more tangible connections with Hannibal, most notably in the form of Mark Twain's own boyhood home, on which Tom's fictional home is closely modeled, and the home of Laura Hawkins, the real-life girl on whom Mark Twain modeled Becky Thatcher. Both houses still stand as fully restored tourist attractions. Nearby are the island and cave that play important roles in *Tom Sawyer*, and a local promontory has been renamed "Cardiff Hill" after the similar fictional hill in the novels. (The latter is a true case of life imitating art.)

*Huckleberry Finn* has some tangible ties to Hannibal, too, beginning with the town itself, the island, the cave, and Cardiff Hill. Another reason Hannibal has emphasized its ties to *Tom Sawyer* rather than *Huckleberry Finn* has been its discomfort with the latter novel's far greater attention to African American slavery—a subject whose local history the town has been uncomfortable addressing. Happily, in recent years, the city has moved to bring *Huckleberry*

*Finn* more fully into its tourist industry. In 2006, a "Huck Finn House" was opened as a replica of the home in which the boyhood friend of Mark Twain who inspired the fictional Huck had lived. Even more significantly, in 2013, Jim's Journey: The Huck Finn Freedom Center opened nearby to honor the memory of the fictional slave who accompanies Huck on his journey down the Mississippi and to commemorate the historical contributions of Hannibal's African American residents.

One of the most important ties of *Huckleberry Finn* to Sam Clemens's youth is the book's language. The novel was highly unusual for its time—indeed, it was virtually revolutionary—in being narrated entirely in the vernacular voice of its unschooled protagonist, Huck Finn. Moreover, not only does Huck tell his story in the often coarse and ungrammatical language of a mid-nineteenth-century backwoods Missouri boy, he also passes along the dialogue of other characters in their own distinct regional dialects—which number seven varieties, according to Mark Twain's count. The most important—and most vocal—other character is Huck's co-protagonist, Jim, who speaks in what Mark Twain labeled the "Missouri negro dialect." The youthful Sam Clemens learned that dialect from long and often close contact with slaves in Hannibal and especially those on his uncle's Florida farm who were his boyhood playmates. Mark Twain had a good ear for language that enabled him to reproduce African American speech accurately. In addition to narrating *Huckleberry Finn*, Huck also narrates *Tom Sawyer Abroad*; *Tom Sawyer, Detective*; and two of the three Tom and Huck stories Mark Twain never finished.

## Mark Twain's Transition to Adulthood

Located on what was then the edge of America's western frontier during Sam Clemens's boyhood, Hannibal was a technologically primitive community, lacking either railroad or telegraph links with other regions during his time. Its main connections to the outside world were through the steamboat packets that regularly stopped at its docks. It was not a promising place to produce a writer who would one day be regarded as one of America's great authors, but the fact that it actually did so invites reflection on *why*. His experiences in Florida and Hannibal clearly planted many of the seeds that would later blossom in his writing. Had he grown up almost anywhere else, he almost certainly would never have written *Tom Sawyer* or *Huckleberry Finn*.

Because of the limited educational opportunities in his community as well as the impoverished condition of his family that required him to go to work at an early age, Sam Clemens received little formal education. Nevertheless, he early became and always remained a prodigious reader who would eventually become one of the great self-educated figures of his time. Between reading adventure stories and daydreaming about traveling to faraway places, while watching steamboats ply the nearby river, he developed a lifelong thirst for travel and especially wanted to venture out on steamboats. A nostalgic passage in *Life on the Mississippi* (1883) recalls that boyhood longing:

> When I was a boy, there was but one permanent ambition among my comrades in our village on the west bank of the Mississippi River. That was, to be a steamboatman. We had transient ambitions of other sorts, but they were only transient. When a circus came and went, it left us all burning to become clowns; the first negro minstrel show that came to our section left us all suffering to try that kind of life; now and then we had a hope that if we lived and were good, God would permit us to be pirates. These ambitions faded out, each in its turn; but the ambition to be a steamboatman always remained (chapter 4).

Although written for *Life on the Mississippi*, that paragraph says a lot about *Tom Sawyer* and *Huckleberry Finn*. Modern film treatments notwithstanding, neither Tom nor Huck ever works on a steamboat, but steamboats play important roles several times in *Huckleberry Finn*. The circuses, minstrel shows, and pirate games Sam Clemens enjoyed as a boy were clearly on his mind when he was writing his novels. Circuses and pirates are mentioned frequently throughout *Tom Sawyer*, and a pretend pirate (the King) makes an unforgettable appearance at a religious camp meeting in chapter 20 of *Huckleberry Finn*. A minstrel show comes to St. Petersburg in chapter 22 of

*Tom Sawyer*, and Huck attends a circus in chapter 22 of his own novel. Sam Clemens himself eventually defied the long odds against fulfilling his boyhood dream by becoming a real steamboatman well before he would become "Mark Twain."

In 1853, Sam Clemens left Hannibal for good to begin several years of working as a journeyman printer in newspaper offices and printshops in the Midwest and East. The fact that he left home and traveled to the East Coast on his own before he even turned eighteen says a great deal about both his desire to travel and his courage in striking out on his own. The next major turning point in his life came in early 1857, when he persuaded a master steamboat pilot named Horace Bixby to take him on as an apprentice. He then spent the four years leading up to the outbreak of the Civil War piloting boats between St. Louis and New Orleans. Bixby remained working on the river until his death at the age of eighty-six. Were it not for the Civil War, Sam Clemens very likely would also have continued in that profession indefinitely. "I supposed—and hoped," he wrote in *Life on the Mississippi*, "that I was going to follow the river the rest of my days, and die at the wheel when my mission was ended. But by and by the war came, commerce was suspended, my occupation was gone" (chapter 21). If that terrible war had any positive outcomes—besides the noble one of forcing an end to human slavery—they included redirecting Sam Clemens to a career that would lead to his becoming "Mark Twain" and writing *Huckleberry Finn*. It is not an exaggeration, therefore, to suggest that without the Civil War, the world would never have heard of Tom Sawyer, Huck Finn, or a host of other memorable fictional creations.

While Mark Twain's years in Missouri helped prepare him to write about his boyhood there, his years of piloting boats on the Lower Mississippi prepared him to write about the river, which he later did, and at length, in many books—most notably *Life on the Mississippi* and *Huckleberry Finn*. The river also figures prominently in *Tom Sawyer*, but what that novel says about it are things that almost anyone who grew up around a river town like Hannibal would have known from their daily experiences of observing the river, taking occasional swims, and boating or rafting to nearby islands. In contrast, what *Huckleberry Finn* says about the river would have been impossible for Mark Twain to write without the deep knowledge he had gained as a pilot. Moreover, it was not a coincidence that he worked on both *Life on the Mississippi* and *Huckleberry Finn* at virtually the same time. The first book grew out of a series of articles titled "Old Times on the Mississippi" that he published in *The Atlantic Monthly* in 1875. Those articles offered a poignant, very personal, and embellished memoir of his experiences as an apprentice steamboat pilot under Horace Bixby. The central theme of the series was that each time, the cub pilot thinks he has finally "learned" the river, he discovers his education has actually only barely begun:

> It was plain that I had got to learn the shape of the river in all the different ways that could be thought of,—upside down, wrong end first, inside out, fore-and-aft, and "thort-ships,"—and then know what to do on gray nights when it hadn't any shape at all. So I set about it. In the course of time I began to get the best of this knotty lesson, and my self-complacency moved to the front once more. . . . (*Life on the Mississippi* chapter 8)

He goes on to recall having to relearn the river yet again from another new perspective. This theme of having to learn something over and over became, in a sense, a metaphor for Mark Twain's life. His experience as a pilot trained him to realize that one's education is never complete, and he never wanted to stop learning. Perhaps the same observation may be made about Huck's experiences in *Huckleberry Finn*, in which each time he learns to adjust to new circumstances, something happens that forces him to start over and relearn how to deal with the people he encounters along the river.

### Writing *Huckleberry Finn*
In 1876, the year after finishing his "Old Times" articles, Mark Twain published *Tom Sawyer*, his first solo novel. He then started on another novel—the one that would become *Huckleberry Finn*. His progress on that book would be slowed by work on other books, travel, and temporary lapses in interest. When he finally completed it

in 1884, he was busy organizing his new publishing firm. Production complications delayed the book's American release until early 1885 (which is why the English edition came out first, at the end of the previous year). Meanwhile, he had returned to the Mississippi River in 1882 to gather new material for *Life on the Mississippi*, which he published the following year. That book expanded *The Atlantic Monthly* articles about cub piloting, adding chapters about his 1882 trip describing how much the river had changed since his piloting days. His return to the river doubtless rekindled his motivation to finish *Huckleberry Finn*, which is replete with moving descriptions of the river, such as this idyllic passage from chapter 19, in which Huck and Jim are relaxing on their raft:

> Sometimes we'd have that whole river all to ourselves for the longest time. Yonder was the banks and the islands, across the water; and maybe a spark—which was a candle in a cabin window—and sometimes on the water you could see a spark or two—on a raft or a scow, you know; and maybe you could hear a fiddle or a song coming over from one of them crafts. It's lovely to live on a raft. We had the sky, up there, all speckled with stars, and we used to lay on our backs and look up at them, and discuss about whether they was made, or only just happened . . .

Lines like those could only have been written by someone with an intimate familiarity with the river—someone like Mark Twain. Mark Twain's deep familiarity with the river, however, occasionally caused him to go a little too far in ascribing a similar familiarity to Huck. In this next passage, from chapter 12, for example, Huck seems to know more about both the river and steamboating than a boy who has apparently never even been on a steamboat should:

> We fixed up a short forked stick to hang the old lantern on; because we must always light the lantern whenever we see a steamboat coming down stream, to keep from getting run over; but we wouldn't have to light it for upstream boats unless we see we was in what they call a "crossing"; for the river was pretty high yet, very low banks being still a little under water; so up-bound boats didn't always run the channel, but hunted easy water.

Terms such as "upstream boats," "crossing," "channel," and "easy water" would have issued easily from the mouth or pen of an experienced pilot, but probably not from an inexperienced boy. It is also doubtful that Huck would be able to read the significance of the river's "very low banks"—the type of skill that *Life on the Mississippi*'s cub pilot struggled hard to learn.

## Mark Twain's Continuing Travels

Visits to St. Louis; Cincinnati; New York; Philadelphia; Washington, DC; and other places during the early 1850s and his years on the Mississippi satisfied part of Sam Clemens's urge to travel, but his wanderlust continued to grow. In 1861, as the Civil War began to rage, he went west with his older brother, Orion Clemens, whom President Abraham Lincoln appointed secretary of the government of the new federal territory of Nevada. In *Roughing It* (1872), the book he later wrote about his experiences in the Far West, he reiterated his dream of traveling, in the words of an inexperienced, young naïf who had never before been anywhere:

> I was young and ignorant, and I envied my brother . . . especially the long, strange journey he was going to make, and the curious new world he was going to explore. He was going to travel! I never had been away from home, and that word "travel" had a seductive charm for me (chapter 1).

This was gross exaggeration, of course, as Sam Clemens had actually been away from home, traveling almost continuously, over the eight years leading up to his journey to the West. It is also, however, an honest reflection of his deep desire to see the world at large. Some of that interest can also be seen in *Huckleberry Finn*, whose ignorant, backwoods title character seems to have inherited some of his creator's interest in reading. Scattered throughout Huck's narrative are numerous mentions of books he reads. In chapter 14, for example, he names "a lot of books" that he and Jim find among the "truck" stolen by the gang of murderers on whose skiff they escape from the wrecked steamboat *Walter Scott*. The next day, they rest "in the woods talking, and me reading the books, and having a general good time." As Huck later settles into the Grangerford home, he talks about the family's books he reads in chapter 17. For a boy who can barely read his own name at the beginning of his narrative, he seems to have progressed surprisingly far in his self-education by this time.

After the scoundrels who call themselves the king of France and the duke of Bridgewater board Jim and Huck's raft in chapter 19, Huck is quick to see them for the frauds they are but does not immediately let on to Jim what he thinks. Later, in chapter 23, he draws on his apparently substantial reading to explain to Jim how "all kings is mostly rapscallions, as fur as I can make out." As he goes on to explain his view, he offers example after example from European history, much of which he mixes up and even throws in irrelevant allusions to *The Arabian Nights*:

> "You read about them once—you'll see. Look at Henry the Eight; this'n's a Sunday-School Superintendent to him. And look at Charles Second, and Louis Fourteen, and Louis Fifteen, and James Second, and Edward Second, and Richard Third, and forty more; besides all them Saxon heptarchies that used to rip around so in old times and raise Cain. My, you ought to seen old Henry the Eight when he was in bloom. He was a blossom. He used to marry a new wife every day, and chop off her head next morning. And he would do it just as indifferent as if he was ordering up eggs. 'Fetch up Nell Gwynn,' he says. They fetch her up. Next morning, 'Chop off her head!' . . . he made every one of them tell him a tale every night; and he kept that up till he had hogged a thousand and one tales that way, and then he put them all in a book, and called it Domesday Book . . . .

Huck clearly exhibits a greater knowledge of the world than a child with his background is likely to have. If that is a false note in the novel, blame it on Mark Twain's own knowledge of the world, which was extensive by the time he wrote *Huckleberry Finn*.

Physical settings were not the only memories that Mark Twain mined in his fiction. His own family members and Hannibal friends and neighbors would also provide models for many of his characters in both his Tom and Huck tales and other writings. Matching Tom

Sawyer with a real-life person has always proven tricky because of Mark Twain's coyness on that subject, though he sometimes claimed he himself was Tom. Other characters are easier to connect with his real-life contemporaries. For example, he explicitly identified his younger brother, Henry Clemens, as the model for Tom Sawyer's younger half-brother, Sid, though he also added that Henry was a finer person than Sid ever was. Sid figures prominently in *Tom Sawyer* but appears only momentarily in *Huckleberry Finn*—on the steam-ferry searching for Huck's presumably drowned body in chapter 8. Later, in chapter 32, when Tom reappears in the narrative, he finds Huck in the home of his Aunt Sally and Uncle Silas Phelps. They believe Huck to be Tom, so Tom then pretends to be Sid from that point.

Mark Twain clearly modeled Tom Sawyer's Aunt Polly on his own mother, Jane Lampton Clemens. Aunt Polly is a major character in *Tom Sawyer*, and she makes a major appearance in the last chapters of *Huckleberry Finn*. Tom's cousin Mary (whose surname is unknown) is modeled on Mark Twain's sister Pamela Clemens. She appears frequently in *Tom Sawyer*, but like Sid, she surfaces only once in *Huckleberry Finn*, in the brief steam-ferry scene in chapter 8. Of much greater interest are Mark Twain's models for Huck himself and for Jim. In contrast to uncertainty about a model for Tom Sawyer, Mark Twain explicitly identified his boyhood friend Tom Blankenship as his Huck in a 1906 autobiographical dictation:

> In "Huckleberry Finn" I have drawn Tom Blankenship exactly as he was. He was ignorant, unwashed, insufficiently fed; but he had as good a heart as ever any boy had. His liberties were totally unrestricted. He was the only really independent person—boy or man—in the community, and by consequence he was tranquilly and continuously happy, and was envied by all the rest of us. We liked him; we enjoyed his society. And as his society was forbidden us by our parents, the prohibition trebled and quadrupled its value, and therefore we sought and got more of his society than of any other boy's (*Autobiography* 2:172)

During Mark Twain's lifetime and afterward, numerous men stepped forward claiming to have been the original Huckleberry Finn, but that honor almost certainly belongs to Blankenship, whose eventual fate is not known. Like the fictional Pap Finn, incidentally, Blankenship's father was notorious as a town drunk.

Evidence for Mark Twain's models for the escaping African American slave Jim is more complicated. He appears to belong to what Mark Twain called "the composite order of architecture" when he described Tom Sawyer as having a combination of the characteristic of three different boys in his preface to *Tom Sawyer*. Three African American men contributed to his creation of Jim. The first was a slave on his Uncle John Quarles's Florida farm whom he knew as Uncle Dan'l. In an autobiographical extract, he described Dan'l as a wise and good friend and adviser:

> whose head was the best one in the negro-quarter, whose sympathies were wide and warm, and whose heart was honest and simple and knew no guile. He has served me well, these many, many years. I have not seen him for more than half a century, and yet spiritually I have had his welcome company a good part of that time, and have staged him in books under his own name and as "Jim," and carted him all around—to Hannibal, down the Mississippi on a raft, and even across the Desert of Sahara in a balloon—and he has endured it all with the patience and friendliness and loyalty which were his birthright (*Autobiography* 1:211).

That endearing tribute to Dan'l would apply equally well to *Huckleberry Finn*'s Jim, whose patience, honesty, simplicity, and warm heart Huck repeatedly describes. Huck also praises Jim several times for having "an uncommon level head" (e.g., chapters 14 & 16). Mark Twain's autobiographical passage, of course, explicitly links Dan'l to *Huckleberry Finn*'s Jim as well. His comment about the journey across the Sahara refers to *Tom Sawyer Abroad*, in which Tom, Huck, and Jim travel across the Atlantic Ocean and North Africa in a balloon craft built by a mad scientist.

A second candidate for Jim's model is George Griffin, a former slave who was the Clemens family butler in Hartford, Connecticut, from the late 1870s until the family left for Europe in 1891. An immensely competent man whom Mark Twain greatly respected, he was virtually a member of the Clemens family at the very time Mark Twain was writing *Huckleberry Finn*. A possibly telling clue is this enigmatic "Notice" that precedes the novel:

> Persons attempting to find a motive in this narrative will be prosecuted; persons attempting to find a moral in it will be banished; persons attempting to find a plot in it will be shot.
>
> By Order of the Author
> Per G. G., Chief of Ordnance

The identity of "G. G" has never been firmly established. Those initials might very well belong to George Griffin.

The third major candidate for Jim's model is John T. Lewis, a free-born African American from Maryland who farmed on the property of Mark Twain's sister-in-law, Susan Crane, outside Elmira, New York. Mark Twain knew Lewis well during the period he was writing *Huckleberry Finn* and had a high regard for him, too—especially after he saw Lewis risk his life to stop a runaway carriage from killing several people. Mark Twain was particularly intrigued by Lewis's strong religious opinions.

## Success and Its Aftermath

In 1885, Mark Twain appeared to have reached a point at which his success was assured. His newest book, *Huckleberry Finn* was a publishing success, and his firm's next publication, General Ulysses S. Grant's two-volume Civil War memoirs would prove to be one of the best-selling works of the nineteenth century. Mark Twain himself was at the height of his creative powers and was one of the highest-paid authors in the world. He lived in a magnificent custom-built home in Hartford, Connecticut, had a loving wife and three adoring daughters. Some significant works still lay in his future—most notably *A Connecticut Yankee in King Arthur's Court* (1889) and *Pudd'nhead Wilson* (1894)—but by the 1890s, his creative powers were beginning to wane. During that decade, he and his wife, Olivia, closed down their Hartford house—to which they would never return—and relocated their family to Europe to cut down on household expenses. Over the next decade, the family moved from country to country, with a major interruption in 1895–1896.

That interruption was caused by the collapse of Mark Twain's most costly business ventures. In 1894, the publishing company he had launched a decade earlier declared bankruptcy. Around the same time, the revolutionary automatic typesetting machine in which he had invested a fortune and had hoped would make him rich beyond his dreams was finally pronounced too unreliable to be marketable, causing him instead to lose his entire investment. Despite having reached a pinnacle of success as an author, he suddenly found himself a business failure, just as his father had been. To recover his fortunes and pay off his publishing firm's creditors, he left from England in May 1895 to undertake an exhausting round-the-word lecture tour that started in North America and took him to Fiji, Australia, New Zealand, India, and South Africa. When he returned to England in August 1896, he wrote *Following the Equator* about his long trip. Meanwhile, he and his wife were shattered by the sudden death of their oldest daughter, Susy. With much of the joy sucked out of their lives, the family continued to move about in Europe until October 1900, when they returned to the United States. There Mark Twain found himself more admired and celebrated than ever before, in large part because of his success in paying off his bankrupt company's creditors in full when he could easily have satisfied most of them with much less.

Mark Twain continued to write through his last decade but little of what he published during those years matched the quality and interest of his earlier writings. On his death in 1910, he left a large body of unfinished writings that would keep editors busy publishing new Mark Twain books far into the future. In addition to volumes with stories such as "Tom Sawyer's Conspiracy" and "Huck Finn & Tom Sawyer Among the Indians," the posthumous volumes included collections of previously unpublished stories, sketches, essays, letters, speeches, notebooks, unfinished novels, and even plays. His autobiographical writings have been published in at least a half-dozen different versions, culminating with the Mark Twain

Project's publication of the first complete edition in three massive volumes in 2010–2015. It may not be an exaggeration to say that more words of his writing have been published for the first time since he died than were published during his lifetime.

## Mark Twain's Legacy

In 1906, four years before Mark Twain died, he observed that over the course of the preceding century, 220,000 books had been published in the United States, but "not a bathtub-full of them are still alive and marketable." That statement may contain a modicum of exaggeration, but its essential point is as true now as it was in Mark Twain's time: Few books outlive their authors, then or now. Indeed, this may have been especially true for nineteenth-century America novelists, most of whom are utterly forgotten today. There are exceptions, of course, and of these, Mark Twain may be the most outstanding example. In the year 2010—a full century after his 1910 death—not only were most of his books still in print, some—including *Huckleberry Finn*— had never gone out of print, even briefly, since their original publication. There may not be another American author of his time for whom the same can be said. That fact raises questions about what accounts for his enduring popularity and whether his popularity says anything about his greatness as a writer.

A simple but incomplete answer to the question of why Mark Twain's popularity has endured is that at least three of his books have entered the realm of acknowledged classics. The title characters and basic story lines of *Tom Sawyer, Huckleberry Finn*, and *The Prince and the Pauper* (1881) have become so deeply ingrained in American culture that many people who know these titles may not even know that it was Mark Twain who wrote them—just as they may know almost everything but the names of the authors of such other famous books as *Pinocchio, Ben-Hur*, or *The Swiss Family Robinson*. Indeed, when the Disney Company used "The Prince and the Pauper" as the title for an animated Mickey Mouse film in 1990, it did not even bother to include Mark Twain's name in the film's credits—an omission that seemed to imply that Mark Twain's story has passed beyond the realm of a mere classic to become a timeless and anonymously created fairy tale. This sort of popularity, however, does not account for why a book such as *Huckleberry Finn* is assigned reading in thousands of high school and college classes every year and is the subject of a seemingly endless outpouring of scholarly theses, articles, books . . . and controversy.

Among scholars, the difference between literary works worthy of study and those that are not lies in the matter of their "interpretability"—or, in simpler language, how much can be read into them. Whereas Herman Melville's *Moby-Dick* (1851) lends itself to nearly endless interpretations of its themes, symbols, and multiple levels, an intelligent, witty, beautifully crafted, and immensely entertaining novel may reveal all it has to say on its first reading, leaving nothing more to be interpreted. One of the things that makes Mark Twain a truly great writer is that many of his books—especially *Huckleberry Finn*—can be read both as high entertainment and as deep works of almost limitless interpretability—as the essays within the present volume demonstrate.

Mark Twain's writings are carefully read, reread, analyzed, reanalyzed, interpreted, and reinterpreted because they continue to have something fresh to say to each new generation. In an essay comparing Mark Twain to Ambrose Bierce in *Critical Insights: Mark Twain*, the distinguished scholar Lawrence I. Berkove called Mark Twain "an unaccountable literary genius, a giant for the ages" (Berkove 132). Berkove's description is apt, as it reflects the growing view that Mark Twain has depths that can never fully be plumbed, that we can go on forever reading and studying him and never fully explain his work. Many who study Mark Twain feel momentarily satisfied when they seem to have answered a question about him, only to find new questions emerging to take its place. Meanwhile, every year sees the publication of perhaps a half dozen new books and even more new articles about him.

If all this makes studying Mark Twain sound like it should be wearing, it is not. In fact, it is exactly the opposite. Most people who have spent years reading and studying Mark Twain—both scholars and "buffs"—relish sharing in the thrill of making new discoveries.

Enough new research is being done to convene international conferences every two years—alternating between Elmira, New York, and Hannibal, Missouri. These conferences are always well attended, and the enthusiasm participants bring generates palpable excitement.

Some years ago, when Shelley Fisher Fishkin, one of the leading scholars in the field, was working on *Lighting Out for the Territory*, she wondered why she never grew bored with Mark Twain and hit on a little epiphany: We cannot get bored with the man, she suggested, because he connects with *everything*. Like Mark Twain's own bathtub anecdote, her remark may contain a touch of exaggeration, but it also expresses an important truth. Mark Twain actually does connect with almost everything. During his nearly seventy-five years on this planet, he lived through one of the greatest periods of social, political, and technological change in human history. When he was born in 1835, fewer than thirteen million Americans were living in the nation's twenty-four states. By the time he died, in 1910, the country had grown to more than ninety-two million people living in forty-six states, and the percentage of them living in cities had more than doubled. Moreover, at the time of his birth, slavery was flourishing in the southern states, steam-powered trains and vessels were still in rudimentary stages of development, medical practices had scarcely advanced beyond those of the Middle Ages, and inventions such as photography, telegraphy, and even typewriters still lay in the future. By the end of his life, American slavery had long since been abolished. Tens of thousands of miles of railroad lines were moving high-speed trains around the country, and gas-powered automobiles were beginning to appear everywhere, iron-hulled steamships were plying the world's seas, and airplanes were taking to the skies. Photography had advanced so far that color film was already being used and motion pictures were being made. The telegraph was carrying messages almost everywhere in the world, and telephonic and radio communication was rapidly spreading. Thanks to a new understanding of germs and other developments, medicine was moving into the modern age.

Mark Twain himself was quick to adopt new technologies, such as typewriters, electrical lighting, modern plumbing, and telephones. He was one of the first people to be photographed in color, and he appears in a brief Thomas A. Edison movie that can be seen on YouTube.

Mark Twain was certainly not the only American to live through all those and other changes, but he was unusual in closely observing and writing about most of them. He was also unusual for his time in being exceptionally well traveled from a relatively young age. He lived for at least a few months in almost every region of the present United States. He also crossed the Atlantic Ocean twenty-five times, visited every inhabited continent, and spent nearly twelve years living in other countries. During his widespread travels, he met many of the world's leading cultural, political, and scientific figures and had close relationships with more than a few of them. As a consequence, he has attracted almost as much attention from biographers as he has from literary scholars.

Mark Twain's interests were so broad and diverse that is difficult to find a subject on which his writings do not touch. He had a rich imagination and incredibly inventive mind that allowed him to foresee future technologies and political and social developments. He left a large body of speculative fictional writings unpublished when he died. Had he finished and published more of those works, he might now rank alongside Jules Verne and H. G. Wells as a pioneer of science fiction.

For all those reasons and more, suggesting that Mark Twain connects with everything may not be as great an exaggeration as it first appears to be. There are, however, other dimensions to Mark Twain that keep readers and scholars returning to him. One of the most important—and perhaps most obvious—is his remarkable ability to make people laugh. Whatever else one thinks about his writing, he very frequently is funny and often in unexpected ways. Indeed, an ironic effect of his humor was that he enjoyed such a great reputation as a humorist during his lifetime that it got in the way of critics appreciating the profundity and his work. It would not be until decades after he died that the full greatness of his writing began to be appreciated.

Is Mark Twain the greatest writer America has yet produced? And is *Adventures of Huckleberry Finn* the great American novel? Many people would answer both questions in the affirmative, but perhaps such questions need not even be asked. Leaving aside the matter of whether it is even possible to answer such questions, it should be enough to say that Mark Twain is a great writer and that *Huckleberry Finn* is a great book. Proof in support of this assertion lies in the fact that fully a century after his death, people continue to read his books avidly—even when they are not assigned in schools—and scholars continue to offer new and often exciting interpretations of his life and work—as the essays in the present volume amply demonstrate.

## Works Cited

Berkove, Lawrence I. "Kindred Rivals: Mark Twain and Ambrose Bierce." *Critical Insights: Mark Twain.* Ed. R. Kent Rasmussen. Pasadena, CA: Salem P, 2011. 110-136.

Fishkin, Shelley Fisher. *Lighting Out for the Territory: Reflections on Mark Twain and American Culture.* New York: Oxford UP, 1997.

Johnson, Merle. *More Maxims of Mark.* New York: n.p., 1927.

Twain, Mark. *The Adventures of Tom Sawyer.* Hartford, CT: American Publishing Co., 1876.

_____. *Autobiography of Mark Twain.* Vol 1. Ed. Harriet Elinor Smith, et al. Berkeley: U of California P, 2010.

_____. *Autobiography of Mark Twain.* Vol 2. Ed. Benjamin Griffin, Harriet Elinor Smith, et al. Berkeley: U of California P, 2013.

_____. *The Innocents Abroad, or The New Pilgrims' Progress.* Hartford, CT: American Publishing Co., 1869.

_____. "Old Times on the Mississippi." *The Atlanta Monthly* (Jan.– June, Aug. 1875).

_____. *Pudd'nhead Wilson* and *Those Extraordinary Twins.* Hartford, CT: American Publishing Co., 1894.

_____. *Roughing It.* Hartford, CT: American Publishing Co., 1872.

_____. *A Tramp Abroad.* Hartford, CT: American Publishing Co., 1880.

Twain, Mark & Charles Dudley Warner. *The Gilded Age: A Tale of To-day.* Hartford, CT: American Publishing Co., 1874.

# CRITICAL
# CONTEXTS

# "Bessie" or "Becky": Should We Care about Text?

Victor Fischer

Several generations of readers familiar with the character Becky Thatcher in *The Adventures of Tom Sawyer* (1876) have been perplexed by the brief appearance of someone Huck Finn calls "Bessie Thatcher," whom he sees aboard the ferry-boat searching for his body in chapter 8 of *Adventures of Huckleberry Finn* (1885). Who is that character? Is she Becky's mother or perhaps her sister? The text provides no answer. The steam-ferry sails by and Bessie is not heard from again.

When members of school classes and book groups are not all reading the same editions of *Huckleberry Finn*, they sometimes notice that the titles of their copies of the book are not all the same. Some say "Adventures of Huckleberry Finn" and others "*The* Adventures of Huckleberry Finn." Moreover, the last words of the novel often differ: Some editions end with "Aunt Sally she's going to adopt me and sivilize me and I can't stand it. I been there before." Others end with six additional words—"THE END. YOURS TRULY, HUCK FINN". Why these differences? How did they come about? Which versions are correct?

Careful readers have noted other discontinuities or anomalies in the text of *Huckleberry Finn* and wondered about them as well but have had no explanations. Does text matter? This essay argues that it does very much matter and that certain editions called "critical editions," which are tasked with investigating variant readings and how the text was transmitted, can and do provide those answers and explanations.

## Choosing Editions

In choosing an edition of a classic novel to read or study, some readers look for the most recent or the least expensive edition available, presumably reasoning that all editions will essentially be the same and differences among them will be minor and negligible. Others know that the texts of first editions are likely to be the most accurate and authoritative and that some scholars consider them the most historically relevant, since they embody not only the words the author published, but also the contributions of the typesetters, editors, artists, binders, and publishers of their time. Such readers often look for a facsimile copy of a first edition—such as those of the 1996 Oxford Mark Twain edition—or one that promises to be closely based on a first edition.

Sometimes, however, it happens that even a first edition has been compromised by unauthorized editorial interventions, inadvertent errors, or an author's inability fully to control the bookmaking process. One way to determine if that is the case— and if it is, to learn what the author meant to publish—is to begin with the earliest extant document containing the text, usually the manuscript, and trace every step of its transmission into a published book. Knowing who had the opportunity and motive to make changes in the text allows one to distinguish between an author's changes and unauthorized ones, leading not only to a more accurate text but to a history of the author's revision of it. The result is what is called a "critical edition."

## First American Edition of Huckleberry Finn

The text of the first American edition of *Adventures of Huckleberry Finn*, published in 1885 by Mark Twain's own firm, Charles L. Webster and Co., is problematic. The transmission of the text from Mark Twain's handwritten manuscript through typed copies of it, which were heavily revised by the author and then used for typesetting, produced a far from perfect text. Mark Twain found the process of seeing the book through the press infuriating and sporadically relinquished control of it. His friend and fellow author, William Dean Howells, read the book before publication. He offered to have a clean, or "fair-copy," typescript made of the heavily revised typescript for the first half of the book. He suggested doing that to make the typesetters' work less prone to error, although adding an extra copying step is actually likely to introduce even more errors.

Howells also offered to read the book's first printed "proof" pages. Mark Twain responded on August 7, 1884, after his own exasperated attempts to proofread the early galleys:

> I have no doubt I am doing a most criminal & outrageous thing—for I am sending you these infernal Huck Finn proofs—but the very last vestige of my patience has gone to the devil, & I cannot bear the sight of another slip of them. My hair turns white with rage, at sight of the mere outside of the package; & this time I didn't even try to glance inside it, but re-enveloped it at once, & directed it to you. Now you're not to read it unless you really don't mind it—you're only to re-ship it to Webster & tell him, from me, to read the remnant of the book himself, & send no more slips to me, under any circumstances. Will you?

## The First Critical Edition

I had the singular privilege of editing a critical edition of *Huckleberry Finn* twice, the first time with coeditor Walter Blair, best known for his pioneering work on *Huckleberry Finn*, especially his book *Mark Twain & Huck Finn* (1960), and his American humor studies. At that time, only the second half of Mark Twain's original manuscript was known to exist. The first half was presumed forever lost. Not long after publication of our critical edition, the "lost" first half of the manuscript was discovered in a Hollywood attic, astonishing the world (and causing Walter, then ninety years old, to tell the Chicago *Tribune* that it was "a scholar's worst nightmare"). Having access to the full manuscript meant our critical edition work would need to be redone, which is why we produced a second critical edition—this time with coeditor Lin Salamo, my colleague at the Mark Twain Project in Berkeley, California. These editions provided the fullest possible record of just how and how much the novel's first edition had departed from the text that Mark Twain had written. It also led to the discovery of how subsequent editions in his lifetime and afterward continued to stray even further from his original text, as new errors were introduced and reprinted.

To produce a critical edition, it is necessary to determine just what documents and documentary evidence bearing on the text survive or can be reconstructed. During the 1980s, the only part of the *Huckleberry Finn* manuscript known to survive had been written in 1883 (what became chapters 22-43), plus an interpolation into the missing first half (what became chapters 12½-14). Mark Twain's extensive literary "working notes" and many of the original illustrations by Edward W. Kemble also still survived. These materials revealed some page numbers of the otherwise lost part of the manuscript and of the lost typescript copies that Mark Twain had revised extensively and submitted to the printers as copy from which to typeset the book. There were also a selection of proof sheets marked by Mark Twain and printer's proofreader; a publisher's prospectus; and extensive but far from complete correspondence among the author, publisher, illustrator, and others.

To reconstruct the journey of Mark Twain's text from his manuscript to first printed edition, we—as editors—drew on all these documents. Close comparison of the manuscript with the first edition revealed extensive revisions to the text that could only have been made by Mark Twain himself. That same journey from manuscript to printed page, however, also had many opportunities for errors and mistranscriptions, and for non-authorial spellings and punctuation (that is, alterations made by persons other than Mark Twain). This was because the text was copied and recopied in three successive typescripts, two of them heavily revised by the author and one that he most likely never saw. All those typescripts, unfortunately, are now lost.

A comparison of the 1883 manuscript, surviving proof sheets, and the first edition revealed that the greater part of authorial revision must have taken place on the lost typescripts that served as printer's copy. It also became clear in comparing another, unrelated, 1883 Mark Twain manuscript, "1,002. An Oriental Tale," with a typescript made of it by the same typists who copied the *Huckleberry Finn* manuscript, that they were prone to eye-skips. Eye-skips occur when typists momentarily look away from the documents they are transcribing, marking their places by holding in mind the last words typed, and then return to those same words, not where they left off but further down in the text, thereby "skipping" over the intervening words. The result is that those intervening words are accidentally omitted from the typewritten copies, without the authors' or typists' knowledge. An example of an apparent eye-skip occurs in chapter 12 of *Huckleberry Finn*, when Huck describes the criminals lurking in the wrecked steamboat *Walter Scott*. Mark Twain wrote:

> I couldn't see them but I could tell where they was, and how close they was, by the whisky they'd been having.

In the first edition of the book, that same passage reads:

> I couldn't see them but I could tell where they was, by the whisky they'd been having.

The words "and how close they was" were probably omitted when the typist's eye skipped from the first to the second occurrence of "they was."

In chapter 13, the first edition created an unintended "jump cut"—the term for an abrupt transition that makes the subject appear to jump from one spot to the other, without continuity—resulting in Huck's going from rowing a skiff to pacing the deck of a ferryboat while searching for someone to help the thieves he and Jim had left on the *Walter Scott*. The first edition omitted two entire sentences from the account as Mark Twain had originally written it. Here is how the passage reads in the book's first and later editions:

> I closed in above the shore-light, and laid on my oars and floated. As I went by, I see it was a lantern hanging on the jackstaff of a double-hull ferry-boat. [*omitted sentences*] I skimmed around for the watchman, a-wondering whereabouts he slept; and by-and-by I found him roosting on the bitts, forward, with his head down between his knees. I give his shoulder two or three little shoves, and begun to cry.

If one rereads the above passage, inserting the following sentences where their omission is marked above, the passage makes greater sense:

Everything was dead still, nobody stirring. I floated in under the stern, made fast, and clumb aboard.

The omission was most likely the result of a typist's eye-skip from "I floated" to "I skimmed."

Errors like these were made in ways that eluded Mark Twain's control, but some errors were caused by his own inattention. For example, even though he had begun writing *Huckleberry Finn* in 1876, just on the heels of reading the proofs of *The Adventures of Tom Sawyer*, he apparently forgot Becky Thatcher's first name and called her "Bessie Thatcher" in her sole appearance in chapter 8. In 1883, when he reviewed the typescript of the first part of the book before beginning to write the second half, he was bothered by that name. Three times he wrote notes to himself, such as "'*Bessie*' or Becky?" He clearly intended to correct the name but never did. As a result, the name in chapter 8 has remained "Bessie" in well over one hundred different editions that have been examined. His manifest intention to fix it was noted and the name was corrected in all the Mark Twain Project critical editions, along with an explanation of how the mistake came about.

## The Second Critical Edition
In late 1990, the long-missing first half of the manuscript of *Huckleberry Finn* was discovered in a Hollywood attic. For the first time in more than a century, it was possible to see how Mark Twain himself had originally written chapters 1-12½ and 15-18½ in 1876 and chapters 18½-21 in 1880. When the discovery was announced in February 1991, it was greeted with extraordinary public interest worldwide. Although the manuscript was essentially a first draft, what it contained was so revealing that it seemed incumbent on the Mark Twain Project editors to include as much information as possible about it in the introduction, notes, and appendixes when we set out to edit the novel for the second time.

Among the biggest surprises the newly found manuscript contained were passages Mark Twain decided to leave out of his book. Among them was a story narrated by Jim that we have called

"Jim's 'Ghost' Story." Dropped from chapter 9, it was first published as "Jim and the Dead Man" in *The New Yorker* magazine in 1995. The manuscript also showed the author at work with extraordinary care and purpose as he revised his first draft of Huck's struggles with his conscience in chapter 16 and in other famous passages that he revised and transformed. Among them was the opening passage of chapter 19, in which Huck describes the sunrise on the Mississippi, a famous and beloved example of vernacular writing and of "showing" not "telling," often used in the classroom. In 1957, Leo Marx said of it,

> Much of the superior power of *Huckleberry Finn* must be ascribed to the sound of the voice we hear. It is the voice of the boy experiencing the event. Of course no one ever spoke such concentrated poetry, but the illusion that we are hearing the spoken word is an important part of the total illusion of reality. . . . [T]he vernacular method liberated Sam Clemens. When he looked at the river through Huck's eyes he was suddenly free of certain arid notions of what a writer should write (Marx 140).

An analysis of the manuscript alterations and those made on a lost typescript before the first edition was set made clear just how much of the style was achieved by Mark Twain's careful revision on the typescript, which, though lost, could now be editorially reconstructed. The evidence of his disciplined self-revision seemed a gift worthy of study, by general readers as well as by students and professors. Here is a small sample of the original manuscript reading followed by Mark Twain's revised reading:

*Manuscript:*

> sometimes you could hear the screak of a sweep, or jumbled sounds of voices, it was so still, & sounds traveled so far; now you could begin to see the ruffled streak on the water that the current breaking past a snag makes; next, you would see the lightest & whitest mist curling up from the water; pretty soon the east reddens up, then the river reddens, & maybe you make out a little log cabin in the edge of the forest, away yonder on the bank on t'other side of the river; then

the nice breeze would spring up, & come fanning you from over the water, so cool & fresh, & so sweet to smell, on account of the woods & the flowers; next you'd have the full day, & everything shining in the sun, & the song-birds just agoing it!

*Mark Twain's revised reading (the first edition, which incorporated Mark Twain's revisions on the lost typescript, is the primary source)*:

sometimes you could hear a sweep screaking; or jumbled up voices, it was so still and sounds come so far; and by and by you could see a streak on the water which you know by the look of the streak that there's a snag there in a swift current which breaks on it and makes that streak look that way; and you see the mist curl up off of the water, and the east reddens up, and the river, and you make out a log cabin in the edge of the woods, away on the bank on t'other side of the river, being a wood-yard, likely, and piled by them cheats so you can throw a dog through it anywheres; then the nice breeze springs up, and comes fanning you from over there, so cool and fresh, and sweet to smell, on account of the woods and the flowers; but sometimes not that way, because they've left dead fish laying around, gars, and such, and they do get pretty rank; and next you've got the full day, and everything smiling in the sun, and the song-birds just going it! (chapter 19)

Both this passage and that of the King's feigned religious conversion and gulling of the camp meeting attendees in Pokeville in chapter 20, which tones down the racial and religious satire present in the first draft, are noteworthy examples of the author at work. We were able to show both stages of Mark Twain's revisions in appendixes in the revised critical editions and online at marktwainproject.org.

As with the 1883 manuscript, a comparison of the 1876/1880 manuscript with the first edition turned up deletions that were almost certainly not authorial. In chapter 6, for example, when Pap is waging a legal battle to get Huck back from the Widow Douglas, two readings were altered, doubtless by Mark Twain himself. The word "cowhiding" was substituted for "raw-hiding" and "like" for Huck's too literate "as if." However, an explanatory clause, bracketed below, was also dropped, more likely a consequence of an eye-skip by the typist or typesetter from "and then" to "and then":

> That law trial was a slow business; appeared like they warn't ever going to get started on it; so every now and then[, all winter, the old man would lay for me and catch me, and then] I'd borrow two or three dollars off of the judge for him, to keep from getting a cowhiding.

## The "Raft Episode"

Access to the 1876/1880 manuscript also shed new light on an old controversy: the deletion from the first American edition of *Huckleberry Finn* of the entire "raft episode." Mark Twain had earlier taken that lengthy passage from his work-in-progress and put it in chapter 3 of *Life on the Mississippi* (1883). There he introduced the episode with this passage:

> By way of illustrating keelboat talk and manners, and that now-departed and hardly-remembered raft-life, I will throw in, in this place, a chapter from a book I have been working at, by fits and starts during the past five or six years, and may possibly finish in the course of five or six more. . . . [A]n ignorant village boy, Huck Finn, son of the town drunkard . . . has run away from his persecuting father, and from a persecuting good widow who wishes to make a nice, truth-telling, respectable boy of him; and with him a slave of the widow's has also escaped. They have found a fragment of a lumber raft (it is high water and dead summer time), and are floating down the river by night, and hiding in the willows by day,—bound for Cairo,—whence the negro will seek freedom in the heart of the free States. By and by they begin to suspect the truth, and Huck Finn is persuaded to end the dismal suspense by swimming down to a huge raft which they have seen in the distance ahead of them, creeping aboard under cover of the darkness, and gathering the needed information by eavesdropping:

Mark Twain clearly intended to publish the episode in its original place in *Huckleberry Finn* when he submitted it in his printer's copy for that book. It came into question in an oblique way when he was planning the door-to-door sales campaign for the book. He had been very disappointed with *Life on the Mississippi*'s sales in 1883, which he attributed to a poor sales prospectus. *Life on the Mississippi* had incorporated the text from his popular 1875 *Atlantic Monthly* articles, "Old Times on the Mississippi." Some of those pages had been prominent in the sales prospectus seen by potential buyers of the subscription book. Thinking that people had recognized the earlier text and concluded the book was a mere "reprint," he worried that *Huckleberry Finn* might meet the same fate if any of the "raft episode" text—which potential buyers might have seen in *Life on the Mississippi*, was included in its sales prospectus. On April 14, 1884 he instructed Charles Webster, his nephew by marriage and his publisher, to exclude the raft episode from the prospectus. Webster, who had been grappling with the problem of making *Tom Sawyer* and *Huckleberry Finn* matching volumes, answered on April 21: "the book is so *much* larger than Tom Sawyer would i[t] not be better to omit that old Mississippi matter? I think it would improve it." Surprisingly, Mark Twain acquiesced the next day:

> Yes, I think the raft chapter can be left wholly out, by heaving in a paragraph to say Huck visited the raft to find out how far it might be to Cairo, but got no satisfaction. Even this is not necessary unless that raft-visit is referred to later in the book. I think it is, but am not certain.

Mark Twain had forgotten, however, that although the "raft-visit" was never referred to later in the book, deletion of the episode created a problem in the text. It left unexplained how, after yet another fruitless attempt to figure out if Huck and Jim had passed Cairo, Illinois, where the Ohio River joined the Mississippi, Huck could tell they had indeed passed Cairo in the fog: "When it was daylight, here was the *clear Ohio water* [italics added] in shore, sure enough, and outside was the old regular Muddy! So it was all up with Cairo." It was in the deleted raft episode that Huck had first learned that the Ohio River's clear water and the Mississippi's muddy water remained in separate channels for some distance below Cairo. Huck did not realize that information would be useful until he saw the phenomenon himself. Mark Twain, incidentally, never wrote the paragraph saying that Huck visited the raft but found out nothing. The first edition reads:

> We talked about Cairo, and wondered whether we would know it when we got to it. I said likely we wouldn't, because I had heard say there warn't but about a dozen houses there, and if they didn't happen to have them lit up, how was we going to know we was passing a town? Jim said if the two big rivers joined together there, that would show. But I said maybe we might think we was passing the foot of an island and coming to the same old river again. That disturbed Jim— and me too. So the question was what to do? I said, paddle ashore the first time a light showed, and tell them pap was behind, coming along with a trading scow, and was a green hand at the business, and wanted to know how far it was to Cairo. Jim thought it was a good idea, so we took a smoke on it and waited (chapter 16).

With the raft episode deleted, the next paragraph suggests a change of plan, with no explanation, namely to just watch for Cairo, the town they worried they had passed in the fog:

> There warn't nothing to do now but to look out sharp for the town and not pass it without seeing it. He said he'd be mighty sure to see it, because he'd be a free man the minute he seen it, but if he missed it he'd be in the slave country again and no more show for freedom.

Webster simply deleted two sentences that originally followed the episode: "I had to tell Jim I didn't find out how far it was to Cairo. He was pretty sorry."

Deletion of the raft episode was questioned even in Mark Twain's lifetime. George Washington Cable, a friend and fellow author who went on a speaking tour with Mark Twain just before *Huckleberry Finn* was published in the United States, urged him to restore the episode. In 1907, the essayist E. V. Lucas remarked of Mark Twain, "I asked him why he had never incorporated in *Huckleberry Finn* the glorious chapter about the boasting bargemen which he dropped into *Life on the Mississippi*. His reasons were not too understandable but I gathered that some copyright question was involved." The episode has remained controversial, although several editors of *Huckleberry Finn* editions have included the *Life on the Mississippi* text, published in place (without the two sentences from the manuscript, unknown to anyone until the missing manuscript was discovered in late 1990), but always set off by notes, changes in type size, or other editorial markers, such as square brackets. Other scholars have continued to argue for and against its inclusion on various grounds, including judgments on whether the book would be "better" with it or without it.

## Are Characters "Trying to Talk Alike and Not Succeeding"?

The 1876/1880 manuscript also showed, as did the 1883 manuscript, how extraordinarily careful and, for the most part, successful Mark Twain was in shaping and revising dialects in his narration and dialogue to make them conform to the seven dialects he delineates in his "Explanatory" note and in making each speaker's dialect consistent. His carefully delineated dialects were, however, systematically endangered in the publication process. Most typesetters and printers' and publishers' in-house proofreaders considered it their responsibility to correct spelling, grammar, and punctuation (called "accidentals") and to maintain overall consistency in copy, often directed by their in-house rules of style, which tended to conform to contemporary printer's manuals and specific dictionaries. Mark Twain's usage was liable to be changed and was so in each reprinting after the first edition.

A comparison of the 1876/1880 manuscript with the first edition revealed several other ways in which Mark Twain's intentions for his text were thwarted in transmission of the text. For example, Mark Twain, who had spent his youth as a journeyman printer, marked the text of both of the handbills for the King and Duke's shows to look like nineteenth-century theatrical posters, using a variety of fonts—FULL CAPITALS, CAPITALS AND SMALL CAPITALS, *italics*, and so on. His novel's handbill for the Royal Nonesuch performance in chapter 22 retained his markings from the 1883 manuscript and typescript. In contrast, the handbill for the "Shakspearean Revival" in chapter 21 from the 1876/1880 manuscript did not,

---

doubtless because the chapter 21 handbill had been first typed on a primitive all-caps TYPEWRITER, on which it was difficult to make such markings comprehensible, and then retyped without Mark Twain's seeing the typescript before it went to press. Following his careful typographical specifications in the manuscript, the first part of the chapter 21 handbill now reads thus:

SHAKSPEAREAN REVIVAL!!!

*Wonderful Attraction!*

———

*For One Night Only!*

———

*The World-renowned Tragedians,*

DAVID GARRICK THE YOUNGER,

*of Drury Lane Theatre, London,*

*and*

EDMUND KEAN THE ELDER,

of the Royal Haymarket Theatre, Whitechapel . . .

## What Happened to the Text during Mark Twain's Lifetime?

After the first American edition was published in 1885, Mark Twain was essentially through with revising his text, even though he made revisions for magazine excerpts published in the *Century Magazine* in 1884–1885 and for his public reading tours of 1884–1885 and 1895–1896. He was most likely not aware that each authorized reprinting during his lifetime, through mistranscription, styling, and editorial changes, got further and further from his intended text:

- The second American edition (Webster, 1891–1894) was set from the first edition
- the third (Harper and Brothers, 1896–) was set from the second edition
- the fourth (American Publishing Company, 1899, 1901, 1903; Harper and Brothers, 1903–; P. F. Collier and Son, 1921–; Gabriel Wells, 1922–) was set from the third edition

A similar evolution unfolded in England: the Continental edition (Tauchnitz 1885) and the second English edition (Chatto & Windus, 1902) were set from the first English edition (Chatto & Windus, 1884), which had been set from the American proof sheets. The general effect of reprinting in this way was that errors were cumulative, with those in the second repeated in the third, and so on.

Some of the more telling changes occurred after publication of the first American edition. For example, on the title page of his 1883 manuscript, Mark Twain had written "Adventures of Huckleberry Finn" as his last word on the matter. That choice was respected on the illustrated covers and title pages of the first and second editions— even though Kemble's illustration opening chapter 1 seemed to indicate otherwise. There the title began with the word "The" because Kemble had been instructed by the publisher to match the opening illustration of the first chapter of *The Adventures of Tom Sawyer* as part of an abortive plan to sell the two books as matched editions. Further confusion was created by the use of *"The* Adventures of Huckleberry Finn" in running heads of the first and second editions (the third edition had no running heads). By the third and fourth editions (Harper, 1896; American Publishing Company [APC], 1899; and Harper, 1903), the book's title included the unauthorized definite article everywhere it appeared. It has continued that way in the vast majority of reprints through the present day. Meanwhile, across the Atlantic Ocean, the very first English edition in 1884 (even before the first American edition appeared) included "The" in its title—on its cover and title page and in its running heads—as did virtually all subsequent English and European editions.

# The Adventures of Huckleberry Finn

## Chapter I.

THE WIDOW'S.

YOU don't know about me, without you have read a book by the name of "The Adventures of Tom Sawyer," but that ain't no matter. That book was made by Mr. Mark Twain, and he told the truth, mainly. There was things which he stretched, but mainly he told the truth. That is nothing. I never seen anybody but lied, one time or another, without it was Aunt Polly, or the widow, or maybe Mary. Aunt Polly—Tom's Aunt Polly, she is—and Mary, and the Widow Douglas, is all told about in that book—which is mostly a true book; with some stretchers, as I said before.

Now the way that the book winds up, is this : Tom and me found the money that the robbers hid in the cave, and it made us rich. We got six thousand dollars apiece—all gold. It was an awful sight of money when it was piled up. Well, Judge Thatcher, he took it and put it out at interest, and it fetched us a dollar a day apiece, all the year round—more than a body could tell what to do with. The Widow Douglas, she took me for her son, and allowed she would sivilize me ; but it was rough living in the house all the time, considering how dismal regular and decent the widow was in all her ways ; and so when I couldn't stand it no longer, I lit out. I got into my old rags, and my sugar-hogshead again, and was free and satisfied. But

The fact that the book should not have a "The" in its title was complicated by the illustration E. W. Kemble drew for the first chapter.

The last line of the book, marked for capital and small capital letters in the manuscript by Mark Twain, reads:

THE END, YOURS TRULY HUCK FINN.

Clearly, as Huck seems to be talking to readers throughout the book, Mark Twain chose to suggest that the novel was a letter or perhaps a performance by Huck. Edward W. Kemble chose to make it the caption for the last illustration, a picture of Huck smiling and doffing his hat to the reader, as if taking a curtain call. Clearly the publisher was torn between leaving it as the last line of the book and repeating or not repeating it just below as a caption, but elected to make it a caption only, a choice presumably approved by the author. As the book got reprinted, even in the authorized editions of Mark Twain's lifetime, particularly as the illustrations got curtailed or dropped, the text read only "THE END" or, more often, the last six words of the text disappeared entirely.

An opportunity for Mark Twain to intervene in the process of reprinting, one that he likely declined, took place in 1899. It was discovered that the typesetting of the American Publishing Company's collected edition had introduced numbers of errors into the texts. A proofreader and former editor of the *Hartford Travelers Record*, Forrest Morgan, was hired by the president of the company, Frank Bliss, to investigate, so that they could make corrections in subsequent impressions. Morgan compared the 1899 edition of *Huckleberry Finn* with the Harper and Brothers 1896 edition, and went through the texts of several of Mark Twain's books in the "Royal Edition," which was identical to the "Autograph Edition," each of them early impressions of the fourth American edition. Bliss marked Morgan's corrections to indicate which corrections to adopt and "whether to charge them to the publishers or to the firm of Case, Lockwood, and Brainard, printers of the original 'Autograph Edition,'" as one scholar, William Todd, who studied the marked volumes, noted in 1969 (Todd 205). Bliss had consulted Mark Twain on his company's edition of *The Prince and the Pauper* (first published by James R. Osgood in 1881) whenever there was a question he could not answer on his own. However, by the time Morgan worked on *Huckleberry Finn*, Bliss was evidently empowered to make all decisions. In a note attached to the flyleaf, Morgan wrote:

> This—Huck Finn—is, take it all in all, the rottenest read book, for combined sluttish carelessness and impudence, that I have struck in the series. From the middle onward, it is *awful*. Look especially at pages *162, 199*, 205, 233, 256, 262-3, *300, 305, 307, 309, 313, 315, 346*, 364[,] 368-9; but there are plenty more.

Morgan's work shows, for the most part, careful attention to the disparities between the Harper 1896 and the APC 1899 typesettings, although he ignored some house stylings (the 1899 "by and by" for the 1896 "by-and-by," which fortuitously brought the 1899 typesetting closer to Mark Twain's manuscript and preferred form). In addition, he sought to impose consistency at times where it did not exist in the 1896 edition: in chapter 19 he marked the King's dialect "h-yer"—meaning "here"— to be reset "h'yer" with the note "see elsewhere" but since the 1896 edition had "h-yer" Bliss evidently disallowed it. Morgan became a defender of Huck's dialect, with a few readings that he followed up consistently throughout the book, for instance, restoring the final "s" to such words as "towards" and "upwards," which appeared in the 1899 typesetting as "toward" and "upward." At the beginning of chapter 2, he wrote:

> This is *Huck* talking—*he* never said "toward"—that is a cultivated frill—*all* uneducated people say "towards", "backwards["] &c.—as well, of course, as many cultivated ones.

He also restored Huck's dialect "actuly" and "he begun" from the 1899 typesetting's incorrect "actually" and "he began" and wrote in the margin, "impudence!" and later "d—!" (167.2/173.10)

## Modern Editions: What Now

The text of *Adventures of Huckleberry Finn* has been in the public domain since 1941, and most modern editions in print do not identify the sources of their texts. The third and fourth American editions served as the copy for a great many editions in the twentieth and twenty-first centuries. Both with limited illustrations, they were doubtless responsible for the persistence of the unauthorized definite article in the title (*The Adventures of Huckleberry Finn*) and for the reduction of the last line of the book to "THE END."

Among facsimile editions of the first American edition still in print is the Oxford edition, edited by Shelley Fisher Fishkin. A reformatted facsimile of the first English typesetting (which was published earlier than the American edition but was based upon the American proof sheets), *The Annotated "Huckleberry Finn,"* edited by Michael Patrick Hearn, is also available. In the more than 130 years since the first edition was published, many artists have provided new illustrations for the book, all worthy of study for readers interested in different depictions of the characters and settings. The artists have included Thomas Hart Benton in the 1942 edition edited by Bernard DeVoto, Worth Brehm in a 1923 Harper edition, Norman Rockwell in a 1940 Heritage Press edition, and Barry Moser in a Fine Press edition by Pennyroyal Press and a trade edition by University of California Press. Editions in translation in many languages have also been illustrated by many foreign artists.

There is no doubt that *Adventures of Huckleberry Finn* is a great book, but it is wise to know which text one is reading. It is clearly best to choose an edition with a text closest to the author's hand.

## Works Cited and Consulted

Blair, Walter. *Mark Twain & Huck Finn.* Berkeley: U California P, 1960.

Hearn, Michael Patrick. *The Annotated Huckleberry Finn.* New York: W. W. Norton, 2001.

Lucas, E. V. "E. V. Lucas and Twain at a 'Punch Dinner.'" *Bookman* 38 (June 1910): 116-117.

Marx, Leo. "The Pilot and the Passenger: Landscape Conventions and the Style of *Huckleberry Finn.*" *American Literature* 28 (Jan. 1957): 129-146.

Morgan, Forrest. Marginalia in *The Adventures of Huckleberry Finn.* Royal Edition. Hartford: American Publishing Company, 1899. This special copy at Yale University was one of a set of Royal Edition volumes marked in 1899 by Morgan who had been hired by Frank Bliss, the publisher, to check the texts for accuracy.

Reif, Rita. "The First Half of `Huck Finn' Manuscript Is Discovered." *New York Times*, 14 Feb. 1991, A2, B1-B2.

Schmidt, Barbara. "A History of and Guide to Uniform Editions of Mark Twain's Works." *TwainQuotes.com*. Barbara Schmidt, n.d. Web. 4 Aug. 2016. <http:/www.twainquotes.com/UniformEds/toc.html>.

Todd, William B. "Problems in Editing Mark Twain." *Bibliography and Textual Criticism: English and American Literature 1700 to the Present*. Ed. O. M. Brack Jr. & Warner Barnes. Chicago: U of Chicago P, 1969.

Twain, Mark. "1,002. An Oriental Tale." MS of 179 leaves and PH of additional five leaves, written between 14 June and 20 July 1883; typed title page and two TSS of sixty-seven leaves, revised by the author, Mark Twain Papers. Published as "1,002" in *Satires & Burlesques*, edited with an introduction by Franklin R. Rogers, Berkeley: U of California P, 1967.

_____. "Jim and the Dead Man." *New Yorker* 71 (26 June and 3 July 1995): 128-130. Previously unpublished excerpt from the manuscript of *Adventures of Huckleberry Finn*.

_____. *Life on the Mississippi*. Boston: James R. Osgood, 1883.

Wilkinson, Tracy. "Missing Twain Manuscript Is Believed Found." *Los Angeles Times*, 13 Feb. 1991, A1, A3.

## Notable Huckleberry Finn Editions

*The Adventures of Huckleberry Finn*. London: Chatto & Windus, 1884 (first British edition, based on proofs of American edition).

*Adventures of Huckleberry Finn*. New York: Charles L. Webster, 1885 (first American edition).

*Adventures of Huckleberry Finn*. New York: Charles L. Webster, 1891 (second American edition).

*The Adventures of Huckleberry Finn*. New York: Harper and Brothers, 1896– (third American edition).

*The Adventures of Huckleberry Finn*. Hartford, CT: American Publishing Company, 1899, 1901, 1903; New York: Harper and Brothers, 1896 and after; New York: Collier, 1921 and later; New York: Gabriel Wells, 1922 and later (fourth American edition, including APC's

1899 "Autograph Edition," "Royal Edition," "Edition De Luxe," "Japan Edition," and "Popular Edition"; 1901 "Underwood Edition" and "Riverdale Edition"; Harper's 1903 "Library Edition"; APC 1903 "Hillcrest Edition"; Harper's 1909–1916 "Author's National Edition," etc.).

*Adventures of Huckleberry Finn.* Ed. Walter Blair and Victor Fischer, with the assistance of Dahlia Armon and Harriet Elinor Smith. Berkeley: U of California P, 1985 (first critical edition; Mark Twain Library trade edition).

*Adventures of Huckleberry Finn.* Ed. Walter Blair and Victor Fischer, with the assistance of Dahlia Armon and Harriet Elinor Smith. Berkeley: U of California P, 1988 (Works of Mark Twain scholarly edition).

*Adventures of Huckleberry Finn.* Introduction by Justin Kaplan. Foreword and Addendum by Victor Doyno. New York: Random House, 1996 (first edition to incorporate previously unpublished material from the long-lost first half of the manuscript).

*Adventures of Huckleberry Finn.* Foreword by Shelly Fisher Fishkin. Introduction by Toni Morrison. Afterword by Victor A. Doyno. New York: Oxford UP, 1996 (facsimile of first American edition).

*Adventures of Huckleberry Finn.* Ed. Victor Fischer and Lin Salamo, with Harriet Elinor Smith and the late Walter Blair. Berkeley, Los Angeles, London: U of California P, 2001 (second critical edition; Mark Twain Library trade edition).

*Adventures of Huckleberry Finn.* Ed. Victor Fischer and Lin Salamo, with Harriet Elinor Smith and the late Walter Blair. Berkeley: U of California P, 2003 (Works of Mark Twain scholarly edition; digital edition published 2009 at www.marktwainproject.org).

*Adventures of Huckleberry Finn.* Ed. Victor Fischer and Lin Salamo, with Harriet Elinor Smith and the late Walter Blair. Berkeley: U of California P, 2010 (Mark Twain Library, 125th Anniversary Edition).

# Huck's Reception during Three Centuries_____

Kevin Mac Donnell

In *Adventures of Huckleberry Finn* twenty-first century readers are confident they have the whole of Huck Finn in the boy's own words. His is a plain-spoken and guileless voice of a boy whose first name signifies insignificance and whose last name implies a presumably ignoble Irish immigrant heritage and the bigotry that was his birthright. Readers are carried along, side-by-side with him, through a series of picaresque adventures as he floats outside the confines of his culture accompanied by a piece of flesh and blood property named Jim—a runaway slave—a "nigger." Jim and Huck engage with the chaos and violence of society on land and must endure an odyssey on the river that is at once life-giving and deadly, until at last the boy finds his common humanity with Jim, whose paternal guidance is unwavering.

In 1895, ten years after the book appeared in the United States, Mark Twain described *Huckleberry Finn* as "a book of mine where a sound heart & a deformed conscience come into collision & conscience suffers defeat" (Smith xvi). He did not explain if that sound heart and deformed conscience both belonged to Huck, or if that sound heart belonged to the piece of property with which he was traveling, but at that moment of human recognition, Huck overcomes his defective conscience and hears his own sound heart clearly enough to transcend his time and place. He is such a good boy that he thinks he will go to Hell for doing what his heart and conscience now tell him to do instead of conforming to the law and social custom. He knows at the end of his narrative that he must light out for the Territory before civilization utterly destroys him because his days of bigotry and heedless conformity are behind him, and he has become an exemplar of the American experience.

We have the whole of Huck Finn thanks to Mark Twain, the visionary humorist who created this good boy whose testimony captivates us, and we have the whole of Mark Twain thanks to

Samuel Langhorne Clemens, whose own life followed a spiritual arc similar to that of his young protagonist. In an 1853 letter to his family, he uttered a racist rant about "niggers" in New York City being "considerably better than white people." That ignorant remark presaged Pap Finn's rant in *Huckleberry Finn* against the government and an African American college professor (chapter 6). Clemens nevertheless ultimately triumphed in the creation of the Great Subversive American Novel, in which two outcasts find themselves cast together in the common cause of escape from the profoundly flawed civilization that has dehumanized and abused them so badly that each is stripped of his own sense of worth. They have each other, however, and the result is that the soul of a white child is freed by an unlettered black adult who, even after being unfettered at the story's end, must still conform to survive. This is how most Mark Twain scholars and modern readers of Twain's masterpiece have responded to Huck's saga in recent years, but readers' responses to this novel have never been in agreement from the day it was first published, and that debate rages right along.

Readers during Mark Twain's lifetime saw things in the novel that modern readers miss. Likewise, they also ignored things modern readers think are essential to an understanding of the story. Some readers have embraced the book, while others—both then and now—have rejected it. Some people have read the book repeatedly, experiencing new insights with each reading, while others have called for its burning or banning after just one reading—or without reading it at all. For some modern readers the entire book can be judged by the presence of a single offensive word—"nigger." For one young Nebraska girl in 1902, however, the book was her bible and could do no harm, and she felt compelled to write Mark Twain and tell him so (Rasmussen, *Dear Mark Twain* 200-203). The book has been edited, explicated, excused, expunged, explained, and re-explained. Huck's story has been staged, filmed, denounced, and defended. It has been taught, translated, abridged, and banned but never ignored. Louisa May Alcott has been falsely invoked to condemn the book, while Ernest Hemingway has been too often quoted to celebrate this landmark in American literature—more about this later. William

Dean Howells, who perhaps knew Mark Twain best and understood his literature was art, bestowed upon him the title "Lincoln of our literature."

## Nineteenth-Century Reviewers

Upon its publication, the book was widely advertised and reviewed. Mark Twain and George Washington Cable embarked on a reading tour, during which Mark Twain promoted *Huckleberry Finn* with more than one hundred advance readings in dozens of cities. He also published three excerpts in *Century Magazine*, a widely read popular journal. More than a few reviewers complained about the extensive advertising campaign and accused Mark Twain of writing for the market, but nearly all reviewers commented favorably on the book's sarcastic injunctions against those seeking a motive, a moral, or a plot in its story, and most who commented on Edward W. Kemble's illustrations were also favorable. There, however, is where their general agreement ended. Also, although Mark Twain was often discussed and praised in African American newspapers, and Jim was a major character in the story, no reviews or notices of the book can be found in the African American press. Only two or three reviews in other publications mention Jim by name, and none discusses his character at length (McParland 126-130).

Although agreement was found on a few things and race was almost ignored, the book still stirred up conflicting reactions that would sound familiar to modern readers. For example, one reviewer thought the evasion chapters were "forced," while another welcomed Tom Sawyer's return to the story in those chapters. A reviewer for the *New York World* called Huck a "Bad Boy" in the title of his review, while one for the *Hartford Evening Post* pointed out that Huck was both a bad boy "and a sharp one" whose "philanthropic act [toward Jim] will long keep his memory green." Other reviewers saw Huck as a bad boy in the tradition of Thomas Hughes's *Tom Brown's School Days* or George Peck's *Bad Boy*. One even said Huck was such a bad boy that the story would have been more effective if Huck had been killed at the end by "indignant citizens." Author and critic Brander Matthews, who penned one of the most perceptive reviews of the book, put it best when he said Huck was "a genuine boy; he is neither a girl in boy's clothes like many of the modern heroes of juvenile fiction, nor is he a 'little man,' a full-grown man cut down; he is a boy, just a boy, only a boy" (see Budd 258-265 for all quotes).

Reviewers also disagreed about whether the book would appeal to both boys and girls, or whether it was even appropriate for children of either sex. With the publication of *The Prince and the Pauper* in 1881, Mark Twain had been widely praised for writing a wholesome story that would benefit all children who read it, and it had elevated him at last to a level of respectability above that of a mere humorist. However, a review in the London *Athenaeum*—probably written by the influential critic and poet William Ernest Henley—rejoiced that "in *Huckleberry Finn* [Mark Twain] returns to his right mind, and is again Mark Twain of the old time" and declares it was written for boys, but that grown men would find it delightful. He does not mention girls. Brander Matthews thought that boys would enjoy the book more than girls, but reviewers for the *Boston Evening Traveller* and the *Boston Advertiser* detected "coarseness" and bad taste and were altogether far less approving. Frank Sanborn, a resident of Concord, Massachusetts, who had been a friend of Henry David Thoreau and a supporter of abolitionist John Brown, declared that anybody could read the book in his *Springfield Republican* review. Joel Chandler Harris, the author of *Uncle Remus* (1880) and one who certainly knew something about slavery and race, defended the book with vigor when he reviewed it for the *Atlanta Constitution* and said that anybody who thought the book coarse could hardly be believed to have read it. The *San Francisco Bulletin* admired the book's satire but was uncertain if boys would benefit from reading it. It was another San Francisco reviewer at the *Chronicle* who more or less anticipated the famous verdict of Howells and crowned Mark Twain "the [Thomas A.] Edison of our literature" because of his "inventive genius." Two weeks later, the same paper, this time prompted by the news that the book had been banned by the Concord Free Library, again distinguished itself by publishing perhaps the only contemporary review explicitly to address Huck's famous crisis of conscience, saying there was "nothing truer in the book." Tom's nonsensical behavior in the evasion chapters was then singled out for praise, noting that it "can only be fully appreciated by one who has read [the adventure tales] it ridicules," and added that anybody could read the book (Budd 259-275).

Other contemporary reviewers expressed insights into the novel that sound quite modern: Brander Matthews observed that in "[*The Adventures of*] *Tom Sawyer* we saw Huckleberry Finn from the outside; in the present volume we see him from the inside." Robert Bridges (*not* the future British poet laureate of the same name), writing as "Droch" for the magazine *Life*, slyly suggests that Pap's delirium tremens will entertain children "on long, rainy afternoons" and that Huck's killing of the pig to create a fake murder scene is a "little joke [that] can be repeated by any smart boy for the amusement of his fond parents." He ends his amusing attack by recommending the "Royal Nonesuch" for "Lenten parlor entertainments and church festivals." The reviewer who best understood the book, however, was Frank Sanborn. Writing for the *Springfield Republican*, he admitted that the book was not appropriate for Sunday school libraries but defended it against the "extreme censure" visited upon it by his townspeople, and spelled out the "vein of deep morality beneath its exterior of falsehood and vice." While other critics repeatedly said they'd leave it to readers to determine what morals were being taught by this book, Sanborn spelled out those morals, saying the book was "an argument against negro-slavery, lynching, whiskey-drinking, family feuds, [and] promiscuous shooting." He added that while some of the book's humor was indeed coarse, it was redeemed by the best parts of the book that were "true to life." Among the best parts he cited were "the young hero's meditations with himself over his duty regarding the runaway slave, Jim." Sanborn then admonished his readers that "Good people must make no mistake about the teachings of this book" (Budd 261-277).

**TRAGEDY.**

At Mark Twain's request, E. W. Kemble drew this picture of the naked King performing in the "Royal Nonesuch" in a way that makes his body paint appear to be a leotard (see page 57).

Critical Insights

## Nineteenth-Century Readers

To what extent did reviewers reflect the reactions of average readers or influence popular opinion? One way to measure such reader reactions is to examine memoirs written by those who read *Huckleberry Finn* in their youth, but a survey of such books from the 1920s through the 1940s yields dismal results. In virtually every case, the authors' recollections are vague, reflecting merely a nostalgic glance back at an authentic American childhood. A second source of readers' reactions is the letters written to Mark Twain himself by his readers. Slightly more than one thousand such letters survive in the Mark Twain Papers at the University of California, and two hundred of them have been published in R. Kent Rasmussen's *Dear Mark Twain* (2013). Although only one-fifth of the extant letters to Mark Twain were included in this volume, most of the letters having to do with *Huckleberry Finn* were included for the simple reason that there were fewer of them than might be expected (Rasmussen, *Dear Mark Twain* 10). At least thirty-one of those two hundred letters comment on *Huckleberry Finn* or the character Huck Finn. Two-thirds of the letter writers wrote simply to praise the book. Typically, they praised the book along with other works by Mark Twain, told him how much they enjoyed the book when they were children, or said how much their own children loved the book. A few readers were more specific, praising Huck for his pluck or his ability to get out of scrapes (Rasmussen, *Dear Mark Twain* 137-138, 200-203).

Although the sex of some letter writers is ambiguous, about one-third were female, and several of them stated that reading the book did them no harm—refuting concerns expressed by (mostly male) book reviewers. Some were curious to know if Huck was based upon various boys Mark Twain himself had known in his childhood or whether the book had been dramatized. One alert member of a reading club asked why the "raft-chapter," previously published in *Life on the Mississippi* (1883) was not in *Huckleberry Finn* (Rasmussen, *Dear Mark Twain* 91-92, 131-132, 147). Two wrote poems (Rasmussen, *Dear Mark Twain* 107-109, 125-126), and another letter may have been written by an African American (Rasmussen, *Dear Mark Twain* 175-176). A young man in Maine addressed his letter of praise directly to Huck himself (Rasmussen, *Dear Mark Twain* 137-138).

One anonymous writer sent a snarky postcard attacking the book, but two other anonymous writers praised it (Rasmussen, *Dear Mark Twain* 110-111, 210-211, 256-258).

Girls wrote the best letters and gave the most specific reasons for praising *Huckleberry Finn*. One young girl, the granddaughter of English novelist G. P. R. James, said she admired both *Tom Sawyer* and *Huckleberry Finn* and "would like to play with them [i.e., the boys] and get into such scrapes"; however, she didn't like the boys playing with a dead cat in *Tom Sawyer* because she loved kitties (Rasmussen, *Dear Mark Twain* 163). It was a young girl from Flint, Michigan, who wrote to ask if Huck was based on more than one boy (Rasmussen, *Dear Mark Twain* 91-92). It was also a girl who, after reading a French translation of *Huckleberry Finn*, bluntly informed Mark Twain what constituted "the Americanism Mark Twain stands for—freedom from tradition, independent judgment, humor & wholesomeness" (Rasmussen, *Dear Mark Twain* 219).

None of the young male readers—even those writing Mark Twain years later as adults—came close to expressing their reactions to Huck as plainly as did the girls. Gertrude Swain, a young girl from Greeley, Nebraska, irked that a preacher had attacked *Huckleberry Finn*, may have said more in her letter than all the rest combined, delivering a verdict that sounds startlingly modern:

I've been going to write to you for a long time, ever since I saw that piece in the paper about Huck Finn being a bad book.

I am a little girl twelve years old. I have read Huck Finn, about fifty times. Papa calls it my Bible, I think it is the best book ever written, and I don't think it would hurt any little boy or girl to read it. I think it would do lots of them a lot of good. I don't think that preacher knew what he was talking about.

I think the folks know it all by heart, I have told them so much about it, especially all of Jim's sign's. Poor Huck, he did get into more trouble, and get out of it so slick. . . .

I think Huck is just fine and I wish there was more like it. (Rasmussen, *Dear Mark Twain* 200)

It can come as no surprise that Gertrude's letter generated Mark Twain's most candid reply to any of the letters he received concerning *Huckleberry Finn*. He told her he "would rather have [her] judgment of the moral quality of the Huck Finn book, after fifty readings of it, than of fifty clergymen after reading it once apiece." He added that he "should have confidence in your moral visions but not so much in theirs, because it is limited in the matter of distance, & is pretty often out of focus" (Rasmussen, *Dear Mark Twain* 201). Critics of his day may have been uncertain and in disagreement over how much boys might benefit from reading *Huckleberry Finn* and fretted even more over the idea of little girls reading it, but it was a plucky little girl who provoked Huck's creator to put on record whose opinion he most valued and why. He intended to tell others what he had told her, jotting down a reminder to himself: "Write this child a note, & add her letter to the introduction of the new Huck." Sadly, he never followed through on his latter intention.

Besides those who formally reviewed *Huckleberry Finn*, other notable critics and prominent readers commented on the book. Shortly after the book was published, Mark Twain's friend and future US secretary of state, John Hay, who had grown up near the Mississippi River at the same time as young Sam Clemens, wrote Mark Twain to say that the book was a "faithful record" of the days when "Huck Finns and Tom Sawyers were my admired and trusted friends" (Zwonitzer 157-158). Irish playwright George Bernard Shaw wrote to Mark Twain in 1907 to report that he had discovered that none other than William Morris, the Pre-Raphaelite socialist, designer, and author, had been a "Huckfinomaniac" (Fishkin 113-114). English author and critic Andrew Lang called the novel a "masterpiece," "a flawed gem," and may have been the first to call it "the great American novel" when he published those judgments in 1891 (Inge 41). Eight years later, the prominent English historian and novelist Sir Walter Besant called Mark Twain "my favorite novelist" and *Huckleberry Finn* "his best book" (Inge 43).

## Twentieth-Century Readers

Praise from prominent authors and public figures continued after Mark Twain's death in 1910. Contributing a letter to a tribute in the *North American Review*, the African American educator Booker T. Washington focused on the character Jim, saying that Mark Twain "succeeded in making his readers feel a genuine respect for Jim, in spite of the ignorance [Jim] displays" and in doing so that Mark Twain "exhibited his sympathy and interest in the masses of the negro people" (Washington 829). Three years later, H. L. Mencken praised *Huckleberry Finn* in *The Smart Set*, ranking Mark Twain as the "full equal" of Miguel de Cervantes, Moliere, Jonathan Swift, and Daniel Defoe and declaring *Huckleberry Finn* "one of the great masterpieces of the world" before crowning its author as "the noblest literary artist who has set pen to paper on American soil" (Inge 71). Ten years after Mencken had his say, influential newspaperman and Progressive politician William Allen White chimed in, calling the book a "symbolic history," "more than a satire," and a "masterpiece of fableizing [*sic*]" (White xi). The twentieth-century canonization of *Huckleberry Finn* was off to a good start.

Through the 1920s, 1930s, and 1940s, praise poured in from such diverse directions as the Argentine master of magical realism Jorge Luis Borges in 1935 (Fishkin 177-180) and *American Gothic* artist Grant Wood in 1937 (Fishkin 200-204). In popular culture, the book continued to be viewed as a nostalgic look back at an idealized American childhood. That image was reinforced and visualized in film adaptations made in 1920, 1931, 1939, 1960, 1975, and 1993, plus numerous television and stage adaptations (Rasmussen, *A to Z* 229-230). Additional reinforcement of that sentimental image came from portrayals of Huck in numerous film, television, and stage adaptations of *Tom Sawyer* (Rasmussen, *A to Z* 466-467). The adaptations were not such radical distortions of Mark Twain's own visual intentions as they might first appear. Mark Twain had taken firm control over the illustrations of the first edition of the book in 1884, reviewing and approving (and often rejecting) Kemble's drawings as the eager young artist sent them to the publisher. Mark Twain repeatedly asked that they be sanitized, softened, or deleted altogether to play down sexuality or violence. At Mark Twain's behest, Kemble made Huck better looking, represented the raucous camp meeting with only one benign courtship image, and carefully posed the naked dancer on stage in the "Royal Nonesuch" to make him look as if he were wearing leotards rather than body paint (David 340-345). The visual Disneyfication of *Huckleberry Finn* had thus begun with Mark Twain himself before the book was even printed.

Perhaps the two most famous reader responses to *Huckleberry Finn* are those of Louisa May Alcott and Ernest Hemingway. Alcott's prissy put-down ("If Mr. Clemens cannot think of something better to tell our pure-minded lads and lasses, he had better stop writing for them") and Hemingway's later proclamation that "all modern American literature comes from one book by Mark Twain called *Huckleberry Finn*" are oft-quoted, but are sorely in need of correction. Alcott may never have said a thing about *Huckleberry Finn*. The earliest print source for her famous quote is Thomas Beer's *The Mauve Decade* (1926), which has now been proven to contain fabricated quotes and source materials (Mac Donnell 21). It is sometimes cited as appearing in *The Critic* in 1885, but this is not verified by a thorough search of that magazine from 1884 to 1889 (covering the year the book appeared in England to the year following Alcott's death).

Hemingway's statement is a bit of a stretcher, as Huck himself might say. It comes from Hemingway's *Green Hills of Africa* (1935), a supposedly nonfiction account of a big-game hunting trip in 1933 in which Hemingway—or a fictionalized version of him—is the chief character and narrator. The conversation in which Hemingway quotes himself talking about the book is preceded a few pages earlier by his statement that he did not want to disabuse his listener of his illusions about "literary people" and is followed a few pages later with an admission that he'd engaged in "verbal dysentery" (Hemingway 19, 22, 29). The opinion Hemingway rendered may, therefore, be an exaggerated version of his views on Mark Twain and should be read (and quoted) with caution and in proper context.

Other writers have had plenty to say about their reactions to *Huckleberry Finn*. Although Hemingway had praised the book in

1935, he had also warned readers that the evasion chapters were "just cheating." William Somerset Maugham echoed that sentiment just five years later when he called Tom Sawyer a "muttonhead" who had ruined those final chapters (Fishkin 5). E. L. Doctorow registered a similar complaint, deploring the "minstrelese" depiction of Jim that Booker T. Washington had accepted at face value (Doctorow 132). On the other hand, V. S. Pritchett (1941), Kurt Vonnegut (1996), and Erica Jong (1996) have all called the novel a masterpiece (Inge 75-79; Vonnegut xxxi-xxxiii; Jong xxxi-xlii). In 1985, Norman Mailer took a different approach and admitted that his first reading of the book was a disappointment, but that his second reading was a revelation. He had felt like he was reading a recent novel by a modern author who had been heavily influenced by—and who had borrowed liberally from—older writers, like Ernest Hemingway, William Faulkner, John Steinbeck, John Dos Passos, J. D. Salinger, Kurt Vonnegut, Joseph Heller, Saul Bellow, James Dickey, and even the actors John Wayne and Burt Reynolds (Mailer 4-5). Kurt Vonnegut's take was also a bit different: After ranking the book with Herman Melville's *Moby-Dick* (1851), Hemingway's *A Farewell to Arms* (1929), Homer's *Iliad* and *Odyssey* (eighth century BCE), Fyodor Dostoevski's *Crime and Punishment* (1866), and the Bible, he concludes that all those books are "about what a bummer it is to be a human being" (Vonnegut 8-9).

## Twentieth-Century African American Readers

The reactions of black writers to *Huckleberry Finn* have also varied. Ralph Ellison echoed Booker T. Washington in 1953, when he wrote that Mark Twain "does not idealize the slave, Jim. Jim is drawn in all his ignorance and superstition, with his good traits and his bad" (Fishkin 259). In 1982, Ellison still saw *Huckleberry Finn* as a "fictional vision of an ideal democracy in which the actual combines with the ideal . . . in which the highly placed and the lowly, the black and the white . . . combine to tell us of transcendent truth and possibility such as those discovered when Mark Twain set Huck and Jim afloat on the raft" (Fishkin 6). Neither Washington nor Ellison discusses the repeated presence of the word "nigger" in the text. Not so, however, with humorist and social activist Dick Gregory, who embraced the word when he used it for the title of his autobiography in 1964. Says Gregory, "Titling my book *Nigger* meant I was taking it back from white folks. Mark Twain threw it up in the air and I grabbed it" (Fishkin 448).

In 1983, Fairfax County, Virginia, school administrator John H. Wallace generated widespread media attention when he produced a heavily sanitized edition of *Huckleberry Finn* that removed the words "nigger" and "hell" from the text, along with entire passages, rendering parts of the story absurd. Although he acknowledged Mark Twain's intended satire, he still saw the book as damaging to young black readers. Law professor Sharon E. Rush, provoked by the pain her young daughter felt when forced to read the book as part of her school curriculum, wrote *Huck Finn's "Hidden" Lessons* (2006), thoughtfully explaining why she felt the book was racist and advocating that it be removed from required curricula and taught instead as an "anticanonical text in American literature" that demonstrates the "limits of whites' goodwill toward blacks and other people of color" (Rush 149).

Nobel Prize-winning author Toni Morrison's reaction to her first reading of *Huckleberry Finn* was similar to that of Sharon Rush's daughter, but she came to view the removal of the book from schools as a "purist yet elementary kind of censorship designed to appease adults rather than educate children" (Fishkin 409). She does not dismiss the evasion chapters or protest the use of the word "nigger" and focuses instead on the relationship of Huck and Jim and notions of fatherhood and childhood. She also suggests that the book is "classic literature" whose "argument at the core" cannot be dismissed (Morrison, Introduction xxxi-xli). What is that core? She wisely observes that

> if we supplement our reading of *Huckleberry Finn*, expand it— release it from its clutch of sentimental nostrums about lighting out to the territory, river gods, and the fundamental innocence of Americanness—to incorporate its contestatory, combative critique of antebellum America, it seems to be another, fuller novel. It becomes a more beautifully complicated work that sheds much light on some

of the problems it has accumulated through traditional readings too shy to linger over the implications of the Africanist presence at its center (Morrison, *Playing* 54).

## Twentieth- and Twenty-first-Century Critics

Those river gods and traditional readings became part of the canonization of the book when critic Lionel Trilling wrote his famous introduction to a 1948 edition of *Huckleberry Finn*, which was soon followed by T. S. Eliot's introduction to a 1950 edition. Both editions were widely used in schools and framed discussions and critical approaches to the book in the following decades. Trilling and Eliot discuss the river gods at play and defend the evasion chapters. Both are also effusive in their high praise of the book as a masterpiece, echoing the verdicts rendered earlier by Lang, Mencken, White, and Pritchett. Trilling called it a "subversive" book and "almost perfect" and declared that it represented "unpretentious truth" (Trilling xv, xviii).

Eliot—like Mark Twain a native Missourian—said Huck gave the book its style and the Mississippi River its form, and that Mark Twain "wrote a much greater book than he could have known he was writing" (Eliot xii, xv). He also makes a candid admission: "*Huckleberry Finn*, like other great works of imagination can give to every reader whatever he is capable of taking from it" (Eliot xiv). Although early Mark Twain critical studies were profoundly shaped by competing schools of thought established by Van Wyck Brooks (1920) and Bernard DeVoto (1932), the popular reaction to the book had remained relatively unchanged and was more influenced by movies until the Trilling and Eliot editions appeared.

The canonization of the book also continued in popular culture and reached mass markets. Four years before the Trilling edition appeared, The Gilberton Company, a comic book publisher, added the title to their extremely popular *Classics Illustrated* series. That series was copied by other comic book publishers as the original series grew to 167 titles. By the time the series ended in 1971, young readers could read a comic book about Huck as well as comics based on other Mark Twain works, and comic book versions of masterpieces by Homer, William Shakespeare, Cervantes, and Charles Dickens. Meanwhile, cheap paperback editions and movies introduced young readers to Huck. By the twenty-first century, the book was even available as a graphic novel. Consequently, not all students confronting Huck, Jim, and Tom in classrooms are meeting them for the first or last time.

After Trilling and Eliot, a host of prominent critics added to the canonization of the novel, with new editions that featured new introductions appearing every few years. There have also been new debates on the evasion chapters, race, censorship, and even the establishment of an authoritative text. Objections to the canonization were raised along the way, most notably by Jonathan Arac's *Huckleberry Finn as Idol and Target* (1997), which argued that the *hyper*-canonization—or *hyper*-idolatry—of the work had resulted in a complacency about race that allowed white readers (including teachers and scholars) to discount the objections of black readers (Arac 13).

In 2011, the NewSouth edition, edited by Alan Gribben appeared, substituting benign euphemisms for "nigger," "Injun Joe," and "half-breed" to overcome objections of school boards that had removed the book from their schools. A storm of controversy erupted before this edition appeared—with Gribben's thoughtful introduction that artfully draws more attention to the issue of racism as a "teachable moment" than any other edition of the book published in decades—leaving early critics looking overwrought.

Another challenge to the status quo came with Andrew Levy's *Huck Finn's America* in 2015. Levy argues that instead of choosing between a reading of the book as a novel about childhood—as most nineteenth-century readers did—or one about race—as most modern readers do—a more rewarding reading of the book recognizes "that Twain found the borders that divide parents and children as false as those dividing black and white" (Levy xvii). Levy makes his case by examining nineteenth-century parenting practices and race relations, as well as modern parenting and race relations. This belated blending of two traditional approaches to the novel results in more than a recognition of its satire; it makes clear that *Huckleberry*

*Finn* is a rebuke of American child-rearing and an indictment of American race relations, both then and now.

## Future Readers

Each generation has seen Jim and Huck anew, and there is no reason to expect future readers to be different. This is how art functions: Leonardo da Vinci's masterpiece *Mona Lisa* (known in Italian as *La Gioconda*) was once regarded simply as the portrait of a lady. However, her smile has transcended the centuries to become something more. She has been copied, parodied, and debated, but her enigmatic smile—widely known as the Gioconda smile—endures. So it has been for Huck Finn. The last page of the first edition of Mark Twain's masterpiece illustrates Huck tipping his hat at his readers and places his right hand over his heart as he leans slightly forward as if about to take a bow. The story has been told and the backdrop of bigotry has receded—but the evasion chapters remind us that bigotry has not vanished. Huck and Jim have finally escaped the bonds that enslaved them both, but Huck's journey has really just begun, and Jim's dignity and freedom are not yet out of danger even if he himself is no longer a slave. In that time and place, he remains a "nigger."

Directly above his portrait on that final page, Huck has boldly announced his intention to escape even further away from American society. A new generation of readers see themselves mirrored in this story. Huck is a reflection of white aspirations, and Jim is a reminder of the perils that linger for blacks and whites who do not conform. Readers may flatter themselves and think they have already—or shall soon—travel in their own lives that same path as Huck, or else imagine that Huck and Jim are truly and wholly free. But there is no territory for an escape. By the time the book appeared in America in 1885, there were few territories left to provide any escape, and those that were left were still dangerous. Mark Twain, ever artful, knew this. Every reader must plot his own path. In the meantime, beckoning readers by his own example, there stands Huck—alone, humble, exceptional, defiant, transcendent, and American—flashing his own Gioconda smile.

---

## Works Cited

Arac, Jonathan. *Huckleberry Finn as Idol and Target: The Function of Criticism in Our Time.* Madison: U of Wisconsin P, 1997.

Budd, Louis J., comp. *Mark Twain: The Contemporary Reviews.* Cambridge, UK: Cambridge UP, 1999.

David, Beverly R. "The Pictorial Huck Finn: Mark Twain and His Illustrator, E. W. Kemble." *American Quarterly* 56 (Oct. 1974): 331-351.

Doctorow, E. L. "Huck, Continued." *The New Yorker* (26 June 1995): 132.

Eliot, T. S., Introduction. *Adventures of Huckleberry Finn.* By Mark Twain. London: Crosset, 1950.

Ellison, Ralph. *Shadow & Act.* New York: Random House, 1964.

Fishkin, Shelley Fisher, ed. *The Mark Twain Anthology: Great Writers on His Life and Works.* New York: Library of America, 2010.

Hemingway, Ernest. *Green Hills of Africa.* New York: Scribner, 1935.

Inge, M. Thomas, ed. *Huck Finn among the Critics: A Centennial Selection.* Frederick, MD: University Publication of America, 1985.

Jong, Erica. Introduction. *1601, and Is Shakespeare Dead?* By Mark Twain. New York: Oxford UP, 1996.

Levy, Andrew. *Huck Finn's America: Mark Twain and the Era That Shaped His Masterpiece.* New York: Simon & Schuster, 2015.

McParland, Robert. *Mark Twain's Audience: A Critical Analysis of Reader Responses to the Writings of Mark Twain.* Lanham, MD: Lexington Books, 2014.

Mac Donnell, Kevin. "Mark Twain Kills a Boy." *Mark Twain Journal* 54:1 (Spring 2016): 17-32.

Mailer, Norman. *Huckleberry Finn Alive at 100.* Montclair, NJ: Caliban Press, 1985.

Morrison, Toni. Introduction. *Adventures of Huckleberry Finn.* By Mark Twain. New York: Oxford UP, 1996.

Morrison, Toni. *Playing in the Dark: Whiteness and the Literary Imagination.* Cambridge, MA: Harvard UP, 1992.

Rasmussen, R. Kent, ed. *Dear Mark Twain: Letters from His Readers.* Berkeley: U California P, 2013.

_____. *Mark Twain A to Z.* New York: Facts on File, 1995.

Rush, Sharon E. *Huck Finn's "Hidden" Lessons: Teaching and Learning Across the Color Line*. Lanham, MD: Rowman & Littlefield, 2006.

Smith, Henry Nash, ed. *Adventures of Huckleberry Finn*. Boston: Houghton, Mifflin, 1958.

Trilling, Lionel. Introduction. *Adventures of Huckleberry Finn*. By Mark Twain. New York: Rinehart, 1948.

Vonnegut, Kurt. Introduction. *A Connecticut Yankee in King Arthur's Court*. By Mark Twain. New York: Oxford UP, 1996.

_____. *A Man Without a Country*. New York: Seven Stories Press, 2005.

Washington, Booker T., contrib. "Tributes to Mark Twain." *North American Review*. 191.6 (June 1910): 827-35.

White, William Allen. "An Appreciation." *Adventures of Huckleberry Finn*. New York: Gabriel Wells, 1923.

Zwonitzer, Mark. *The Statesman and the Storyteller*. Chapel Hill, NC: Algonquin Books 2016.

# Huck Finn and Tom Sawyer Expelled: Censorship and the Classroom

Alan Gribben

Mark Twain's pair of young adult novels that entertained junior and high school students—*The Adventures of Tom Sawyer* (1876) and *Adventures of Huckleberry Finn* (1885)—have recently been expelled from the approved reading lists in hundreds of public school districts. No longer can school teachers introduce Becky Thatcher, Cardiff Hill, Jackson's Island, McDougal's Cave, Pap Finn, the wrecked *Walter Scott*, the Grangerford-Shepherdson feud, the Duke and the King, Colonel Sherburn, the Wilks sisters, or the Phelps farm in the classroom. The unstated reason for the books' disappearance consists of a racially offensive, two-syllable word—"nigger"— employed by Twain's uneducated characters, young and old. Within the past decade, American society has deemed the word to be so culturally objectionable that only an abbreviated euphemism, "the n-word"—is acceptable in public discourse.

During the 1980s, three decades after the US Supreme Court's decision in the *Brown vs. Board of Education* case ended racial segregation in public school facilities in 1954, the parents of African American students began to challenge the mandatory assignment of Twain's novels, which repeatedly used the n-word. School administrators became increasingly uncomfortable with requiring his books in racially integrated English classes. In April 1984, I personally witnessed an emotional incident resulting from this mounting conflict. Arriving at a scholarly conference devoted to "American Comedy" held on the Pennsylvania State University campus, I and the other attendees were greeted by African American parents marching with protest signs outside the building where we were to meet. Their target, as it turned out, were our sessions commemorating the centennial of *Huckleberry Finn*'s publication. We soon learned that a dispute had arisen in the local public schools after a teacher, endeavoring to bring the novel to life for her class, asked the only African American student in her class to read Jim's lines aloud in a class skit. I remember being vaguely sympathetic to the parents' resentment and having pity for the well-meaning school teacher swept up into this community imbroglio, yet also feeling complacently confident that I would be able to continue teaching that novel at the college level with complete impunity. One merely needed to justify the historical necessity for Twain's utilizing the n-word, I thought, as well as explain the reason for Jim's illiterate folk speech—namely, that slaves had been barred by law from learning to read or write in nearly all Southern states.

## My Change of Heart

But fate had transformations in store for my life and my thinking. In 1991, I left my full professorship at a large southwestern university that had nearly 50,000 students and approximately a 3 percent African American enrollment. I accepted a departmental headship at a 5,000-student campus located in Montgomery, Alabama. More than one-third of the students at my new institution were African American. Many of them were descendants of the slaves once owned in that region, and some of the students probably had forebears who had picked cotton on the vast plantation where our college campus stands. Forty-four percent of the population of the state of Alabama had consisted of slaves by 1850, and although many thousands of those emancipated by the Civil War elected to migrate to northern cities, other thousands chose (or may have been coerced) into staying behind.

The city to which I moved is so rooted in the tragedies of southern history that Montgomery attracts large numbers of tourists who are curious about its legitimate reputation as both "The Cradle of the Confederacy" and "The Birthplace of the Civil Rights Movement." To its credit, Montgomery has confronted the burden of its heritage and erected large historical plaques throughout the community designating sites such as the downtown slave market; the signage does not spare the details of a shameful practice. It also has monuments to the martyrs of the voting rights drive and to the Freedom Riders who were beaten at the Greyhound Bus

Depot; a downtown museum chronicles the larger story of political subjugation and eventual liberation.

My teaching assignments at my new campus principally consisted of American literature survey courses, which tended to draw the majority of the African American students (as seeming more relevant to their lives than the other choices of British literature or Western World literature). Thus my course enrollments were often half black and half white. Consequently, I began to look at Twain's novels in a different light than I had viewed them in my teaching experiences in Berkeley, California; Austin, Texas; and (during a few summers) Elmira, New York. My students now included an audience whose grandparents had bequeathed a legacy of bus boycotts and marches against hostile mobs, policemen, and state troopers so that their children and grandchildren would never again be subjected to abuse such as being called "niggers," perhaps the vilest word in the English language because it conveys a stamp of permanent, inescapable inferiority. I found that Twain's electrifying themes in *Adventures of Huckleberry Finn*—rebellion against authority, resistance to conformity, friendship across racial boundaries—were becoming obscured by my students' palpable pain at being forced to read this word more than 200 times. I noticed that on the days when my reading syllabus assigned Twain's novel, the absenteeism rate soared among my African American students.

Another memorable experience affected my attitude toward this impasse. In 2010, I agreed to undertake a statewide speaking tour to promote *The Adventures of Tom Sawyer*. Librarians had designed these "Big Read" events to remind younger readers that engrossing literature predated the Harry Potter series. What shocked me was the number of middle and high school teachers who approached me after my presentations to explain that they were prohibited by their school districts from teaching *Tom Sawyer*, let alone *Huckleberry Finn*. According to them, both novels are now off limits in most integrated public school classrooms because of one inflammatory word. Later, I found that school districts across the entire country, most of them careful not to make headlines by any outright "banning" of the two classics, have quietly allowed these books to slip off their approved curriculum lists of assignable readings.

Driving home at night through the forests of southern pines and hardwoods after delivering those *Tom Sawyer* library talks, I contemplated the prospect of generations of students being prevented from encountering Twain's masterpieces. In today's multipurpose colleges, it is frequently possible to earn a bachelor's degree without completing any course containing nineteenth-century American literature. Eventually large numbers of Americans will lack any first-hand knowledge about the greatest author our nation produced after Hawthorne and Melville. On one particular trip along the winding, moonlit highway leading from Eufaula, Alabama, to Montgomery, I began to formulate an idea that went against my doctoral education at the University of California at Berkeley as well as my training in scholarly publishing at the Mark Twain Project at Berkeley, where I had been employed as a research editor for eight years during my graduate school years.

It occurred to me that I was equipped by my lifetime of studying and teaching Mark Twain to prepare an edition of his two novels that could offer teachers and school districts a workable alternative to simply ignoring these books. After all, I had already reconstructed Twain's personal library and reading in a 1,000-page catalog, coedited a collection of his travel writings, and published dozens of scholarly articles investigating his biography, prose style, and celebrity image. What if I now produced editions of both *Tom Sawyer* and *Huckleberry Finn* that retained every phrase, sentence, and chapter in them *except* the offensive racial slurs?

In 2010, *Huckleberry Finn* was the fourth most-frequently challenged, pre-twentieth-century title in the United States, and *Tom Sawyer* was the fourteenth. This optional edition could reflect our emerging sensitivity to racially disparaging words in authors' texts. Astrid Lindgren's *Pippi Longstocking*, P. L. Travers's *Mary Poppins*, and Hugh Lofting's *Doctor Doolittle* have undergone extensive makeovers to remove their racist stereotypes so that modern-day parents can buy the books. Of course, the n-word epithet also occurs in Harper Lee's *To Kill a Mockingbird* (1960), a title still assigned in numerous high schools, but it appears there only a few times and with a greater consciousness of its racial animus. In *Huckleberry Finn*, the flow of n-words is incessant, whereas Scout Finch employs it only occasionally in her narrative and for a powerful effect.

## Finding a Publisher

I approached Suzanne La Rosa and Randall Williams, cofounders of NewSouth Books, an intrepid press known for its titles on southern culture, civil rights, and race relations, and proposed a duplicate set of editions. In one version, only the racial aspersions would be emended and the text otherwise left the same; the other edition would be entirely faithful to Twain's original language. The volumes would have identical paginations, enabling students and instructors to have their choice of reading *Tom Sawyer* and *Huckleberry Finn* with or without the n-word. I outlined to La Rosa and Williams how the alternative NewSouth Edition would substitute the word "slave" for the nine n-words in *Tom Sawyer* and the 215 usages of the same racial epithet in *Huckleberry Finn* (counting the ones in the tables of contents and the captions for illustrations in Twain's first edition). Ironically (as it turned out), the publishers' initial concern was whether they would be able to make enough teachers and readers aware that this optional edition was available. Nevertheless, NewSouth recognized its importance to schools and agreed to become the publisher for this series. They decided to start with an n-word-free edition, combining both novels in a single volume, since their research indicated that a composite format would have less competition in the textbook market. An original language edition would then follow within a few months.

## Initial Condemnation

Before I could even get my manuscript to the press, a *Publishers' Weekly* reporter noticed NewSouth's announcement and wrote an article anticipating the book's forthcoming release. Within hours, my email inbox (and the "Contact Us" address at my publishers) began to clog up with furious objections, some of whose similarities of language suggested that an Internet campaign was underway to discourage its publication. I soon shared Huck's situation when he arrived at the Phelps farm, where "in a quarter of a minute I was a kind of a hub of a wheel, as you may say—spokes made out of dogs." Some of the responders threw the racial slur around so freely that they resembled Pap Finn on one of his worst drunken tears. Most, however, stepped fastidiously around the very term they were castigating our edition for excluding.

The *Wall Street Journal* reported nearly 60,000 posts about the NewSouth Edition on Twitter and Facebook within a four-day period in January 2011. Debate teams at high schools and colleges eagerly took up the subject. College and community newspapers tussled with the issues involved. News outlets in Canada, Australia, the Republic of Ireland, and the United Kingdom treated the matter like an international crisis and solicited interviews with me and my publisher. The furor made it appear that I was dislodging a cornerstone of Western civilization. Even my hometown paper scoffed at the idea, asking editorially whether I would next rewrite Melville's *Moby Dick* to eliminate any cruelty to whales. National cartoonists weighed in, gloomily predicting the end of free speech in America. Several prominent commentators attacked the edition because it originated from a press located in the Deep South, as though this fact by itself lent the matter a sinister aspect. Newspaper letter writers and Internet bloggers insisted—nearly always without bothering to read my Introduction to the forthcoming edition that I posted at www.newsouthbooks.com—that I was about to desecrate a pair of literary monuments in an act of heedless sacrilege.

Cartoonist Jim Day's take on the NewSouth controversy for the *Las Vegas Review Journal*. (Jim Day Courtesy Cagle Cartoons)

Three widespread misconceptions became noticeable. The first of these arose because media pundits and entertainment personalities on radio and television exaggerated the news to make it seem as though all other existing editions of the two novels would hereafter be abolished. Despite the limited press run planned for our experimental edition, many people outside academe wrote to me in consternation, fearful that they would never again be able to read the original versions of Twain's novels.

A second error was typical among those who had evidently never read *Huckleberry Finn*. They insisted that by substituting the term "slave" for the n-word I was essentially "sanitizing" Huck Finn's narrative, glossing over the plight of antebellum African Americans and thereby depriving instructors of valuable "teachable moments"—whereas, as any reader of the novel knows, it is hard to open any chapter of *Huckleberry Finn* without encountering the institution of slavery and the unsavory racial attitudes of the 1840s. Besides, where is the logic in alleging that injecting the designation "slave" avoids the abject condition of those enmeshed in slavery? The NewSouth Edition merely translated the offending racial insults; it did not write human slavery out of Twain's novels. Completely intact are the representations of his disgust for an institution he was ashamed of having supported in and beyond his adolescence. (Twain's family had owned as many slaves as they could afford, and his father sat on a trial jury that gave lengthy penitentiary sentences to three abolitionists who came across the river from Illinois in an effort to help slaves escape.) A case could be made that *Huckleberry Finn* was largely a gesture of atonement for the author's unenlightened views during his youth.

In a third erroneous assumption, politically conservative columnists indignantly concluded that this edition represented another instance of caving in to "political correctness." By contrast, political liberals for their part deplored the loss of a racially insulting word that to them proved America's eternal prejudices. Amid all this turbulence, I could at least take some satisfaction that my small action had achieved a nearly impossible feat: our NewSouth Edition had temporarily united America's prickly Far Right and contentious Far Left.

Early comments about the edition at least took into account my scholarly record and credited me with possessing good motives. An influential reviewer for the Mark Twain Forum, a popular Internet discussion board, acknowledged the chorus of disapproval the NewSouth Edition had met with but noted that its editor is commendably "passionate in his conviction that *Adventures of Huckleberry Finn* belongs in the classroom." One of my former students, the young adult fiction series author Rick Riordan, gave me the benefit of the doubt in a blog on January 7, 2011:

> Dr. Gribben was an excellent teacher. He was very conscious of the racially charged language in Huck Finn, and was careful to put the novel in its historical context and explain Twain's choice of words. . . .
> I don't have any problem with offering teachers, students and general

readers more choices, especially if it makes the texts more accessible and causes less unease for students (and parents). . . . I have no doubt Alan Gribben understood that he was in for a storm of criticism . . . , but he did it with the best of intentions, and I applaud his courage.

However, as other bloggers fanned the flames with falsehoods and innuendoes, the subsequent commentators were not so fair. My campus email address continued to register forty or fifty messages a day, most of them in the form of protests, the majority of them ill-informed and vituperative. Within a few weeks I received 1,082 personal email messages addressing the NewSouth Edition—443 (roughly 41%) of them extremely negative and ranging from polite disagreement to out-and-out aspersions; 469 (approximately 43%) of them ambiguous in tone, expressing concerned curiosity or requests for interviews and more information; and 170 (about 16%) of them positive, taking the form of supportive comments or (at the extreme) wishing they could get into a boxing ring with the negative critics.

## Academic Disfavor

I had to anticipate that I would receive a few bruises for altering, however slightly, the text of a beloved author, but some of the revilement came from unexpected directions. The gibes of my fellow scholars on the Mark Twain Forum were the most wounding, coming as they did from colleagues whose work I had encouraged and praised and from whom I expected a fair shake. A major Twain scholar lectured me in the 2014 edition of the *Mark Twain Annual* about the author's motives: Twain had "decided to make the word a dominant component of his text," he reminded me; what is more, "Twain is fully obvious in his intentional use of the 'n-word'"; finally, "Twain's manipulation of the n-word is not accidental, but rather is part of a coherent plan to show racism as so integral and pervasive as to be inescapable." In other words, I must be blind to transparent truisms. My lessons regarding textual orthodoxy did not end here; I received a chilly reception at three scholarly conferences I attended after 2011, and strong objections were voiced from the floor when I tried to explain my reasoning at the Seventh International State of

Mark Twain Studies Conference in 2013. Even professors I rated as among my close friends tactfully avoided the subject of my unpardonable *malum*.

After several weeks of public clamor I saw that the textual purists, very often ensconced in elite universities or private prep schools with relatively small minority enrollments, would prefer that these novels *not* be taught at all in public schools rather than make any compromise about a degrading name in them. That outcome, let it be noted, enables these professors and instructors to function like high priests chosen to interpret Twain's writings to a privileged few. To them, the n-word is not merely crucial to the two books—it is virtually their entire point. So what if this supercilious attitude denies other students a vital portion of their common literary heritage? To my mind, such perverse stubbornness registers an enormous and telling disconnect between the private academy/university/media intelligentsia and the real world of the beleaguered public school teacher. Certain defenders of the status quo were distinguished African American authors and critics; this development baffled me until an African American woman employed on my campus took me aside and explained, "The ones who like that word in the books are the ones who have it made."

## Media Hypocrisy

I had to laugh whenever the professional commentators avoided printing or pronouncing the very word they were mocking me for substituting and that they were expecting public school teachers to read aloud in racially integrated classrooms. Newspapers routinely reject any letters to the editor that contain this word, and media broadcasters and columnists know that their own jobs would be forfeited if they dared to violate a tacit protocol by uttering or publishing the dreaded word. All of us can recall the names of various television celebrities who have had their careers damaged or ended for using the n-word, even in private conversations.

Some objectors charged that I was second-guessing Twain's artistry and demonstrating little respect for his ability with phrasing. One of my favorite sayings of his—about the difference between lightning and a lightning-bug—was often sarcastically quoted back to me. I found this notion to be downright comical, since I am on record, in articles and encyclopedia entries, as praising Twain's knack for using exactly the right words in the right places. It was indeed the right word for the nineteenth-century audience, but (for many readers) no longer for our twenty-first-century world. The salient issue is not whether he knew what he was doing when he employed the n-word; the point is whether his books can effectively transport and enlighten in the public schools *without* those racial epithets in the dialect that Twain recalled being spoken by uneducated people during the days of slavery. I contend that these novels are so well-crafted that they do retain their impact.

## Hardly "Censorship"

More serious were the accusations that I was practicing "censorship." I would answer that exactly the opposite is the case. I have devised a means by which these novels can return to public school classrooms from which they are currently barred. "Censorship" is normally defined as prohibiting the publication, sale, or reading of a work and having the enforcement of a governmental mandate behind that policy. For example, after a military junta seized control of Greece in 1967, it forbade any distribution of *Huckleberry Finn*, among many banned books. In other words, censorship historically involves a state or institutional action. My edition has no state or institutional power behind it. Whereas censorship is aimed at suppressing speech or ideas, the NewSouth Edition of Twain's novels is trying to promote and circulate his books and ideas rather than suppress them. As Randall Williams of NewSouth Books has said, "What we have done is translation, not censorship. Our translation has not deprived anyone of reading Twain's original language, nor did our translation affect the millions of copies of the work already in circulation or yet to come." In fact (although the media resolutely ignored this), within a few months in 2011, NewSouth Books carried through with its plan for the series and issued Original Text Editions of both *Tom Sawyer* and *Huckleberry Finn* in identical formats to the NewSouth

Editions. Each edition explicitly stated on its cover whether or not the racial pejoratives were included.

Did we not, then, in effect *circumvent* the prevailing system of silent but effectual censorship? The step we took can significantly enlarge the younger audience for Twain's brilliant works. And those teachers and curriculum directors who are comfortable using the standard editions of *Tom Sawyer* and *Huckleberry Finn* are still entitled to continue doing so.

A third solution also presents itself. In my college courses, I offer the students their choice of the identically paginated NewSouth Editions or the original language editions. Most African American students (and a surprising number of the other students) opt for the texts that translate the n-word as "slave." We then waste little time agonizing over the racial slurs, but rather invest our class hours in digging deeper into these provocative novels.

### *60 Minutes* Diminishes the Vitriol

My publishers resolutely refused to halt or postpone the NewSouth Edition in spite of the warnings and invectives hurled at them, and more than a month after the book finally reached print, a national television program probed the controversy. On March 20, 2011, *60 Minutes* and its CBS television affiliates aired a segment partly filmed at a Minnesota high school in which one teacher acknowledged the "pain" that the n-word inflicts in high school classrooms. When interviewed, an African American student admitted that he hid his extreme discomfort as his classmates turned their heads to watch his reactions each time the word surfaced in the teacher's remarks. The NewSouth Books editor-in-chief, Randall Williams, himself a civil rights historian, was interviewed by Byron Pitts in the *60 Minutes* segment and spoke movingly about slavery's having been "a sin." For the most part, acrimonious commentary about the edition waned after this television program made its impact. Moreover, readers were now able to obtain copies of the book and see for themselves its explanatory introduction and useful notes.

What to make of the foregoing wave of righteous hysteria? Judging from the fury aroused in many emailers, bloggers, and media professionals, one would have thought I had *inserted* the hated n-word into two famous novels rather than subtracted it. I hoped that when the actual book became available, a number of these critics would be struck by the helpful erudition, affection for the novels, and respect for other scholars that the edition reflected. This did not come to pass; only a handful of the hardcore objectors ever bothered to look at the book and retract their earlier remarks. One of the few who did rethink her comments was a columnist for the St. Louis, Missouri *Post-Dispatch*. She admitted in 2013 that she had been involved in the "the national hand-wringing [that] greeted a revised edition of the novel. . . . I was part of the crowd crying about the sacrosanct nature of Twain's original text." However, after her fourth-grade daughter heard the n-word uttered repeatedly in a dramatization of Twain's "A True Story, Repeated Word for Word," this writer conceded that she began to grasp "how reading the work impacted racial relations within a class. I didn't realize the novel could be taught in a vacuum of the racial tension surrounding it." A university professor in New York City sent me an email testimonial: "I found it so difficult to teach *Huckleberry Finn* that I removed it from the basic American Lit. course and use it only for advanced or graduate courses. I just didn't want to spend half of the time allotted to the book to be used to deal with arguments about the use of the 'n' word!"

## Gratifying Personal Reactions

Although one member of my campus department personally chided the NewSouth editor-in-chief for altering the text, most of my other colleagues seemed to comprehend this effort to reintroduce Twain's novels into the classroom. Professors in the fields of medieval and Renaissance literature even mentioned to me the many concessions in translation necessary to make the Pearl Poet, Chaucer, Shakespeare, and other authors intelligible to students. In 2015, my campus made a gesture toward vindicating my action by awarding me its inaugural Excellence Through Diversity Award.

There were local responses of another nature, too. At noon one day, an African American cashier at a local delicatessen in

Montgomery recognized my name on my credit card, asked me if I was the professor who had just edited a new Mark Twain book, came around the counter (to my initial apprehension), wrapped her arms around me, and said that now she could introduce Twain's novels to her children. A middle-aged African American man who was having his car repaired at a Montgomery paint and body shop heard the proprietor call me by name; he broke off a conversation, walked over to where I was standing, pumped my hand, and thanked me profusely for taking a step toward making school classrooms more friendly to young African Americans during a formative period in their emotional development. Several older African American men across the country wrote to tell me that the day these novels were discussed in class amounted to one of the worst days of their lives. The publisher and I soon received grateful letters of support from classroom teachers who had previously given up on assigning *Huckleberry Finn*. "It is a great move on your end," wrote one high school instructor, who continued:

> I completely stopped teaching this book because of the effect it had and has on African American students. Any person who disagrees with your version should be forced to assign and teach the old version . . . , just so they can experience the difficulty and discomfort of such hateful language in a scholastic setting. . . . It simply isn't worth teaching because the n-word becomes the focus. Not only does it hurt feelings, but it can also spark hostility. . . . I think it's a good option and I'm glad you did it.

Another teacher agreed, writing:

> I suspect that not one of your critics has stood before an integrated classroom. . . . I also doubt that they have seen the expressions of humiliating discomfort of students in a classroom where the novel is used as an excuse to repeat the n-word over and over. Thank you for your efforts to return the most important novel in the American literary canon to its rightful place in high school curriculums.

A public school teacher in North Carolina initially opposed the NewSouth Edition, but after hearing me speak at a national conference, he decided to try it with his predominantly African American high school class. Although the students "remained aware of the word" and found themselves "mentally substituting Clemens's original word" wherever they saw the term "slave," the instructor testified that "as a class, we found that the NewSouth approach actually opened up the possibilities for discussion," that "the general reaction of students was positive," and that he is "grateful the option is available" (Hugh H. Davis, "On Teaching *Huckleberry Finn*," *Mark Twain Journal* 54.2 [Fall 2016]: 60-70).

At this point, I could imagine how Twain must have felt in the unforgettable episode he described in *Roughing It* when his campfire accidentally touched off a gigantic forest fire on the shore of Lake Tahoe. Unable to put it out, he concluded that his only recourse was to row his boat out into the lake and watch with rapt awe the magnitude of the immense conflagration he had unintentionally sparked. I have devoted the entirety of my academic career to understanding and promoting Mark Twain's writings, and I still have faith that conscientious journalists, scholars, and teachers will ultimately perceive the value of this optional edition. It will not, of course, end the controversy over the n-word in *Tom Sawyer* and *Huckleberry Finn*, but it might enable instructors to set aside this unproductive issue for the time being and focus instead on Twain's enthralling narratives, powerful satires, and haunting messages about the price of unthinking social conformity (as exemplified most notably by Huck's unexamined view of slavery as natural and defensible, but with implications for all of us in our everyday lives).

No university press or large commercial publishing house could have withstood the barrage of hostile publicity that preceded this book's arrival. Only an independent press with a philosophical commitment to ameliorating our civil discourse about race relations would have been capable of honoring the contract they had signed and seeing the project through to publication despite a concerted media effort to prevent its release. NewSouth's alternative edition removes the last possible excuse for public schools not to include these works in their curricula again. Students are no longer held captive to the n-word in assigned Mark Twain readings.

Many columnists seemed to believe that Mark Twain, if he were alive today, would have strenuously objected to any tampering with his texts, however minimal. I can only reply that no one, myself included, can channel the mind of an author more than a century after his death. We *do* know, however, that Twain was probably the most commercially minded literary artist our nation ever produced. He employed an army of salespeople to knock on doors in cities and farmlands, his latest book in hand, because that method of marketing was more lucrative than the retail bookstore system.

We are also aware that he was capable of undergoing enormous and continuous changes. He drastically modified his views about religion, Native Americans, slavery, history, philosophy, evolution, financial investing, Shakespeare, politics, colonial imperialism, and dozens of other subjects. He altered his public costume repeatedly, arriving on the East Coast in a shockingly unconventional sealskin coat and concluding his days on earth by donning white linen suits that became his final trademark. Who is to say that this chaser of fortunes and public attention might not smile upon a translation that revokes the expulsion of his boy books, welcomes them back into school classrooms, and gains new readers for these novels?

# Huckleberry Finn vs. Uncle Tom's Cabin as Antislavery Novels_____

Jocelyn A. Chadwick

Always a novel of controversy, import, and looming censorship, *Adventures of Huckleberry Finn* (1885) continually begs several questions. Just what does it contain that many high school teachers see as important for students? Why has it endured when so many books once considered "standards" in high school curricula have not? *Uncle Tom's Cabin* (1852), on the other hand, has maintained its status as a literary icon since its original publication. That novel clearly fomented significant and lasting impact on the slavery issue. Many Americans regard *Uncle Tom's Cabin* as fiction that crystallized the inhumanity of slavery and demanded change, which came with the Civil War.

Published two decades after the Civil War, *Huckleberry Finn* is the more visceral of the two novels. It relies on a subtle, yet complex form of satire to immerse readers in a reality of slavery, freedom, challenge, and survival—all contextualized within a blackness-and-whiteness paradigm. Mark Twain's novel is a change-agent wrapped in fiction for views and feelings internalized and externalized, positive and negative for Twain's nineteenth-century audience, as well as for audiences today. Stowe's novel provides safe, pleasant, even likable slaves surrounded by a diverse population of owners—both benevolent and horrid. *Huckleberry Finn*, by contrast, focuses on the development of a relationship between two unlikely individuals who are themselves microcosms of the nation during the nineteenth century. What continues to make *Huckleberry Finn* a novel one can neither put away nor discount lies with its continually putting a finger on the pulse of racism and racialist discourse. In her introduction to Oxford University Press's 1996 edition of *Huckleberry Finn*, Nobel Prize-winning author Toni Morrison wrote that the novel addresses and articulates our nation's "muffled rage."

Antislavery novels made up a respected and prescient genre during the nineteenth century. This essay will examine how *Huckleberry Finn* and *Uncle Tom's Cabin* function as examples of that genre. It will also examine the two novels as examples of the social media of both their time and our own.

## Antislavery Novels as Early Social Media

Were there eighteenth- and nineteenth-century equivalents of modern social media? How did earlier Americans connect on local, national, and international issues? As tension and atrocities emanating from slavery and abolition increased, "social media" of the period played a critical role in both the North and South to advocate for each side's cause, using illustrated and serialized magazines, newspapers, journals, flyers, and photography. Fiction, too, was a growing part of social media during that time. In the South, novels and short stories were particularly important in supporting the "naturalness" and "right order" of slavery, exemplified by writers like Thomas Nelson Page.

The North was influenced by both fiction and nonfiction, particularly in the forms of antislavery novels and slave narratives—both of which have persisted in relevance to this day. Slave narratives provided audiences with powerful, first-person, primary sources that immersed readers in the day-to-day struggles of surviving slavery, enduring unimaginable atrocities, and dodging the dangerous hazards of winning freedom. As antislavery novels *Uncle Tom's Cabin* and *Huckleberry Finn* exemplify two very distinctive pathways into this tumultuous period in America's literary history. Both remain groundbreaking social commentaries that still resonate. Stowe's novel perpetuates the ongoing and nagging stereotype of racial inferiority, despite its assertions to the contrary. Twain's *Huckleberry Finn* thrusts readers into the visceral brutality of slavery while at the same time introducing both free and enslaved black people as conscious, thinking, reflective human beings—real individuals with voice and choice. The black professor from Ohio in chapter 6 and Jim and the slaves on the Grangerford plantation in chapter 17 illustrate these traits.

Slave narratives and antislavery novels addressed specific audiences, occasions, and purposes. Slave narratives—often ghost written or written by former slaves themselves, such as Henry "Box" Brown, Josiah Henson, and Harriet Jacobs—first became popular in the late eighteenth century. Their readers were interested mostly in issues of slavery, freed slaves, and the often traumatic "journeys" to freedom. Antislavery novels offered fictional adaptations of slave narratives, making possible more diverse stories. Writers developed thematic threads with life-changing situations readers ordinarily would never experience themselves. From a modern perspective, the same thematic threads emanating from writers during the period of slavery morph to reflect current concerns through the lenses of not only such writers as Toni Morrison, William Faulkner, George Schuyler, Langston Hughes, Zora Neale Hurston, and Henry Louis Gates Jr., but also the concerns of students who read the novels.

## Uncle Tom's Cabin Examined

In *Uncle Tom's Cabin*, Harriet Beecher Stowe introduced in an extended piece of fiction her own ideas about the daily lives of slaves and about African Americans as individual people. The views she expressed differ keenly from the stark and unsettling reality recounted in the narrative of Josiah Henson, who escaped slavery in 1830. In her follow-up book *A Key to Uncle Tom's Cabin* (1853), Stowe claimed she had based her character Uncle Tom on Henson himself. However, any comparison of *The Life of Josiah Henson* (1849) with Stowe's novel reveals a stark difference in the temperaments of the fictional Uncle Tom and the real-life Henson. Stowe's novel emphasizes a gentle, innocent, child-like nature of slaves, their ready embracing of Christianity, and their need for the guidance and care of their benevolent masters. Tom and his wife, Chloe, accept their enslavement and, therefore, also accept their own dehumanization and minimization. Uncle Tom lacks the will to act in any sort of resisting way. Because of the huge success of Stowe's novel, "Uncle Tom" has come to personify all slaves, indeed all black people. In spite of Stowe's assertion that Josiah Henson had inspired her character, her rendering of Uncle Tom created in its wake a negative stereotype that has been a demeaning racial albatross to this day, not only among African Americans but also among other cultures as well.

Some readers and literary critics fail to see the harm of this sustained stereotype. The respected novelist Jane Smiley is an example. In January 1996, she published "Say It Ain't So, Huck: Second thoughts on Mark Twain's 'Masterpiece'" in *Harper's Magazine*, comparing *Huckleberry Finn* unfavorably to *Uncle Tom's Cabin*. She saw Stowe's rendering of African Americans of the slave era was positive and profound, as Stowe's slaves are "thoughtful, autonomous, and passionate black characters." Some contend Stowe created weak, suppliant black characters, which evolved into stereotypes that continue to loom darkly over African Americans today. To them, Smiley countered that Stowe's book is an "adept characterization of a whole world of whites and blacks . . . whose names have entered the American language as expressions. . . . The characters appear, one after another, vivified by their attitudes, desires, and opinions." Sambo, Uncle Tom, and other characters in Stowe's novel do indeed "all live," as Smiley asserts. Among African Americans of later generations, however, their names have lived as unwanted badges of shame and ignominy.

Clarence Major's book *From Juba to Jive: A Dictionary of African-American Slang* (1994) defines "Uncle Tom" as a "derogatory term for African-American; a servile 'Negro' . . . a black person who is culturally disloyal" (492). Major defines a "sambo" as a "white pejorative term for any person of African descent" that is now used ironically by black Americans (396). In *A Key to Uncle Tom's Cabin*, Stowe herself wrote,

> The negro race is confessedly more simple, docile, child-like and affectionate, than other races; and hence the divine graces of love and faith, when in-breathed by the Holy Spirit, find in their natural temperament a more congenial atmosphere (25).

Stowe went on to acknowledge that white and black children begin life at an equal pace, with the black children actually:

---

often superior to, the white children . . . but that there came a time when they became indifferent to learning, and made no further progress. This was invariably at the age when they were old enough to reflect upon life, and to perceive that society had "no place to offer them for which anything more would be requisite than the rudest and most elementary knowledge. (50)

Stowe's rendering of Uncle Tom has provided readers of both her time and the present with compassion and empathy, but at what cost? Nineteenth century pro-abolitionists read about escaped slaves who were vibrant and determined in their personal narratives and whose goal was freedom at all costs. Stowe's Uncle Tom, in contrast, does nothing to show any concern about freedom, not only for himself but also for his family. Stowe's citing the experiences of Josiah Henson's family as her primary foundation rings hollow in light of Henson's actual account, which is permeated with determination, anger, and a clear goal of freedom. Henson's views of master-slave relations stand in stark contrast to Uncle Tom's conversation with Chloe about their "blessings" of servitude in chapter 10 of *Uncle Tom's Cabin*.

In contrast to Uncle Tom, Henson talks about the maltreatment and dehumanization of "fellow beings" under slavery (*Life of Josiah Henson* 5). With disdain of his "coarse," "vulgar," and "licentious" owner, Henson describes the daily brutalities slaves faced, as they were underfed and without personal rights. "The natural tendency of slavery," he wrote, "is to convert the master into a tyrant, and the slave into the cringing, treacherous, false, and thieving victim of tyranny" (5). Henson eventually became sufficiently angry to consider killing his masters but relented after much reflection and thought:

I was about to lose the fruit of all my efforts at self-improvement, the character I had acquired, and the peace of mind which had never deserted me. All this came upon me instantly, and with a distinctness which made me almost think I heard it whispered in my ear; and I believe even turned my head to listen (48).

Instead of trying to kill his masters, Henson turned his attention solely to leading his family to freedom.

Stowe made an earnest effort to write a novel that would help end slavery and change the nation itself but simultaneously germinated and sustained racial and cultural stereotypes. Contemporary southern writers, such as Thomas Nelson Page, utilized those stereotypes in their own books, which championed the southern position on slavery.

Describing slave life for children and their masters' white children on plantations in an essay in *The Old South* (1892), Page wrote, "There were the busy children playing in groups, the boys of the family mingling with little darkies as freely as any other young animals, and forming the associations which tempered slavery and made the relation not one to be understood save by those who saw it" (11). Readers have found little difference between Page's and Stowe's depictions of African Americans, despite the latter's benevolent intentions. Stowe's modern readers thus find her work neither positive nor redeeming.

How did Stowe's African American contemporaries react to her novel? Black leaders supported *Uncle Tom's Cabin* during the nineteenth century but not without reservations. An excerpt from a letter black journalist Martin Delany wrote to fellow journalist Frederick Douglass offers a clear point of view:

> although Mrs. Stowe has ably, eloquently and pathetically portrayed some of the sufferings of the slave, is it any evidence that she has any sympathy for his thrice-morally crucified, semi-free brethren any where, or of the African race at all; when in the same world-renowned and widely circulated work, she sneers at Hayti—the only truly free and independent civilized black nation as such, or colored if you please, on the face of the earth—at the same time holding up the little dependent colonization settlement of Liberia in high estimation? I must be permitted to draw my own conclusions, when I say that I can see no other cause for this singular discrepancy in Mrs. Stowe's interest in the colored race, than that one is independent of, and the other subservient to, white men's power (*Frederick Douglass' Paper*, 6 May 1853).

In this same correspondence, Delany chides Douglass for "praising" Stowe's work, as so many did during the time, and notes Stowe's support for "colonization"—a term then used for transporting African Americans away from the United States to colonize lands elsewhere, such as in Liberia in West Africa. Douglass's reply to Delany is revealing. After reminding Delany of his own past support of a colonization scheme, he dismissed a chapter in *Uncle Tom's Cabin* advocating colonization, and went on to defend Stowe:

> Whoever will bring a straw's weight of influence to break the chains of our brother bondmen, or whisper one word of encouragement and sympathy to our proscribed race in the North, shall be welcomed by us to that philanthropic field of labor. . . . Who doubts that Mrs. Stowe is more of an abolitionist now than when she wrote that chapter? — We believe that lady to be but at the beginning of her labors for the colored people of this country. (*Frederick Douglass' Paper*, 6 May 1853)

As an antislavery novel, *Uncle Tom's Cabin* raised white feelings against slavery but did not necessarily move them to consider racial equality. Stowe's depiction of black characters lessened fear and resistance to African Americans, whom she portrays as mostly meek and malleable. Stowe made the strong and rambunctious Topsy seem safe by transforming her into a Christian missionary to Africa. Indeed, by the end of the novel, every black character with anything like an independent spirit has left the United States. Jane Smiley argues that "The power of *Uncle Tom's Cabin* is the power of brilliant analysis married to great wisdom of feeling." However, if Stowe's white readers had been aware of her book *A Key to Uncle Tom's Cabin* and of her liberal modification of Josiah Henson's real narrative, would they continue to regard her novel as a champion of ending the oppression of slaves?

Although not one mid-nineteenth-century African American thinker is known publicly to have dismissed *Uncle Tom's Cabin*, we can understand that silence. At that time, well before the Civil War, no other piece of fiction existed that codified and showcased the plight of slaves—benign or otherwise. At the same time, however, Stowe does not wholly depict the bifurcated nature of the United States at a time when the presence of a growing number of free and vocal African Americans was being felt. These individuals supported the Underground Railroad and published newspapers and journals and traveled on the lecture circuit, explaining their experiences, anger, and frustrations.

After publication of *Uncle Tom's Cabin*, the complexities of slavery and racial relations still waited to be explored in fiction. Meanwhile, the wounds of the coming Civil War and its aftermath also waited to be written. Most significantly, perhaps, the human face of African American slavery was also waiting to be rendered in fiction. That task would fall to an unsuspecting Mark Twain, who changed everything.

### *Huckleberry Finn* Examined

In 1874, nine years after the Civil War ended and twenty-two years after *Uncle Tom's Cabin* had first appeared, Mark Twain published "A True Story: Word for Word, As I Heard It," a 2,175-word narrative in *The Atlantic Monthly* that marked a conscious step into more realistically rendering African Americans in nineteenth-century fiction. Within those two decades, many African Americans—both free and freed—had entered his personal life and helped inspire his writing. They included not only luminaries, such as Frederick Douglass, but also humbler folks, such as John T. Lewis, whom he later used as a model for Jim in *Huckleberry Finn*, and Mary Ann Cord, his sister-in-law's cook, on whom he modeled the central figure in "A True Story."

Thanks to Mark Twain's relationships with these individuals and others, America's understandings of the antislavery novel, the significance of the slave narrative, and the country's very literary heritage would forever change. "A True Story" and Mark Twain's first solo novel, *The Adventures of Tom Sawyer* (1876), foreshadowed what was to come in a dynamic way. These were, however, but primers that allowed Mark Twain to find his own voice, his own place, his own protean perspective on pivotal social issues that would take form in *Huckleberry Finn*, which was first published in

---

America in 1885. Up to that time, most antislavery novels had been serious, even tragic, not allowing for reader distance. To create this readerly distance, Mark Twain utilized a different form of satire for this novel—a form that he began exploring in "A True Story."

Mark Twain's masterful control and style with satire powers *Huckleberry Finn*. His use of satire is at once protean and organic in that it allows for reader adaptation in inviting exploration and continuous audience identification. Stowe wrote her novel *before* the Civil War. Mark Twain wrote his *after* the war, as Reconstruction was failing. Twain utilizes an extended-condensed metaphor to scaffold and contextualize his rhetorical message. All metaphors have two parts: The vehicle part packages, or conveys the message; the tenor part—whether stated (explicit) or implied (condensed)—develops the metaphor's meaning and message. The vehicle that carries *Huckleberry Finn*'s metaphor is the journey on the Mississippi River with brief sojourns ashore. Huck and Jim's interactions with "organized" civilization and, more importantly, with each other provide the tenor, the idea or thematic message.

Jim and Huck represent the central microcosm of the nation—both then and now, yes, with regard to race but not solely. They also represent other comparisons to the human condition that shift with time and audience. Moreover, Huck does not simply treat Jim as an object lacking feelings, as Smiley suggests. Americans reading *Huckleberry Finn* during the 1880s would have known about such issues as slavery, abolition, the Emancipation Proclamation, and the horrific war. They also would have been all too familiar with the hope of President Abraham Lincoln's Reconstruction plans that died with his assassination.

The need for the elaborate metaphor Twain incorporated in his novel was not, however, merely for his contemporary audience alone but also for future audiences. The familiar antislavery thematic threads nineteenth-century audiences readily understood would demand more investment from later audiences seeking to understand nineteenth-century language and contexts. The "backstory" of slavery and slave juxtaposed with nineteenth-century racial dichotomies of black and white would require more critical thinking and immersion.

Jim, for example, is decidedly not—as Smiley and other critics have asserted—muted, lacking autonomy, a passive individual. Twain's audience would have immediately grasped Jim's depth. Under Mark Twain's deft, stylistic layering of metaphor, modern audiences, too, can experience both historical and immediate messages of his text.

The last fourteen chapters of *Huckleberry Finn*, in which Tom Sawyer directs an unnecessary and absurdly complicated plan to effect Jim's escape from the Phelps farm, are highly controversial because of the indignities to which the plan subjects Jim. Mark Twain's subtle irony and satire in those chapters, however, vindicate them. As Jim makes his final turn toward full independence—exerting his right to choose and chart his path—he decides to remain with Tom Sawyer, fully realizing the dangerous consequences. In addition, as Jim again *chooses* to remain silent rather than "give up" Huck and Tom when he is recaptured, readers begin to see this book as something more than the traditional antislavery novel. What some readers and critics have failed to comprehend lies with Jim's final decisive movement into establishing his own, separate voice, regardless of the consequences. When Tom is shot in chapter 40, Huck tells Jim to leave him and take what is surely his final chance at freedom. Jim, however, responds,

> "Well, den, dis is de way it look to me, Huck. Ef it wuz *him* dat 'uz bein' sot free, en one er de boys wuz to git shot, would he say, 'Go on en save me, nemmine 'bout a doctor f'r to save dis one?' . . . No, sah—I doan' budge a step out'n dis place, 'dout a doctor; not ef it's forty year!"

Slaves often used a speaking technique known as double-voicing—essentially a defensive measure they used to tell whites what they wanted to hear. By this point in the novel, however, Jim knows he can express himself freely to Huck and no longer needs double-voicing. As a result, audiences read and hear Jim's authentic free and independent voice.

The novel ends with Huck's declaring his intent to "light out for the Territory . . . because Aunt Sally she's going to adopt me and sivilize me and I can't stand it. I been there before." Huck refuses to be "civilized" as he has come to understand what the term means. Modern readers can grasp the irony not only in such statements but also in the novel as a whole. Nothing is fixed, resolved, or happy.

*Huckleberry Finn* is a keenly different, universal, and unshakable antislavery novel because it far exceeds the parameters of traditional slave narratives and antislavery novels. It charts and crystallizes for future audiences "an unlettered slave, clinging to the hope of freedom," as Langston Hughes wrote in *A Pictorial History of Black Americans* (235). Readers of *Tom Sawyer* had looked forward to Huck and Tom's further exploits in Twain's much-anticipated sequel. To the surprise, dismay, and even anger of some readers, *Huckleberry Finn* utilized the boyish exploits as contextual window-dressing in order to pursue a thematic thread he subversively interweaves into *Huckleberry Finn*. Huck recounts his own narrative. He and Tom are still the best of friends—at least, at the novel's beginning—but quite quickly, the boyish sequel morphs into a serious and nuanced slave narrative, embodying the visceral impact many of the primary-resource slave narratives contain.

Huck and Jim drive *Huckleberry Finn*, while pivotal roles are played by such peripheral characters as the free black Ohio professor, Pap Finn, the slave community on the Grangerford plantation, Colonel Sherburn, a mob, and Aunt Sally. Using these characters as backdrops, Mark Twain captures with unrivaled clarity and deliberateness diverse personalities and voices of free, freed, and enslaved African Americans. Because he renders those voices consistently, he organically illustrates a real dynamic lacking in monolithic, docile, and nonresistant black voices that Stowe's Uncle Tom typifies. Twain even allows readers to hear and experience slaves' masterful manipulation and use of double-voicing—a language manipulation they found necessary in order to communicate among themselves.

An obvious example of double-voicing occurs in chapter 18 when Huck's "assigned" Grangerford slave, Jack, entreats him (using Huck's assumed name): "Mars Jawge, if you'll come down into de swamp, I'll show you a whole stack o' water-moccasins." There are no water-moccasins, there is only Jim—Jim and a rebuilt raft! Another, more subtle double-voicing occurs between Huck and Jim in chapter 16. Here and in earlier chapters, readers experience Jim's mastery of language, logic, and persuasion. In that chapter, Huck leaves the raft with the intent of doing the "right thing" by turning Jim in before he can steal his family from their legal owners. Huck feels resolved to do that, but what Jim then says shakes him badly:

> "I's a free man, en I couldn't ever ben free ef it hadn' ben for Huck; Huck done it. Jim won't ever forgit you, Huck; you's de bes' fren' Jim's ever had; en you's de *only* fren' ole Jim's got, now."

What stops Huck cold without his even understanding why is Jim's arrangement and manipulation of language and argument: "Dah you goes, de ole true Huck; de on'y white genlman dat ever kep' his promise to ole Jim." In both classical and modern rhetoric, such lines persuasively play on both Huck's sense of ethics and his personal feelings. The logic is inescapable, too. Consequently, as Huck tries his best to deconstruct what happens when he consciously elects to go against his intention of turning Jim in, readers see and experience with him the result of powerful rhetoric and relationships that emanate from it as he muses on his dilemma:

> Then, I thought a minute and says to myself, hold on,—s'pose you'd a done right and give Jim up; would you feel better than what you do now? No, says I, I'd feel bad—I'd feel just the same way I do now. Well, then, says I, what's the use you learning to do right, when it's troublesome to do right and ain't no trouble to do wrong, and the wages is just the same? I was stuck. I couldn't answer that.

Huck decides to do nothing, save what he and Jim are already doing because going against Jim would *feel* ethically and morally wrong. Jim drives this scene and its results, as he does in many scenes throughout the novel. With many similar scenes, modern students view archetypal thematic threads as they were in the past and, more importantly, as those threads relate to them today—whiteness vs. blackness, stereotypes vs. archetypes, hero vs. antihero, docility vs.

resistance, voice vs. voicelessness, identity vs. invisibility, maturity vs. immaturity, freedom vs. enslavement, freedom of choice vs. lack of choice. It is this protean adaptability and resonance that Mark Twain's novel possesses that transcends Stowe's novel.

## The Novels Today

Today's students naturally draw comparisons and contrasts between *Uncle Tom's Cabin* and *Huckleberry Finn*. The former is an early antislavery novel from a time period well familiar with the genre. The novel extends the impact of the century's "social media," just as the African American periodical press did. While much of northern social media focused on slavery and its abolition, the African American press also addressed racial independence and uplift in newspapers edited by Frederick Douglass and others. Stowe's novel specifically examines and immerses readers in America's history with its "peculiar institution."

While Stowe's novel brought attention to the issue of slavery, it also brought with it a broad-brush of mono-character-typing, the import of which yet permeates the American language today. Not from this novel alone, but with its northern stamp of approval, it has helped perpetuate stereotypes of African Americans as unable to think critically, not desiring independence, having a docile and childlike nature, being unable to understand family, and needing to serve. Stowe herself further reifies this perception in her follow-up book, *The Key to Uncle Tom's Cabin*.

As time has passed, so has the sustained impact of *Uncle Tom's Cabin*. In 1949, the African American novelist James Baldwin called the book "a very bad novel" describing it as "self-righteous" and filled with "virtuous sentimentality" ("Everybody's Protest Novel," *Zero*, spring 1949). In a March 17, 1963 television interview, black nationalist leader Malcolm X called civil rights icon Martin Luther King Jr. "a twentieth century . . . Uncle Tom who is doing the same things today to keep negroes defenseless in the face of attacks that Uncle Tom did down on the plantation". Harvard scholar Henry Louis Gates Jr. both praises and critiques the novel, first in regarding it as a text that must not be excluded from the literary landscape if readers are to understand the nineteenth century. Secondly, Gates maintains the necessity of this text because of what and how Stowe renders her perspective and position on African Americans as a people: "no one respectable can represent race in the way Harriet Beecher Stowe did as a real thing that exists in these sort of blocs or categories that are perpetuated biologically and be taken seriously." (*Uncle Tom's Cabin Reconsidered*, 2006).

In contrast, Mark Twain's *Huckleberry Finn* made use of the archetypal family structure and then expanded it into a variety of blends. Finally, he interwove all these blends into configurations that our students today not only understand but with which they also resonate and engage. Twain's kneading and reworking the paradigms within the thematic threads intrigue today's students. He piques their curiosity and interest from gender representation to parenting, to types of extended relationships. Race, of course, has been the most traditional point of departure of discussion and analysis. But even with this thread, students today, coming from myriad cultures and ethnicities, view the issues differently, even with more complex filaments than in the past. Because of all that has historically and socially transpired, students today are a different audience altogether: more focused, less romantic, demanding texts to speak to them and their experiences. Toni Morrison concluded her 1996 introduction to Oxford's *Huckleberry Finn* with this appraisal: "For a hundred years, the argument that this novel *is* has been identified, reidentified, examined, waged, and advanced. What it cannot be is dismissed. It is classic literature, which is to say it heaves, manifests, and lasts."

Some have described *Huckleberry Finn* as America's epic, while others have decried it as trash. Still others have described it as racist. Some have sought to rewrite it, arguing such bowdlerization is undertaken for the sake of African American children—children who somehow require the aid of benevolent white and black critics to think and reflect for them. This novel lives and will continue to live because Mark Twain created a work of art whose very skeleton is, for Americans of all dispositions, an ongoing and irresistible dialectic about ourselves and Other—how we view Other, our relationship to Other, our space and place with Other, our sharing and living with Other. That Other can be white or black or Asian; straight, gay, or transgender; man or woman; Protestant or Catholic; Christian or Muslim; and the diverging patterns continue to grow.

Today's students are proving more than capable of having these hard conversations; indeed, they flourish in them because they want to think and break apart and analyze and understand. In 1950, T. S. Eliot summed up the monumental impact of *Huckleberry Finn* succinctly:

> *Adventures of Huckleberry Finn* is the only one of Mark Twain's various books which can be called a masterpiece. I do not suggest that it is his only book of permanent interest; but it is the only one in which his genius is completely realized, and the only one which creates its own category (Introduction to Cresset edition of *Huckleberry Finn*, 1950).

We need both *Uncle Tom's Cabin* and *Huckleberry Finn* to remind us of where we were, to warn us away from sentimentality fraught with preconceptions, to prepare us for where we are going, to provide a literary context that foments exploration and conversation without the necessity of pointing fingers at ourselves until we are ready. Mark Twain's book accomplishes this task generation to generation— visceral, at the moment, minute by minute visual, close, immediate, and sometimes unrelenting. Simply put, the novel still proves to be irresistible.

# CRITICAL READINGS

# Animating the Unsaid: Between the Lines in *Huckleberry Finn*

Jon Clinch

A few years ago I had the opportunity to take an unusual look at *Adventures of Huckleberry Finn*. Inasmuch as Mark Twain's most important novel has been examined from most every direction, the idea of anyone's taking "an unusual look" is probably suspect on its face. Yet the world is always full of new angles and new possibilities, especially concerning a subject as deep and rewarding as *Huckleberry Finn*.

My project was the writing of a novel called *Finn* (2007), which set out to be "the dark, secret history of Huckleberry Finn's father." Essentially, the aim of the novel was to explore some important things that Twain suggested but left unsaid in *Huckleberry Finn*. Developing it called for a reading of Mark Twain's novel that was both close and expansive, an approach that instead of being critical or scholarly was engaged and deeply sympathetic. It would be the willful act of a reader prepared to enter Twain's world via both the text on the page and the text left unwritten.

As an act of sympathetic imagination, such a reading of *Huckleberry Finn* could not focus directly on Twain's technique or methods. Quite the contrary: my intent was to be captivated only by the narrative, immersed completely in Huck's story as if it had actually taken place and could be discovered in full by a kind of visionary belief.

I had reasons. First, I needed to avoid the trap of *reimagining* Pap Finn. He'd already been fully imagined; to alter him so as to suit some purpose of my own would be to violate the original material and dishonor Twain. Not that that kind of thing is not done all the time, of course. Gregory Maguire's popular 1995 novel *Wicked: The Life and Times of the Wicked Witch of the West*, which inspired a smash-hit Broadway musical, for example, gives us a misunderstood and sympathetic Wicked Witch of the West. Could someone have

made Pap Finn into the wronged hero of his son's story? Certainly. But it would have perpetrated an injustice upon the memory of Mark Twain. (We shall let L. Frank Baum's defenders make their own stand, should they ever be so inclined.)

Second, insisting that behind Huck's naïve and perhaps unreliable telling of his own story in Twain's novel is a cohesive reality with conditions and consequences of its own provides a useful way to understand the narrative as Huck gives it to us. No story ever told is complete, after all. And by doing *Huckleberry Finn* the honor of taking it for Gospel (however transmuted by the voice of a child with objectives of his own), we gain a lens for interpreting not only what is on the page, but what is not.

Third, it has always seemed to me that while Twain left holes in Pap's story, he also left a number of clues with which we might fill them in. Consider the scene in chapter 9 in which Huck and Jim find Pap's body in a floating house:

> [Jim] went, and bent down and looked, and says: "It's a dead man. Yes, indeedy; naked, too. He's ben shot in de back. I reck'n he's ben dead two er three days. Come in, Huck, but doan' look at his face—it's too gashly."

> I didn't look at him at all. Jim threwed some old rags over him, but he needn't done it; I didn't want to see him. There was heaps of old greasy cards scattered around over the floor, and old whisky bottles, and a couple of masks made out of black cloth; and all over the walls was the ignorantest kind of words and pictures made with charcoal. There was two old dirty calico dresses, and a sun-bonnet, and some women's underclothes hanging against the wall, and some men's clothing, too. We put the lot into the canoe—it might come good. There was a boy's old speckled straw hat on the floor; I took that, too. And there was a bottle that had had milk in it, and it had a rag stopper for a baby to suck. We would a took the bottle, but it was broke. There was a seedy old chest, and an old hair trunk with the hinges broke. They stood open, but there warn't nothing left in them that was any account. The way things was scattered about we reckoned the people left in a hurry, and warn't fixed so as to carry off most of their stuff.

If we trust Twain completely, and we must, then none of those objects—not the scrawled words and pictures, not the black cloth masks, not the speckled straw hat—are in that room by accident. And even though Huck does not grasp that the body in the corner is that of his father, we must ultimately reckon with the objects surrounding it if we mean to chart the course of Pap's life and death.

## A Machine for Constructing Stories

In constructing *The Castle of Crossed Destinies* (1969; trans. 1977), Italo Calvino arranged and rearranged a deck of tarot cards as a means of generating his book's multiple narratives, letting the cards function as what he called "a machine for constructing stories." In the course of imagining *Finn*, I set out to use the contents of Pap's death room in much the same way.

The objects present at the scene of Pap's death in *Huckleberry Finn* led me to some unexpected places and sometimes even forged connections with other bits of Huck's narrative. The crime suggested by the pair of black masks, for example, led to a black woman and her child who serve as doubles for Huck and his mother, as well as to an encounter with the scoundrel known as the King in his life beyond the pages of *Huckleberry Finn*. The broken wooden leg conjured a fatal encounter with a Philadelphia lawyer, representative of the lost heights of Pap's family background. The words and pictures graven on the walls became a combination confessional and roadmap of Pap's guilty conscience (chapter 8 and elsewhere). And the boy's speckled straw hat grew into a sad memento and fateful clue to the story of Pap's bloody death.

That these and other objects led where they did is anything but a tribute to my own imagination. It is a statement on the power inherent in the selective authority of fiction.

## Leaving In, Leaving Out

Fiction accumulates power by convincing us that it is true, and one way that it does so is by telling not *everything*, but only *the crucial things*. Thus it lures the reader into making an investment of his own, supplying lesser details, helping to tell the story as it moves forward. In *Adventures of Huckleberry Finn,* Twain did an especially masterful job of leaving things out. Pap, for example, appears only sporadically in the text—and is gone entirely by the close of chapter 9—and yet he manages to remain in our minds even during his absences. Huck is obsessed with him, naturally, and mentions him often when he is not on stage in person. But it is more than Huck's response that drives our interest in him. He is the first hint we have that the world in which our beloved narrator exists is no carefree idyll. Pap is vividly and stinkingly alive, depraved and debauched, a figure of unknowable evil and bottomless threat. By portraying him so—and by granting him life in the way that great literature can— Twain makes his absences as compelling as his appearances.

Where has he been when he materializes in Huck's room at the widow's in chapter 5? Where does he go when he leaves? These are not idle questions, not for Huckleberry Finn and not for us, since wherever Pap may be, he is forever haunting the margins of this book.

Twain gave us one more notably absent character in *Huckleberry Finn:* the boy's mother. She is mentioned only once, when Pap describes her during that scene at the widow's, and we know her only as illiterate and dead. That is it. And yet Huck is so real, and Pap is so real, that we wonder in spite of ourselves what kind of woman she might have been. Those two questions—"Where does Pap go?" and "Who was Huck's mother?"—were among those that *Finn* sought to answer.

Huck himself, as a child and as a first-person narrator, can be a source for only so much. First, his knowledge is limited. Second, he may well be concealing things or at least coloring them. His voice itself—humorous, naïve, abundantly tolerant—actively softens any sequence he narrates, however grim or brutal its content may be. I suspect that on Twain's part, this was in some measure a means to excuse his own inability—given the Victorian culture of his time and his presumed audience of boys—to recreate on the page the kind of violence and cruelty known to him from his childhood in the Mississippi valley. Consider this, from his *Notebooks & Journals* of the time: "I can't say, 'They cut his head off, or stabbed him, etc.,'

& describe the blood & the agony in his face" (notebook 18, page 312). Neither could, nor would, Huck.

A novelist writing today faces no such strictures, of course. So other, more explicit, readings of the events good-naturedly narrated by Huck become possible.

## Filling in the Details: A Four-Part Approach

As I strove to fill in the gaps—both in Pap's appearances during *Huckleberry Finn* and in his larger life story—it became clear that at least four different approaches were available to me. In retrospect, they derive from choices made by Twain as he constructed the novel, particularly as the result of Huck's character and first-person narration. Let's group them as matters of limitation, naiveté, shading, and concealment and take a closer look at examples of each.

### *Limitation:*

When any first-person narrator tells his story, the events that he can credibly describe (to the extent that his narration is itself credible) are limited to those that he has personally witnessed. It is perilous enough to trust him on these matters, without extending our trust to things he has only heard about second-hand. In Huck's case, it is particularly risky to trust anything he may have heard—even verbatim—from his manipulative miscreant of a father. Thus Pap's adventures in town *minus Huck*—the encounter with the black professor, for example (chapter 6), or his attempted rehabilitation at the hands of the new judge (chapter 5)—provide enormous opportunities for development.

My method was always the same: to trust the general outline of the story as told by or to Huck (new judge, fresh clothes, broken arm; black professor, voting rights, fury) while dramatizing the material so as to explore particulars of character. In the first case, a fuller exploration of Finn's overnight at the house of the new judge provides a chance to contrast civilized child-rearing methods with his more primitive ways; to work out a fully satisfying version of the broken-arm story that Huck can only telegraph; and to present a close-up description of frontier medicine at work—setting the stage for a similar but more brutal scene to follow toward the book's end. In the second case, putting Finn himself face to face with the black professor lets us witness at close range his ignorance, his arrogance, his entitlement, and his dangerously wounded dignity. It also provides a set of interrelated links among Finn's desperate poverty, his constant engagement with the legal and penal systems, and the economic and legal underpinnings of black/white relations in slave states vs. free.

Here's the entirety of Huck's version, narrated at second-hand by Pap himself (chapter 6).

> There was a free nigger there from Ohio—a mulatter, most as white as a white man. He had the whitest shirt on you ever see, too, and the shiniest hat; and there ain't a man in that town that's got as fine clothes as what he had; and he had a gold watch and chain, and a silver-headed cane . . They said he was a p'fessor in a college, and could talk all kinds of languages, and knowed everything. And that ain't the wust. They said he could vote when he was at home. Well, that let me out. Thinks I, what is the country a-coming to? It was 'lection day, and I was just about to go and vote myself if I warn't too drunk to get there; but when they told me there was a State in this country where they'd let that nigger vote, I drawed out. I says I'll never vote agin. Them's the very words I said; they all heard me; and the country may rot for all me—I'll never vote agin as long as I live.

Here's part of the expanded version from chapter 6 of *Finn*, in which Pap questions the black professor's white companion:

> "New in town?" says Finn from his seat by the fencepost. "Your friend I mean." Looking straight at the white man and the white man only, with an intensity that makes a show of excluding the other.

> The white man has been so long so far beyond contact with an individual like Finn that he accepts his question without reservation. . . . "Why, yes," he says, and again: "Why, yes indeed."

> "Thought so."

"You fixing to sell him?"

"I beg your pardon?"

"Not that he's likely to fetch much." Here he permits his gaze to wander over the black man's regally slim figure. "Not by the look of him."

"Sir."

"Ain't nothing worth any less than a puny nigger. Other'n a puny nigger in a ten-dollar suit, putting on airs."

"Come along, professor," says the white man to the black. "We're late for your introductions at the church." He takes his associate by the elbow but finds him immovable, for the professor has been turned to stone by Finn's effrontery. He spreads wide his legs and cocks his head to one side and leans forward upon his cane, transfixed by their interlocutor as he would be by a Siberian tiger in a circus parade.

"You mind your master," says Finn with a dismissive wave of his hand. "Git along now, boy."

## Naiveté:

If he is like most children, we can count on Huck to overestimate his own capabilities. He is certainly resourceful; we see that particularly in his escape from the shack where his father holds him prisoner (chapter 7). Yet there is a self-aware, Tom Sawyeresque theatricality to the crime that he fakes to cover his tracks: the submerged sack of rocks, the bloodied axe, the sacrificed pig. He takes pride in it all, though. And he persuades himself (and thus probably his readers) that the affair is a complete success.

Here's Huck's self-narrated version, from chapter 5:

I took the axe and smashed in the door. I beat it and hacked it considerable a-doing it. I fetched the pig in, and took him back nearly to the table and hacked into his throat with the axe, and laid him down on the ground to bleed . . Well, next I took an old sack and put a lot of big rocks in it—all I could drag—and I started it from the pig, and dragged it to the door and through the woods down to the river and dumped it in, and down it sunk, out of sight. You could easy see that something had been dragged over the ground . . .

Well, last I pulled out some of my hair, and blooded the axe good, and stuck it on the back side, and slung the axe in the corner. Then I took up the pig and held him to my breast with my jacket (so he couldn't drip) till I got a good piece below the house and then dumped him into the river.

If, however, we believe fully in the Pap that Twain has given us— his innate cunning, along with the wilderness skills of a man who draws his living from the river—we ought to be less certain about the success of Huck's charade. Thus in *Finn* (chapter 6), Huck's father instantly detects the many fabrications of the crime scene, and although he draws a tainted conclusion based on his longstanding hatred for Judge Thatcher and the Widow Douglas, he gets closer to the truth than Huck in his innocence would ever presume.

When Finn returns to the squatter's shack, he finds the place transformed by violence:

"You Huck."

No answer comes from within or without, and the single room lies empty not just of his son but of his own every earthly possession. Food and fishlines and matches, skillet and coffeepot and jug. All of them gone. Only the axe remains, bloodied all over and with a bit of hair stuck to the back of it as if from a blow to the boy's head, and from this significantly ostentatious detail he deduces not Huck's actual plan for counterfeiting his own murder and stealing away under cover of it, but a different and more cunning plan altogether— this one contrived by Judge Thatcher and the widow Douglas.

"They think they can steal him that easy," he says to himself as he rubs the axehead clean with the heel of his hand. "They think I'll give him up for dead like a goddamned beast." He plucks away the tuft of hair and brushes it off on his pantleg.

His instincts serve him well, drawing him onward to discover and discount the rest of Huck's planted evidence.

> He walks the path to the riverbank and discerns there in waist-deep water all he needs for confirmation: A sack, a perfectly good and useful sack, filled with rocks by that wasteful Thatcher or some other in his employ and drawn across the grass to the water as if Huck's body itself had been there dragged. He vows to deny Judge Thatcher the satisfaction of misusing his property, and wades in to recover it less its burden of rocks. Sitting to wring it out upon the bank he catches sight of further sign, footprints in the dirt and a drop or two of blood, and he scouts down along the waterside until he comes upon marks where someone looks to have nearly lost his balance throwing some other thing into the water, some other thing that proves to be a half-grown pig with its throat cut, nearly bled-out and still foggily abloom and staining the Mississippi a vague dark red. . . . He wallows it out and skins it and cleans it with his clasp-knife, and he pledges that none shall have a bite of it save himself. Surely not that son of his who probably went off without a fight and is now living high on some other hog at either the judge's table or the widow's.

### Shading:

As noted earlier, the innocence and childish joy in Huck's voice colors every aspect of the book—including, necessarily, reports about his relationship and interactions with his father. Thus it is easy—and perhaps inevitable, given the difficulty of telling the worst about your only living relative—for Huck to narrate even the scene where his father returns home drunk and furious (chapter 6) as a kind of slapstick comedy:

> Pap was agoing on so he never noticed where his old limber legs was taking him to, so he went head over heels over the tub of salt pork and barked both shins, and the rest of his speech was all the hottest kind of language—mostly hove at the nigger and the govment, though he give the tub some, too, all along, here and there. He hopped around the cabin considerable, first on one leg and then on the other, holding first one shin and then the other one, and at last he let out with his left foot all of a sudden and fetched the tub a rattling kick. But it

warn't good judgment, because that was the boot that had a couple of his toes leaking out of the front end of it; so now he raised a howl that fairly made a body's hair raise, and down he went in the dirt, and rolled there, and held his toes; and the cussing he done then laid over anything he had ever done previous. He said so his own self afterwards. He had heard old Sowberry Hagan in his best days, and he said it laid over him, too; but I reckon that was sort of piling it on, maybe.

Peeling away the warmth of Huck's voice and substituting an elevated and nearly biblical tone, *Finn* reveals something darker—and more dangerous and more deeply unhinged—in that very sequence (chapter 6):

> Bit by bit he descends to the level of drunkenness that he had attained previous to arriving home and then he proceeds beyond it. . . . He rages against the blacks and the government and the law, all of which he insists have conspired to bring him to ruin. Something about his drunkenness gives him the idea that he must stand up in order to orate properly, and every time he attempts to do so he loses his balance and falls, spilling his drink and catching himself with his sore left arm. This only fuels his wrath and his urgent sense that remaining successfully upon his feet is essential to his thwarted purpose and so he rages against the table and against the chair and against the tub of salt pork over which he takes a tumble for they too just like the blacks and the government and the law have been laying for him since the day he was born.

### Concealment:

We have seen how Huck may, wittingly or otherwise, color the facts of his story, but might it ever be possible that he is actually lying? If so, there's no more likely subject for untruth than his uncomfortable relationship with his father. Which is why the one event in *Huckleberry Finn* that I chose to take as entirely manufactured—as something I ought to ignore entirely or even actively refute—was the sequence where Huck awakens on Jackson's Island and finds a great search party in pursuit of his corpse (chapter 8).

Well, I was dozing off again when I thinks I hears a deep sound of "boom!" away up the river. . . . I hopped up, and went and looked out at a hole in the leaves, and I see a bunch of smoke laying on the water a long ways up. . . . And there was the ferryboat full of people floating along down. I knowed what was the matter now. "Boom!" I see the white smoke squirt out of the ferryboat's side. You see, they was firing cannon over the water, trying to make my carcass come to the top.

I was pretty hungry, but it warn't going to do for me to start a fire, because they might see the smoke. So I set there and watched the cannon-smoke and listened to the boom. The river was a mile wide there, and it always looks pretty on a summer morning—so I was having a good enough time seeing them hunt for my remainders if I only had a bite to eat. Well, then I happened to think how they always put quicksilver in loaves of bread and float them off, because they always go right to the drownded carcass and stop there.

Is it likely that such efforts might be made to raise the corpse of an outcast like Huck? Perhaps, given his newfound wealth and his presence in the life of the widow. And yet I have doubts. Further evidence that this episode could be a fabrication comes a few paragraphs later, as Huck names some of the people aboard the ferry.

By-and-by she come along, and she drifted in so close that they could a run out a plank and walked ashore. Most everybody was on the boat. Pap, and Judge Thatcher, and Bessie [Becky] Thatcher, and Jo Harper, and Tom Sawyer, and his old Aunt Polly, and Sid and Mary, and plenty more.

Huck reports that his own father—the town drunk, who prizes him only for the $6,000 fortune that he acquired from Injun Joe at the end of *Tom Sawyer*—has joined forces with Judge Thatcher to hunt for him. If we have been reading at all closely, this act of paternal concern is well nigh unbelievable. (I can imagine one credible reading of it, but it is unlikely because it requires Pap to have analyzed, correctly or incorrectly, some link between finding Huck's body and accessing the boy's fortune.) Regardless, this is the one spot where I felt compelled to diverge from Huck's narrative, and send Finn off in an entirely different direction.

### Forbidden Fruit: Imagining Huck's Mother

For many readers, the most shocking development in *Finn* is the revelation that Huck's mother is black. I blame Twain himself, who raised the question of her identity in the first place: what kind of woman, under what circumstances, would have a child by the monstrous Pap Finn?

I saw a woman under duress. A woman anything but free to exercise her own will. A woman friendless, powerless, far from home, and perhaps even imprisoned. Finn was always a great imprisoner of those he loved—or of those he ought to have loved. Think again of the scenes in the shack where he holds Huck captive (chapters 6 and 7). He has his eye on the boy's $6,000, but all he can get his hands on is the boy himself. Such is his frustration. Such is his fatherhood.

Which brings us to Mary, my imagined mother of Huck. She is a slave girl, shanghaied from aboard a steamboat in the middle of a slave revolt (chapter 7). Might Huck Finn's mother be a slave? More to the point: Might Huck Finn's mother be a black woman?

For me, it suggested answers to a number of other questions I had been asking. For one, how did Huck acquire his deep intimacy with slave lore and superstition? For another, why was Finn not an ordinary racist, but an extraordinary and absolutely virulent one?

The usual answer to the first question is that Huck, a poor child lacking much in the way of family, spends his time in the back lots of the village associating with slaves like Jim at their work and at their leisure, assimilating their culture as his own. Fair enough. That is a more likely scenario than the way an ordinary boy of the town would gain such knowledge: through observing slaves at work in his own household. Huck, whose father sometimes sleeps with the hogs and does not seem to mind, clearly does not come from a slave-holding family.

But what if there were another answer? What if Huck gained his intimacy with slave customs through the most intimate relationship that he could have enjoyed—that of mother and son? It would explain a lot—including the source of his good heart. We know it did not come from his old man.

Speaking of Finn returns us to that second question: why was his racism so potent? Racism is generally a set of learned beliefs, so we can presume that he got the raw materials from his parents or at least from his community. But learning or passing on racism as outsized as Finn's would be quite an achievement.

So I thought it would be worth exploring how a triggering event could turn ordinary, tap-water racism into the surging Niagara that we see in Twain's fully realized Pap. A triggering event like falling in love—after a fashion and against his will—with the very incarnation of his culture's most powerful taboo: a black woman. It would come as a surprise to everyone and especially to himself.

Whether Twain dreamed that we might pursue such a conclusion is unknowable, of course. He certainly did not forbid it. And above all, the nature of his work as a novelist—putting this in, leaving that out, convincing us of the reality of the world and circumstances that he (through Huck) describes—makes it utterly possible. That is just one of the gifts inherent in a deeply realized work of the imagination like *Adventures of Huckleberry Finn*.

# "How a body can see and don't see at the same time": Reading Humor in *Huckleberry Finn*_____

Tracy Wuster

From the very beginning of *Adventures of Huckleberry Finn*, readers are presented with a puzzle of a book. The book's introductory Notice, for example, issues this stern warning:

> Persons attempting to find a motive in this narrative will be prosecuted; persons attempting to find a moral in it will be banished; persons attempting to find a plot in it will be shot.
>
> By Order of the Author<br>Per G. G., Chief of Ordnance

Those admonitions seem like mighty high stakes for a book many students have been assigned to read in classes and asked to make sense of in reports. The warnings, of course, are obviously a joke. They point up the importance of remembering that the book is the work of a figure called "Mark Twain," who was actually a humorous character crafted by a man named Samuel L. Clemens to produce humor. While his book deals with serious cultural issues, the entire volume can and should be read through the lens of humor.

For more than a century, critics and readers have been trying to find motives, morals, and plots in *Huckleberry Finn*. This essay will not do that. Instead, it will point out ways in which reading the book as humor can make it both clearer and more fun. The essay will first focus on Mark Twain's role as a humorist and consider his position in American literature. Readers have always expected to find humor in Mark Twain's writings and have thus approached *Huckleberry Finn* with that expectation in mind.

The essay will then examine how Mark Twain uses the character of Huck Finn as a vernacular narrator to create humor through his descriptions and perceptions of his story. Incongruities between Huck's limited view of events and our own understanding of them as readers create the humor of the novel in a way that both produces pleasure for readers and subtly satirizes the serious issues that Huck's story contains.

A third section in the essay will examine how reading the book's humor shapes interpretations of the moral dilemmas Huck faces in relation to Jim and considers ways in which Mark Twain might be satirizing issues of racism and morality. When it comes to slavery and race, *Huckleberry Finn* shows how "a body can see and don't see at the same time," as Huck says in chapter 34.

Finally, the essay will briefly touch on the book's ending to ask how understanding the book's humor can help readers interpret both that controversial section and the book as a whole. Mark Twain's humor helps us understand how others—and maybe how even we ourselves—may become laughable when we ignore how one's perceptions of the world might be limited by the historical and cultural context in which stories are told.

## "The best of our second-rate humorists"

Readers approach *Huckleberry Finn* with a wealth of cultural associations related to Mark Twain—the famous humorist—and to "American humor" as a tradition. Readers picking up Mark Twain's new novel during the 1880s would not have done so in schools. At that time, the idea of teaching something called "American literature" in high schools or colleges would have seemed peculiar, if not downright laughable. For the vast majority of readers in America and around the world, Mark Twain was a popular and best-selling humorist, one whose inclusion in the world of high-culture literature would have been highly controversial.

From the time Samuel L. Clemens adopted his "Mark Twain" pseudonym in 1863 through much of the 1870s and into the 1880s, that name was mostly classed with fellow humorists who also went by pseudonyms. These humorous figures, such as "Artemus Ward" and the "Reverend Petroleum Vesuvius Nasby," took advantage of societal changes to create the new vocation of professional humorists. In the mid-nineteenth century, expanded communication and transportation networks led to increased opportunities for people to publish and perform as humorous characters, even enabling a few of them to make their livings as humorists.

Earlier humorists were classified hierarchically in three basic categories. On the bottom were minstrels and clowns, whose performances aimed for mass success and were viewed as low quality. At the top of the hierarchy were authors—such as James Russell Lowell and Nathaniel Hawthorne—who wrote at times as "humorists" or "satirists" in order to produce stories or poems that mixed humor with pathos and aimed at moving cultured audiences to either action or deep feeling. Humorists between these poles were largely men—although a few women found fame—who wrote humor for newspapers and magazines, with occasional figures gaining popularity and having their work collected into books.

Mark Twain rose to fame as a professional humorist of this middle type, known for short periodical pieces and for the popularity of his travel books, which provided his unique humorous perspective on locations ranging from Europe and the Middle East to the American West and Hawaii. His most popular works were *The Innocents Abroad* (1869) and *Roughing It* (1872). His books were sold mostly by subscription, meaning they were peddled door-to-door for customers who were often more interested in acquiring large books to show off than in owning quality literature.

Mark Twain coauthored his first novel, *The Gilded Age* (1873), with his friend Charles Dudley Warner. The first novel published as a subscription book, it was an uneven and now largely forgotten satire of contemporary government and business. The novel was a curiosity because of its dual authorship, but its sales quickly dropped off in comparison to Mark Twain's travel books. His first solo-written novel, *The Adventures of Tom Sawyer* (1876), was also a puzzle as a book written for a younger audience in which the trademark character of Mark Twain was absent, although the narrative voice was familiar. The book initially sold poorly and did not have a major impact on American culture until much later.

Critics had classified Mark Twain with his fellow popular humorists in the 1860s, with his reputation growing to become, according to a critic writing in the San Francisco *Daily Evening*

*Bulletin* in 1867, "the best of our second-rate humorists." In the early 1870s, some critics began to argue that Mark Twain should be viewed as a "quality" humorist who deserved attention as a part of American literature. Most crucially, William Dean Howells used his editorial position at *The Atlantic Monthly*, a magazine that played a central role in defining American literature, to argue for Mark Twain's inclusion in "the company of the best." On the other hand, influential critics such as Josiah Holland argued that humorists like Mark Twain were a danger to society. The reactions to Mark Twain's next books—*A Tramp Abroad* (1880), *The Prince and the Pauper* (1881), and *Life on the Mississippi* (1883)—followed a pattern of some critics arguing for the quality of the books, others dismissing or ignoring them, and many critics falling somewhere in between as they tried to puzzle out the meaning of the humorist.

Meanwhile, Mark Twain continued to win a popularity separate from his presence in literary debates. From 1868 to 1873, he took advantage of a growing desire for public performance by lecturing for crowds from Red Dog, Nevada, to London, England. These lectures spread both the fame and the image of Mark Twain, first across the United States and then around the world. His well-received performances made him the living embodiment of American humor. In addition, improved technology for producing and reproducing illustrations meant that the image of Mark Twain was more and more widely distributed in the press and in his travel books, which featured a large number of pictures in which images of him as characters was central. These factors helped make him one of the best-selling authors of his time and cemented the figure of "Mark Twain" as one of the biggest celebrities of the era.

WARMED UP INTO A QUARREL.

Although the narrator of *Life on the Mississippi* never identifies himself by name in the book, illustrations like this one in chapter 32, showing the narrator brawling with his traveling companions, made it obvious that the narrator was indeed Mark Twain.

The name Mark Twain thus existed in two worlds. In literary conversations, his position as an author was controversial. In the realm of popular culture, his celebrity made him more like a stand-up comedian of our time than a literary author of his own time. Modern readers undoubtedly come to *Huckleberry Finn* with their own image of Mark Twain as a literary and popular figure. Keeping the historical context of the novel and its author in mind helps readers see the ways in which the relationship between its author and its humorous narrator both built on and expanded American humor to humorously examine key moral quandaries of American life.

## "You don't know about me, without you have read a book"

Readers who have picked up *Huckleberry Finn* expecting a humorous novel by Mark Twain have gotten a unique take on the tradition of American humor. One of the major trademarks of that tradition was the use of vernacular speakers—characters whose speech was represented in written dialect as a source of fun. Sometimes vernacular figures were city dwellers, but the dominant thread was vernacular speakers of the southern, western, and other rural areas of the rapidly expanding country. They were often presented through frame tales in which educated narrators related stories of encounters with them—making fun of those characters, in both senses of the phrase.

As a vernacular character, Huck Finn was thus part of a longer tradition of American humor. However, he was also unique in that his narrative is told entirely in the voice of its title character and features very little framing by Mark Twain. Only the very first line of the book mentions Mark Twain, when Huck, as narrator, announces:

> You don't know about me, without you have read a book by the name of "The Adventures of Tom Sawyer," but that ain't no matter. That book was made by Mr. Mark Twain, and he told the truth, mainly. There was things which he stretched, but mainly he told the truth. . . .

For readers, Mark Twain's almost total absence may have been surprising, as his comic voice had been so central to the success of his humor that giving his novel's voice over to a young boy was an artistic and commercial risk. Moreover, the book was nearly unique in literature; rarely, if ever before, had a vernacular narrator been so central to a novel. Readers must interpret the puzzling link between Mark Twain as an author of books and Huck Finn as an ostensibly "real" person who was the subject of one of those books (*Tom Sawyer*) and who is now framed as the creator of the book they are reading. Mark Twain is thus either transported into Huck's fictional world or Huck is transported into our world—at least theoretically. Either way, readers must reckon with the fact that all the action of the book is presented through the voice and consciousness of Huck Finn. In contrast to *Tom Sawyer*, nowhere does Mark Twain enter as a narrative voice to comment on, correct, or otherwise provide his own humorous voice to the book.

Throughout the book, readers should keep an eye out for moments when Huck's narration creates humor and for ways that Mark Twain might be subtly satirizing his culture through this humorous device. While Huck Finn is an entertaining narrator, readers should be careful to regard him as an unreliable narrator whose version of events is limited by his own experiences, his own scanty education, and his own prejudices. Vernacular speakers create incongruity between their quaint and often even rude language and behavior and "proper" language and behavior. In the academic field of humor theory, incongruity is one of the major explanations of the source of humor. The difference between what one sees or expects and what happens, when a certain type of surprise is created, can cause pleasurable reactions ranging from smiles or chuckles to outright laughter. The range of possible reactions, however, is modulated by the content of the humor, which can range from frivolous to serious.

Incongruities in *Huckleberry Finn* work on three levels: linguistic, situational, and moral. Linguistic incongruity occurs when the language of vernacular speakers deviates from conventional English in ways that make readers laugh at the manner in which a character is speaking. In the first chapter of *Huckleberry Finn*, for example, Huck describes the challenges of living a "respectable" life in a way that highlights his uneducated upbringing:

> The Widow Douglas she took me for her son, and allowed she would sivilize me; but it was rough living in the house all the time, considering how dismal regular and decent the widow was in all her ways; and so when I couldn't stand it no longer I lit out. I got into my old rags, and my sugar hogshead again, and was free and satisfied. But Tom Sawyer he hunted me up and said he was going to start a band of robbers, and I might join if I would go back to the widow and be respectable. So I went back.

Huck's misspelling of "sivilize" is an unintentional joke on his part: What could demonstrate a lack of "civilization" more than an inability to spell that word? While good for a momentary chuckle here and other places where the word recurs throughout the novel, the humor points to Huck's major concern with the difference between good and bad, freedom and constraint.

Huck's humorous dialect often points to his larger misperceptions of situations in which he finds himself—what may be called "situational incongruity." For example, in chapter 22, he is fooled by a circus performer, who pretends to be a drunken member of the audience and insists on riding one of the horses used by skilled acrobats. The man flies around the ring, hanging on for dear life, the rest of the audience laughs and cheers, but Huck does not find it funny and is "all of a tremble to see his danger." When the drunk finally reveals himself to be one of the acrobats, Huck then feels pity for the ringmaster who acts as though the man had tricked him. This scene, sandwiched between the attempted lynching of Colonel Sherburn and the King and Duke's first performance of their "Royal Nonesuch" show, casts a light on Huck's deficiencies in understanding one of the key themes of the book: performance. Huck is an intelligent boy and a good performer himself at times, but he consistently describes situations in ways that give rise to humor through his incongruous view of what he is actually observing and experiencing.

Many of the stories Huck relates involve incongruities of a moral dimension, such as discussions of religion and Providence, issues of race and slavery, and questions of right and wrong. The first part of the book concerns Huck's reactions to the Widow Douglas and Tom Sawyer, who both represent to him different sources of proper authority. For example, the passages about Tom's gang of robbers in chapters 2 and 3 present a humorous contrast between Tom's reliance on the authority of books to determine proper behavior and Huck's literalism. Thus, Huck resigns from the gang because they "hadn't robbed nobody, we hadn't killed any people, only just pretended." In chapter 3, Huck ponders, in a similarly humorous way, the issues of prayer and Providence, and he dismisses both the religion of the widow and the fantasy world of Tom. After a caravan of "Spanish merchants and rich Arabs" promised by Tom turn out to be a Sunday-school picnic, Huck reflects, "I reckoned he [Tom] believed in the A-rabs and the elephants, but as for me I think different. It had all the marks of a Sunday school." Questions of the authority of religion and of books in determining morality return at numerous points in ways both lightly humorous and deadly serious. Mark Twain is thus using his narrator to make fun of the perceptions of Huck Finn, both in the sense of being fun to read and in the sense of satirizing readers who fail to see the "stretchers" in the narration of an uneducated fourteen-year-old.

Readers enjoy *Huckleberry Finn*, in part, because of the distance between their own perceptions and those of Huck as they recognize the linguistic, situational, and moral incongruities present in the story, even though those categories are often intertwined in the flow of Huck's narration. Huck's limited view of the world is especially apparent when it comes to the adult world of violent authority that Pap brings to the book. As a vernacular speaker who veers from humorous to dangerous, Pap is at first humorous mainly in his drunken badgering of Huck and his effort at "reform" in chapter 5, which ends with his drunkenly rolling off a judge's roof and breaking his arm. After Pap kidnaps Huck in chapter 6, however, the humor darkens as Huck attempts to calm him; to avoid his drunken rages; and, finally, to escape altogether. The very real threat of violence Huck faces, as opposed to the pretend violence of Tom Sawyer's gang of robbers, takes the book into the realm of dark humor—that is, humor that deals with matters such as violence, captivity, death, and sex.

The incongruity between Huck's view of the world and the world of adult morality and violence he encounters offers an opportunity to ponder the distance between Huck as narrator and his readers. Readers should see a satiric distance that calls into question what the author—meaning Mark Twain—might be accomplishing with his use of Huck as a vernacular narrator. For example, Pap Finn's drunken, profanity-laced tirade against the educated, free black man; the law; and the "govment" in chapter 6 might be read as making fun of a character whose racist, antigovernment rhetoric mocks ideas of white privilege. Pap's tirade combines linguistic and moral incongruity to create a humorous incident at which readers can laugh because Pap's ridiculous sense of self-worth is based solely on his skin color, rather than any inherent worth of his education or admirable behavior.

The contrast between proper and vernacular in *Huckleberry Finn*, is created not from the proper/vernacular split in narration but from the variety of contrasts between the proper characters and the less educated characters whom Huck narrates. The vernacular narrator—along with the variety of characters seen through his eyes—helps create consistent incongruity between the way he sees the world and what is actually happening in that world. Because Mark Twain's voice is not heard in the novel directly, readers are left to interpret the ways in which Huck's story might be commenting on American history, on Mark Twain's own time, and on human nature writ large. That task, however, is a type of speculative interpretation that, when done carefully, can lead to a deeper enjoyment of the novel and, with any luck, might not get us shot.

## "Alright, I'll go to hell"

Linguistic and situational incongruity create moments of humor throughout the book, but *Huckleberry Finn* is not read and taught because of these moments alone. The humorous moral incongruities that Huck faces as the book progresses frame serious issues with real-world ramifications as topics of humorous perception. As Huck and Jim float down the river away from St. Petersburg, through the Grangerford-Shepherdson feud, along with the King and the Duke, and into the "Evasion" on Aunt Sally Phelps's farm, individual lines, incidents, and whole sections can be interpreted through the lens of humor in profitable ways, although never to find a moral or a plot, of course. These humorous passages explore many issues, from gender and race to family and childhood. They also operate on several levels of historical understanding—providing insight into the mid-nineteenth century of the novel's action, the 1880s of its publication, and on American history and literature more generally. Readers can interpret these humorous incidents as a way to help better understand the novel, its time, or both through the lens of humor. The book might thus be best perceived not so much as a serious book but as a humorous one that explores serious issues through its humor.

For many readers, Huck's relationship with Jim is the central puzzle of the novel. By focusing on the humor of Huck's narration, readers can better understand the ways in which the concept of race is made fun of and how Huck's humorous morality distorts his perceptions of race, as well as the ways in which Mark Twain might be satirizing conceptions of right and wrong regarding race. In chapter 16, Huck ponders the implications of his helping Jim escape to freedom. Huck is tortured by his "conscience," which voices the logic of his society that holds helping a slave escape to be wrong. Jim's talk of getting abolitionists to help steal his wife and children out of slavery after he gains his own freedom further stabs at Huck's conscience: "I was sorry to hear Jim say that, it was such a lowering of him." Here, we might chuckle sadly at his "conscience" having become so distorted by slave society as to dehumanize Jim by valuing his status as property over his status as a husband and father. The dark joke of Jim's "lowering" himself for wanting to free his children from bondage satirizes the logic of racism that supported slavery. Astute readers might, incidentally, wonder why Mark Twain would satirize the logic of slavery when writing at a time decades after its supposed end.

In chapter 16, Jim counters Huck's social conscience by telling him "you's de *only* fren' old Jim's got now" and calling him "de ole true Huck; de on'y white genlman dat ever kep' his promise to ole Jim." Huck's subsequent decision to lie to the slave catchers—for which he is, ironically, rewarded with forty dollars in gold—might be cheered, but in a major moral incongruity, Huck is ashamed at his inability to do "right." His internal debate over society's expectations versus his feeling kindness toward Jim sets up the central dilemma of the novel, as Huck phrases it: "what's the use of learning to do right, wen it's troublesome to do right and ain't no trouble to do wrong, and the wages is the same?" Of course, the wages are not necessarily the same, as Huck and Jim are enriched by Huck's "immoral" lie.

Readers can see the humor of this situation, even if the joke is darkly ironic rather than laugh-out-loud funny.

What of Jim? Readers have often commented upon how Jim is portrayed as an unintelligent or foolish character who conforms to humorous minstrel stereotypes. Minstrelsy was a form of popular entertainment that influenced white perceptions of black Americans in the nineteenth century and well into the twentieth. By framing black characters as childlike, uneducated, and laughable, minstrelsy provided a major ideological justification for the existence of slavery before the Civil War and for continued racism after the war. Because *Huckleberry Finn* is filtered through Huck Finn, readers know Jim only through Huck's viewpoint, which is often highly distorted by the slaveholding culture that has shaped his perceptions. Readers should thus not be surprised that Jim is portrayed through the minstrel stereotypes created for the entertainment of white audiences. Some white readers of *Huckleberry Finn* may have found Jim's portrayal entertaining for that reason. Another interpretation, however, holds that readers should look beyond Huck's limited view and speculate on the possibility of Jim's employing a minstrel mask—that is, readers might see Jim as performing the racial role he knows Huck expects from him in order to influence Huck's actions. For example, in the chapter 16 scene discussed above, Jim's flattery of Huck as his only friend might be a response to the very real danger the slave catchers pose to Jim. In that case, the joke is on Huck. Here and in other places in the book, Jim's actions create a possible incongruity between the situation and Huck's understanding, allowing some readers to laugh with, rather than at, the seemingly simple escaped slave who might be wiser than he appears.

Without an authoritative narrative voice, readers are left to interpret the meanings of Jim's portrayal. Mark Twain might be using the humor of Huck's narration to satirize aspects of race in American culture. For example, the period in which the novel was written saw an increased interest in stories about race in the southern United States. The dominant mode of this genre, often called "plantation literature," portrayed the antebellum period with nostalgia and looked with trepidation on the freedom of African

Americans. These works employed minstrel stereotypes to make black characters laughable in order to devalue their humanity. Critics have debated whether Mark Twain's novel was part of this trend or satirized it. Some have pointed to Mark Twain's (or Samuel Clemens's) own actions, while others have focused on the ways the text works, regardless of its author's intentions—of which we really know very little. With Mark Twain, as with other authors, we must tread carefully with questions of intentionality.

The key scene of humorous moral incongruity is Huck's decision to "go to hell" instead of informing Jim's owner, Miss Watson, of Jim's location in chapter 31. Here, Huck is again pondering the morality of his situation. Huck is torn between the "authorities" and Jim, with his conscience "grinding" him and making him feel "wicked and low-down ornery" for helping Jim escape. According to Huck's interpretation, telling the truth of Jim's whereabouts would result in Jim's disgrace for his being "ungrateful" to his owner and in Huck's own shame for "stealing a poor old woman's nigger that hadn't done me no harm. . . ." Note that statement's dangling modifier, which leaves unclear who had not harmed Huck: Jim or the poor old woman. That linguistic slip humorously highlights the key moral dilemmas Huck faces in pondering right and wrong.

Consistently and through the remainder of this passage, Huck holds to the view that slavery is right both socially and spiritually. Huck's feelings of shame at how white people would view him, his distorted version of Providence, and his attempts at prayer do not result in his conversion to a view of morality that a majority of his readers might wish for him. The letter he writes to Miss Watson to reveal Jim's whereabouts washes him "clean of sin for the first time." Again, however, he thinks of Jim's actions as a person, especially the memory of the incident discussed earlier. The scene climaxes with Huck holding the letter and pondering the clash between social morality and personal loyalty and deciding his path: "'All right, then, I'll go to hell'—and I tore it up."

It is tempting to view Huck's decision as a moral victory, but if readers take this moment as "the moral" of the book, they are missing the humor of the moment and might deserve to be "banished." Instead, this moment might be viewed as a supreme moment of moral incongruity. Huck is not pondering the moral quandary he faces and seeing the correct option, as post-Civil War morality would have it. Instead, he is consciously choosing to do wrong, remarking, "I would take up wickedness again, which is in my line, being brung up to it, and the other warn't." He then vows to steal Jim and do worse, if he could think up anything worse. The humor here is dark.

Huck has not overcome society's moral logic of racism; he has reaffirmed it. He has not chosen to do "right"—although that is how modern readers might see his actions—he has chosen the "evil" of stealing a human being out of bondage. We might laugh at this moment in which such an intense moral decision is narrated in such skewed terms, and we might chuckle at the thought that a fourteen-year old might have the wisdom to understand and reject his society's most deeply held views. Such moments of moral victory might seem possible at fourteen, but Mark Twain, who was nearing fifty when he wrote that passage, may have been satirizing the desire to so easily transcend prejudice in a culture where racism was, and still is, so deeply imbued.

## "Because right is right, and wrong is wrong"

The final section of the book—the "evasion" chapters—sees the return of Tom Sawyer and the narrative world of boyish pretend, now mixed with the real-world seriousness of Jim's desire to escape slavery. Some readers find the ridiculous antics of Tom Sawyer unfunny or tiring, especially those who are disappointed that Huck would go along with Tom's increasingly cruel plan to help Jim escape. While some argue that the writing or plotting at the end of the book is poor, complaints about the ending are most often framed in moral terms, as many readers find it difficult to square the Huck who seems to see the humanity of Jim with the Huck who allows Tom to turn Jim into a prop in an absurd adventure.

The desire for Huck to transcend the racist morality of his time causes many readers to hope that his friendship with Jim has changed him more than the text indicates. Throughout the evasion section,

Huck's narration shows that he does not reject the logic of slavery or racism but instead acts kindly toward Jim as a fellow human being. For example, in chapter 40, Huck approves Jim's logic for getting a doctor for Tom—who has been shot—by saying "I knowed he was white inside." The humor here of equating goodness with whiteness might be uncomfortable. By seeing Huck as a hero of the story—in the sense of his doing the right thing for the right reasons—readers run the risk of missing a key moral incongruity and the joke being on them.

In the end, readers do not know—in fact, cannot know—what Mark Twain meant with the puzzle of his novel. We can, however, try to interpret by looking closely at Huck's vernacular narrative and asking what we know and what we do not know about the story, then exploring the literary and historical contexts of the novel in order to better understand both. We might start by asking why Mark Twain wrote about slavery in America almost twenty years after its legal end. We could also ask how the book might be satirizing racial politics of the 1880s, when Jim Crow segregation and the increased threat of violence toward African Americans were erasing the freedom African Americans had gained through Emancipation and Reconstruction. What, we might further ask, does it mean to set a free man free, as Tom and Huck attempt to do? How does the humor of this novel challenge the ways readers might think about their own views on morality, race, freedom, and evil? How can we keep the book's humor in mind while discussing such serious questions?

In addition to making people laugh, and often getting them to pay good money to do so, humor has a special ability to call into question one's certainties and to make fun of those characters— fictional or real—who misinterpret the world in ways small or big. Reading *Adventures of Huckleberry Finn* as humor, then, means being open to the interpretive possibilities that are raised by storytelling while being aware of our own sometimes limited view of the world and its meanings. Thus, we must avoid reducing this book to a serious and singular "moral" while enjoying the ways Mark Twain mixed humor and morality to plumb the ways in which we come to understand our world.

# The Reluctant Author: Huck Finn's Metafictional Partnership with Mark Twain⎯⎯⎯⎯⎯⎯⎯⎯

John H. Davis

Although Huck Finn does not claim to be the author of *Adventures of Huckleberry Finn* (1885), he seems determined to tell his own story. His very first statement implies that he is not entirely pleased with the way his story's predecessor, *The Adventures of Tom Sawyer* (1876), was told:

> You don't know me without you have read a book by the name of "The Adventures of Tom Sawyer," but that ain't no matter. That book was made by Mr. Mark Twain, and he told the truth, mainly. There was things which he stretched, but mainly he told the truth (chapter 1).

Despite that disclaimer, Huck is unsure how to produce a book. Consequently, *Adventures of Huckleberry Finn* is much concerned with books and the writing process. This concern, Huck's talking to readers, his awareness of himself as a character, and self-referential fiction constitute metafiction. Having decided to experiment with narration in a longer work, Mark Twain must share Huck's wariness, which leads to a metafictional and metaphorical shared authorship. It is metafictional because the fictional Huck acknowledges that an actual person wrote a prequel. That person thereby becomes both a character and a person existing outside the narrative. The joint authorship is metaphorical because the outside person (Mark Twain) never appears, and Huck never says he has met or even knows him. Authorship is shared because that person's presence, even intrusion, is felt or implied in Huck's text through ideas expressed and allusions to his and others' works. Focusing on literariness and conventions of the novel through authorship by a fictional and a factual author, especially a pseudonymous writer who is himself a creation, delineates metafiction, which emphasizes fictionality *within* fiction. The authors' joint effort is paradoxical, discrepant, and puzzling but ultimately a fruitful collaboration.

## Framing the Story

Mark Twain's understandable caution about beginning a novel with the innovation of a vernacular narrator complements Huck's nervousness at becoming that narrator. Not leaving the matter entirely to Huck, the senior author uses a favorite device, the framework. This framework is similar to one he modified in "A True Story" (1874). In it—as is typical in framework stories—an educated opening narrator, "Misto C————" (a fictionalized Samuel Clemens), introduces a situation and an uneducated second narrator, Rachel (like Huck, a vernacular speaker), who tells a story. Untypically, however, in that story, he does not return to close his frame after it ends, so Rachel has the last word, just as Huck does in his own story. Rachel gains and retains control of that earlier narrative, but the purpose in *Huckleberry Finn* is different. With contrasting attitudes in separate frames, Misto C———- and Rachel are both in "True Story." In *Huckleberry Finn*, Mark Twain as outside author maintains modified control as Huck becomes the inside author. Together they explore ways to tell a story. Huck briefly notes the first author's existence but not his physical presence and does not indicate knowing him except as the writer of a book about Tom Sawyer that includes Huck. However, an educated person outside the narrative—a metafictional presence—is evident even before Huck as narrator appears.

Though not in the story itself, this outside person remains part of its creation. With diction certainly not that of the ill-educated Huck, Mark Twain asserts his control, declaring his authorship by placing several prohibitions on readers immediately following the book's title page. The first is this "NOTICE":

> Persons attempting to find a motive in this narrative will be prosecuted; persons attempting to find a moral in it will be banished; persons attempting to find a plot in it will be shot.
>
> By Order of the Author
> Per G. G., Chief of Ordnance

Mark Twain's second prohibition is an "Explanatory" note about dialects in the text that is signed "The Author." Preemptively limiting criticism of second-author failings, these warnings directed at readers form the outside frame of the story-structure while highlighting first-author existence.

The editors of the University of California critical editions of *Huckleberry Finn* (1985, 2001, 2003) offer biographical interpretations for "G. G." in "Notice," suggesting the initials might refer to either "General Grant" (whose memoirs Mark Twain's own publishing firm was about to publish) or George Griffin, the Clemens family butler. If accurate, these names suggest another fiction-actuality clash by linking the novel to Samuel Clemens's life.

The novel's second frame begins with Huck's introducing himself and updating Tom's story in the first two paragraphs of chapter 1. The third frame—the narrative—begins in the third paragraph, describing Huck's situation in the Widow Douglas's home. It ends with the penultimate paragraph of the novel. Huck then concludes his remarks and the second frame in the final paragraph with

"THE END, YOURS TRULY HUCK FINN."

Combining the conclusion of a novel with that of a letter, Huck reiterates his uncertainty about writing a book. Mark Twain does not formally end the novel or conclude the opening frame. By now, Huck's voice, if not Huck the reticent writer, dominates the book's telling. Nevertheless, his ghostwriter is present throughout the narrative, looking over Huck's shoulder. This situation is the reverse of Rachel's, in which she thematically and metaphorically towers above Misto C——- as she ends "True Story."

In the "Conclusion" of *The Adventures of Tom Sawyer*, the author says:

> So ENDETH this chronicle. It being strictly a history of a *boy*, it must stop here; the story could not go much further without becoming the history of a *man*. When one writes a novel about grown people, he knows exactly where to stop . . . but when he writes of juveniles, he must stop where he best can. . . .

---

The open-ended framework of Huck's own story serves two purposes. Unlike the title of Tom's story, in which "The" implicitly restricts Tom's adventures to his book, Huck's title does not limit Huck's adventures. Like the framework, the title hints at further adventures (which the two authors would actually soon begin). More importantly, metafictionally, it metaphorizes a continuation of the life in the novel and an open door, a broken fourth wall, into that world outside the novel initially referenced by both authors.

## The Broken Wall

Other factors point to a breach in the fourth wall. Prior to the title page in the first American edition and many editions since appears a photograph of sculptor Karl Gerhardt's bust of Mark Twain, probably inserted because Mark Twain thought it would help sales. Both it and his signature beneath it call attention to his prominence as an author beyond this book. Another possible motivation was that he may have wished to prevent his being confused with an undereducated interior narrator. Such links to a nonfictional world are metafictional.

The editors of the latest University of California Press critical edition of *Huckleberry Finn* agree that Huck's role must have perplexed Mark Twain because he phrased the title on his manuscript—rediscovered in 1990—"HUCKLEBERRY FINN | Reported by | MARK TWAIN." His original title for the novel, scratched over in the manuscript, was *"'Huckleberry Finn'—Autobiography."* His puzzlement lingered in his later stories narrated by Huck, indicated by such subheadings as "BY HUCK FINN. EDITED BY MARK TWAIN" for *Tom Sawyer Abroad* (1894) and "BY MARK TWAIN AS TOLD BY HUCK FINN" for *Tom Sawyer, Detective* (1896). Ironically, in the first edition of *Huckleberry Finn*, Edward W. Kemble's first drawing of Huck and the photo of the bust face each other, as though foreshadowing their authorial relationship within the novel that follows. That juxtaposition also reminds readers that, although both images are imaginative creations, the bust is three-dimensional, an object from the multidimensional nonfictional world, while the drawing is two-dimensional. The mind's eye may see the latter as more than a flat depiction, but it remains primarily an illustration of a fictional character in a book, not a person existing outside that book. This distinction again separates the book world from the real world. Whether or not readers note the book's copyright citation to "Samuel L. Clemens" (the only appearance in the book of Mark Twain's actual name), they should realize that, as Huckleberry Finn is a creation of Mark Twain, "Mark Twain" himself is a creation of Clemens. Mark Twain is thereby metafictional in *both* worlds.

As another sales tactic, Mark Twain subtitled *Huckleberry Finn* "Tom Sawyer's Comrade," identifying Huck in relation to the main character of another novel. That connection thus gives Huck a context before Huck himself does in his story while playing on the popularity of the previous book, emphasizing that *Huckleberry Finn* is also a book, and reminding readers that both are fiction. This exterior author stands between the fictional boundaries of the two works to clarify that they are separate, each an imagined world within an actual world. Further emphasizing the distance between the two authors, "Comrade" is a word Huck himself would probably not use to describe Tom. If Huck had composed a title, he would likely have used the first person, as in "My Adventures" or "My Friend Tom Sawyer." "Comrade" does not appear in Huck's story, but numerous appearances in *Tom Sawyer* testify to its metafictional source.

## Era or Error: The Age Factor

The time-setting of the novel is both metafictional and contradictory. Written in one era, the story occurs in another. Stepping from one era to the other is confusing. If Huck tells the story, *when* does he do it? The "Preface" of his reference point, *The Adventures of Tom Sawyer*, published in 1876, says that it is set thirty or forty years in the past, a period corresponding to "Time: Forty to Fifty Years Ago" that appears below the title of Huck's story, first published in England in 1884. Outside the novel proper, the information is significant because it gives a necessary historical context to a fictional story and connects the novel to its writing, a blending of fiction and reality. Huck recaps Tom's story and begins his own

---

where Tom's ends, extending a story he indicates he has read, and in which he participated, that appeared eight years earlier than his own book.

In chapter 17 of *Huckleberry Finn*, Huck says he is about Buck Grangerford's age—"thirteen or fourteen or along there . . ." More interested in presenting boyhood than a specific time within boyhood, the omniscient narrator of *Tom Sawyer* never reveals Tom's age, which seems to vary. In both books, Tom and Huck seem to be about the same age, but in *Huckleberry Finn*, Huck behaves as if he is older than he is in *Tom Sawyer*. Readers encounter a time traveler's paradox. *When* is Huck thirteen or fourteen—at the time of the book's publication or during the 1830s or 1840s? Certainly he is about fourteen in the novel, but he is placed beside Mark Twain, who—if the counterpart to Samuel Clemens—was forty-nine in 1884. Mark Twain's age poses no difficulties, but in relation to it, Huck's age does. If Huck is fourteen in 1834, he is fifteen years older than his not-yet-born associate, who is apparently an established author by 1876. If Huck is fourteen (a real-world/real-time possibility is sixty-four) at publication—the time of telling—which obviously he is at the time of happening, the time line is not only askew but chaotic.

The words "HUCKLEBERRY FINN | Reported by | MARK TWAIN," on the manuscript fragment found in 1990 could indicate that Mark Twain meant to imply that he had discovered, and figuratively edited, a manuscript written earlier by a fourteen-year-old boy. He later wrote a similar description for his unfinished and posthumously published novel *No. 44, The Mysterious Stranger* (1982). He subtitled that book, "Being an Ancient Tale Found in a Jug, and Freely Translated from the Jug." However, even if he is as inconsistent an editor as he is a translator in *No. 44*, that discovery would not explain the adolescent's having read the previous novel, which was not available before 1876. *Tom Sawyer* and *Huckleberry Finn* are not simply the connected fictional stories of two boys. Metafictionally mixing fictional and actual, Huck Finn and Mark Twain bring each other together in the telling of the second book. Excluding reading time, readers confront two present times: the dates of publication and setting. However, if *Huckleberry Finn*'s main character exists inside and outside the novel, further suspension of disbelief is required.

## Other Metafictional Issues

Other questions occur. How does Mark Twain know the boys outside their stories? Who is the "you" whom Huck addresses in his story's very first sentence? Mark Twain presents himself as author before Huck Finn presents himself as telling the story. Did Huck previously tell him the story, arousing his interest? Even if Mark Twain is "editor," "translator," or "reporter," he is not the person addressed because Huck refers to him in the third person in his second sentence. Did he, as editor, arrange chapters and create the contents page? Would Huck assume that task as part of making his book? Presumably, "you" refers to readers or listeners. They may be, one might imagine, like Jim Blaine's auditors in "The Story of the Old Ram" in chapter 53 of *Roughing It* (1872), gathered around Huck to listen, as he seems to be talking rather than writing. Huck's storytelling habit—like that of many southerners—is oral, so his writing method approximates that tradition. Can an ill-educated, poor, misfit, backwoods son of a drunkard and thief be or even become a gifted stylist and skilled storyteller? The notion appears less implausible as one reads the book. More extraordinary is that whatever Huck says—even if drawn from Mark Twain's or Samuel Clemens's mature knowledge—proves not only plausible but unpretentious. Indeed, it is plausible because it is unpretentious.

Despite his plausibility, Huck doubts his own storytelling ability. Describing the river in chapter 7, for example, he hesitates, "You know what I mean—I don't know the words to put it in." Nevertheless, he finds the words repeatedly:

The sky looks ever so deep when you lay . . . on your back in the moonshine . . .

Jackson Island . . . big and dark and solid, like a steamboat without any lights (chapter 7) freckled places on the ground where the light sifted through the leaves . . . (chapter 8)

Huck's style is natural and free-flowing. He says he trusts "to Providence . . . for I'd noticed that Providence always did put the right words in my mouth, if I left it alone" (chapter 32).

## Reading and Writing

Huck (and senior author Mark Twain) must still remove doubts he can read and write. In chapter 2, when other boys sign their names in blood to join Tom Sawyer's gang, Huck can only make a "mark." However, Miss Watson has already begun working with him in a spelling book. Several times afterward he refers to attending school and learning to "spell, and read, and write . . ." Eventually, he feels he is "learning my lessons good." When his Pap threatens him if he attends school, he continues anyway (chapters 1, 4, 5, 6). Several references to Huck's ability to read and write appear throughout the text. Reiterating that Huck is from a family of illiterates, Pap complains, "You're educated, too, they say . . . Who told you you might meddle with such hifalut'n foolishness, hey? . . . Your mother couldn't read, and she couldn't write, nuther . . . None of your family couldn't . . . ." Pap then demands Huck prove he can read (chapter 5).

When Huck later forgets the false name he has told the Grangerfords, he taunts Buck to spell it in chapter 17. Then he writes down Buck's misspelling, "G-o-r-g-e J-a-x-o-n," in case he might later need it. Earlier, however, he had written (spoken) the name's correct spelling to readers and the Grangerfords (chapter 17). This apparent discrepancy is explicable as an intrusion by the other author. The first spelling may be his editing, the other an instance of what is called eye dialect— deliberate misspelling without altering pronunciation—to emphasize Huck's speech and weak literacy.

Later, when Sophia Grangerford asks Huck if he can read handwriting, he lies, "no, only coarse-hand," meaning hand-printed, not cursive writing (chapter 18). In a still later parallel event, Huck remarks of the old Englishman who may be the true Harvey Wilks that nobody could read his handwriting. Using handwriting samples to undo the King and Duke's efforts to defraud the Wilks girls, lawyer Levi Bell says, "fact is, the scratches he makes ain't properly *writing*, at all" (chapter 29). This comment is perhaps an authorially inserted inside joke commenting on the vernacular narration.

Despite Huck's comparing his captivity by Pap early in his narrative as being "lazy and jolly . . . and no books nor study" to "forever bothering over a book" at the Widow Douglas's (chapter 6), Huck recognizes the value of writing, reading, and books. Beyond what he knows of books from Tom Sawyer, he has read material one might not expect and seems to enjoy reading. In describing a later scene on the raft he shares with Jim, he says, "We laid off . . . talking, and me reading the books, and having a general good time. . . . I read considerable to Jim about kings, and dukes, and earls, and such . . ." (chapter 14). The latter reference, possibly an inclusion by the more experienced writer, foreshadows the coming of the Duke and the King. Explaining to Jim that kings are "a mighty ornery lot," Huck not only illustrates that he has read European history and *The Arabian Nights* (although he conflates them) but also argues his fellow writer's low opinion of royalty (chapter 23). He also says he has "read considerable in [*Pilgrim's Progress*] now and then," Henry Clay's speeches, a book of family medicine, and a miscellany, among others at the Grangerfords (chapter 17).

Jim and Huck base their arguments about the biblical King Solomon on what they have been *told*, not what they have *read*. Mistaking intelligence for racial inferiority, Tom has given up on Jim (chapter 35), but he has pounded into Huck that final authority derives from reading and books: "'I've seen it in books; and so of course that's what we've got to do'" (chapter 2). This belief that books must be authorities on making books exposes a metafictional inclination in book-writing.

## Allusions

Allusions to books and literature occur throughout *Huckleberry Finn*, linking it to both literary and literal worlds. Some allusions are direct, some implied, some unconscious, at least metaphorically on Huck's part. These references occur in diverse ways. Tom names

*Don Quixote* and, without giving titles, draws from Renaissance, Restoration, Georgian, and contemporary works, usually romantically adventurous, a range wide enough to create wonder about accessibility for a rural boy. Some have dates that cast doubt he even could have been able to read them in the time frame of the story. Huck also mentions the Duke's references to William Shakespeare's plays *Richard III*, *Romeo and Juliet*, *King Lear*, and *Hamlet*. The Duke parodies *Hamlet*'s most famous soliloquy and mentions the "unities" of Greek drama.

In footnotes to chapter 5 of the 2008 Bedford edition of *Huckleberry Finn*, Gregg Camfield writes that "Contemporary readers would probably have noticed the similarity between Pap and Gaffer Hexam from Charles Dickens's *Our Mutual Friend* (1864–1865)." Camfield also notes that Mark Twain reworked a story from *The Arabian Nights* into the episode in which Huck apologizes after Jim shames him for trying to make him believe he has dreamed Huck was lost in chapter 15 and that, in chapter 40, Tom borrows ideas from two Alexandre Dumas novels (chapter 35) and Dickens's *A Tale of Two Cities* (1859). Given the time-frame of *Huckleberry Finn*, only Mark Twain or Clemens—not Huck or Tom—could know those Dickens references, which are thus metafictional, factual outside the novel.

Much subtler is an homage in chapter 8 of *Huckleberry Finn* to Daniel Defoe's *Robinson Crusoe* (1719). There Huck's sudden discovery he is not alone on Jackson's Island recalls Crusoe's finding a human footprint on his island. As allusions, these references owe more to Mark Twain than to Huck, as must the romance of Harney and Sophia in the Grangerford-Shepherdson feud that recalls the romance amid the Capulet-Montague feud in *Romeo and Juliet*. Also not coincidental is name of the wrecked steamboat in chapter 12: "*Walter Scott*," symbolizing the state of romantic writing, as represented by a romantic writer whose influence Mark Twain condemned. The writer looking over Huck's shoulder thus has purposes for these allusions that are ironic, symbolic, satiric, and thematic. Huck misses these points, creating or increasing irony.

Tom overlooks everything but adventure and romance, emphasizing that romanticism obscures reality.

Allusions that mock or denigrate other literature must result from the influence and prejudices of the exterior author, for here Huck lacks knowledge and critical ability. Indeed, Huck savors the sentimentality that poured from the dead Emmeline Grangerford, even trying to imitate it. While he has reservations about Tom's bookish notions, he admires and bows to Tom's knowledge. Anti-romanticism mainly appears in Tom's tangled schemes to free Jim, such as his demands for the prisoner to have wall scribblings, a coat of arms, a pet, and his leg sawed off (chapters 37-38, 35) that parody a mélange of romantic stories. Satirizing the sentimentality of temperance literature is the call in chapter 21 for Boggs's young daughter to take her drunken father home and of religion in the placing of a heavy Bible on the chest of the father struggling to breathe after he is shot. The language and tone of "vale of sorrors" (chapter 25), "water it with your tears" (chapter 38), and the funereal "Ode to Stephen Dowling Bots, Dec'd" (chapter 17) contribute to the senior writer's satire. Huck may be writing, but he distills the other author's views and reasons for these attacks in the phrase, "all tears and flapdoodle" (chapter 25).

Passages in *Huckleberry Finn* that most obviously come from Mark Twain are allusions to his knowledge and his own works. Huck's description and explanation of a streak that indicates a snag in a swift river current, for example, more likely derive from the experience of a former steamboat pilot like Sam Clemens than from a boy who has previously only swum in the river (chapter 19). Like Huck, Mark Twain can never forget the sight of mourning slaves sold away from their families (chapter 27). Huck's description of a camp meeting and the boastful language of Boggs and the raftsmen (chapters 20, 16, 21) recall Southwest humor, a favorite genre and a major influence upon the older writer.

Notable, sometimes subtle, are references to the professional author's own writings. For example, while discussing a superstition about the new moon in chapter 10, Huck slips into a stream-of-consciousness similar to the speech pattern of Jim Blaine telling of his grandfather's ram in *Roughing It*. Buck Grangerford's patter after tricking Huck with a riddle sounds much like the non-sequitur talk of Mark Twain's "Sociable Jimmy" (chapter 17). Colonel Sherburn's description of a single man robbing a packed stagecoach in chapter 22 may be Mark Twain's remembrance of the daring gunman Slade in *Roughing It*. Slade and Sherburn are similar in that each commits both horrible and admirable acts. Unlike Sherburn, Slade is successfully lynched by the mob that comes for him in chapter 11 of *Roughing It*.

Suspicious of the King and Duke's chicanery, Dr. Robinson says in chapter 25 that "any man that pretended to be an Englishman and couldn't imitate the lingo no better than what he did, was a fraud and a liar." That statement recalls Mark Twain's 1877 Whittier birthday speech about three tramps who pretend to be three famous poets. In that story, the author-character—nervous, like Huck, about his authorial status before the literati—is asked if he too is an impostor. Metaphorically, and unconsciously, prophetic of tragic results in later dream stories is Huck's explanation of Tom's wound, "'He had a dream . . . and it shot him'" (chapter 41), but their essence appears when Huck jokingly convinces Jim that reality is dream and dream is reality (chapter 15). The evolving imagination behind Huck's incidents shows through.

### How Much Book Knowledge Is Enough or Too Much?

Despite his interest in books as a professional author, Huck's partner does not believe that all answers, particularly about writing literature, are there. As his friend William Dean Howells would later write in "Criticism and Fiction" (1891), too many writers derive visions of life from books rather than from observing life, creating "book-likeness," not "life-likeness." Asked by Jim how he knows that Frenchmen talk differently from them, Huck replies, "'I got some of their jabber out of a book'" (chapter 14). However, book-talk, here intended more for humor than for accuracy, typically lacks the vividness gained by an observant ear, as portrayed, for example, in the raftsmen's speech, and the accuracy in dialects "The Author" declares as his intent in

*Huckleberry Finn*'s "Explanatory." "The Author" and observant ear is Mark Twain, who has preemptively claimed credit.

Underscoring the importance of books and their content, Huck mentions "book" or "books" more than four dozen times in his narrative. He typically notes the presence of books, as in "a lot of books" thieves have stolen from the *Walter Scott* in chapter 14 and the many books he sees in the Grangerford house in chapter 17. He also names many specific book titles, usually literature. Because of Tom Sawyer's influence, he frequently cites them as rationale, explanation, and pattern for situations. Books are thus prevalent in the novel Huck may not know he is writing. After Tom reappears and takes charge of events in chapter 33, Huck does not question that authority, despite his own and Jim's misgivings. His main justification for actions comes from books. Tom remakes his world through books. Huck and Mark Twain present and represent the world (Huck's world) through a book, telling a story via literary means found in books.

## What Is Truth and Who Is Writing It?

Whereas the senior writer twice ("Notice"; "Explanatory") calls himself "Author," capitalized for emphasis, Huck does not claim that role, but it becomes his. As a character in a book he is writing that largely concerns writing a book, Huck steps outside the fiction to acknowledge the other writer of that book. Using Tom's book as a starting point. With a mild criticism of its author's "stretchers," he implies that his own narrative will be more forthright but allows room for his own stretching, as "I never seen anybody but lied, one time or another . . ." The thus suggests that his object is "mainly the truth" as he launches into what seems to be straight talk rather than overstated writing. Face-to-face conversation is, to such as Huck, more reliable and believable than what syntax may conceal. Despite his comment about Mark Twain's "stretchers," he does not challenge anything in the earlier story. Instead, he indicates that he intends to set or keep the record straight by telling the full truth, presumably before the other can distort it. However, he eventually learns that truth is sometimes found in lies and gained by deception, but "you can't pray a lie" (chapter 31).

Ironically, Huck's own stretchers, the content of his lies, qualify him to tell a story. While their purposes differ, Tom's and Huck's lies usually take the form of stories. Tom lies for adventure, Huck for survival. Demonstrating their creativity, a priority for authors, he and Tom construct characters, episodes, and backgrounds. Repeatedly, Huck finds himself telling "stretchers," some by necessity, some not, some crucial to his circumstances or his struggle between "a sound heart and a deformed conscience," as Mark Twain put it. For Huck, that struggle mainly involves Jim, as when he tells himself he "warn't man enough" to turn Jim over to slave catchers in chapter 16. When asked by the slave catchers if the man on his raft is white or black, he lies that his "pap"—actually Jim on the raft—is white. Although Jim may symbolically have become his father, Huck also misleadingly hints that "pap" and "mam and Mary Ann," his fictitious family, have smallpox (chapter 16). Deformed by its culture, his conscience relies on beliefs inbred by perverted truth—about race, honor, religion, justice, tradition, and freedom. Huck's "sound heart" responds with a stretcher. His stretchers demonstrate creativity, which becomes stronger and more frequent as the novel progresses, with Huck's growing realization that deceptions and lies are representations of reality and unconscious acknowledgement that storytelling is such a representation.

The most expanded "stretcher" in *Huckleberry Finn* is Tom's scheme to rescue Jim in the final chapters. It serves as though it is a climax, or anticlimax, to many previous stretchers. The ideas are Tom's but their telling, inclusion, and degree of detail are Huck's, as what to include or omit is an author's prerogative. Their presence in the completed work suggest Huck's qualified acceptance of them and the older author's belief in their symbolic necessity to make a point (a truth) about the extended enslavement of black people and to intensify the irony that, although freed—like his formerly enslaved kindred after the Civil War—Jim is not truly free. Likewise, his society is not free from superstition, custom, tradition, honor codes, and religious blindness. When Huck denies lying—that is, telling a story—to Joanna Wilks about being an English "valley," she says, "Lay your hand on this book and say it." Appropriately, in a work devoted to telling a story, the book on which Huck lays his hand is a dictionary, a writer's bible (chapter 26), fuel for lies and truth.

Joanna Wilks asking Huck to swear he is not lying, using a dictionary instead of a Bible.

Although the narrative is a joint effort in paradoxical and contradictory ways, Huck is conscious he is producing a book. In its final paragraph, he writes, "if I'd a known what a trouble it was to make a book I wouldn't a tackled it . . ." In doing so, he and his fellow author must consider the nature of literature. Actually, as the latter writer often does, he is testing the boundaries of storytelling— such as the involvement of readers in his 1865 jumping frog story, complexities of plot in "A Medieval Romance" (1870), and reliability of narrators in "A Curious Experience" (1881). As Mark Twain explores, Huck as teller learns what is necessary and essential to writing a long story.

## Huck as Observer

Huck admires Tom's "style," his manner and attitude, which—as "author" (storyteller)—Tom largely derives from books, but Huck as author and as character/narrator must observe, in the manner later described by Howells. Huck's style is subdued. From the King's naming Huck "Adolphus" in chapter 24 to calling him his "valley" in chapter 26, Huck is unmentioned, largely unseen, and figuratively outside his story. Just as he eavesdrops on the con men in chapter 26, so he does elsewhere. He watches robbers arguing aboard the *Walter Scott*, the Grangerfords attending church, the Shepherdsons shooting Buck, Colonel Sherburn killing Boggs and taunting the mob, and the scoundrels conning the Wilkses. Essentially a third-person narrator, not a participant, Huck tells their stories within his.

Huck practically disappears as Sherburn's language—really that of the elder author—replaces his own. Huck explains that he learned the Duke's *Hamlet* soliloquy "while he was learning it to the king" (chapter 21), but he does not explain how he recalls Sherburn's long speech. Recognizing importance in accurately rendering talk, Huck, however, does not risk imitating British speech (chapters 24, 29), but close-listening generates diverse speech patterns (see "Explanatory"), such as female chatter at the Wilkses (chapter 41). "Author" listens; Huck "writes."

Without transitioning, Huck abruptly breaks the fourth wall (via a symbolic tent-flap) to attend a circus in chapter 22. When the circus audience laughs at an apparently drunken man riding a horse, Huck fears for him. Mistaking performance for reality, Huck as an observer shows empathy—marking his reappearance as a character—thereby illustrating compassion and unconscious irony, and the theme.

## Huck and Literary Devices
Through Jim, Huck encounters criticism, interpretation, and symbolism. As Huck and Jim analyze the biblical story of Solomon in chapter 14, Jim proposes biographical criticism: "'de real pint is down furder . . . in de way Sollermun was raised.'" If Huck interprets, he judges by practicality. Unaware that Tom misinterprets the satire of *Don Quixote* in chapter 3, Huck discounts Jim's ominous "dream" interpretation in chapter 16 by pointing to debris on the raft as representing reality, but grasping Huck's joke, Jim interprets "'what . . . dey stan' for'" as people (Huck) who mistreat friends. Huck's symbolic interpretation is straightforward: The "big clear river . . . was the free states"; the raft is satisfaction, rightness, kindness (chapters 15, 19). Jim's "dream" questions what is and is not real. Writers simulate reality with words. Miss Watson's biblical interpretations are no more literal than Jim's, or Tom's romantic ones. The same subject can yield different interpretations. Because of sisters Douglas and Watson, Huck sees "two Providences" in chapter 3—one with positive and the other with negative possibilities.

Providences (symbolically chance, coincidence, or improbability) in plot pose problems for authors. Huck depends on providence for words, the Duke and King depend on it for victims. Tom's "plan" to rescue Jim represents plot, often improbable despite Huck's comments. Rejecting Huck's notions as too simple and not "romantical enough," Tom prefers complicated plots, so he lengthens, alters, and further complicates his plan with new difficulties (chapters 34-35). With anonymous letters, Tom reveals the plot, but *not* that Jim is legally free. Tom knows that outcome; character Huck does not. Author Huck—knowing Jim's and Pap's final status—chooses to divulge neither. Learning throughout, Huck understands grabbers, perhaps from the Duke: "'if that line don't fetch them, I don't know Arkansaw!,'" and pacing (anticipation): "read on and see what more [the snakeskin] done for us" (chapters 22, 16).

### Concluding a Story, Beginning a Career?

Huck's addressing readers encapsulates the metafictional approach. Figuratively partnered with his nominative creator, a character in a novel writes the novel, heeding literary conventions while acknowledging a literal world. Despite the trouble of making a book—and continuing uncertainty, suggested by Huck's frequent "long think[s]" (chapter 3)—his numerous musings scattered throughout the novel—Huck has succeeded, but not alone. The experiences are Huck's; the ideas are Mark Twain's. Notwithstanding his promise that he "ain't agoing to" make more books, Huck has become an author. Escaping to the territories promises more authorial collaboration and holds the door open to the wider world.

# Is *Huckleberry Finn* a Picaresque Novel?_____

Robert C. Evans

Determining the "genre" of a literary work is crucial to interpreting the work appropriately. This is especially true when a work may fall into the genre (or kind) of literature known as "picaresque." Determining whether Mark Twain's *Adventures of Huckleberry Finn* (1885) is a true "picaresque" novel is not as easy as it might seem at first. This is because the term "picaresque" has been defined in numerous ways. In fact, some scholarship about the term may lead one to wonder if almost *any* work has ever truly been picaresque by any exacting definition since a few original sixteenth century Spanish works. The one work that everyone seems to agree is picaresque is the book that began the tradition: an anonymous 1550 Spanish novel whose English title is *The Life of Lazarillo of Tormes*. For a variety of reasons, however, the one work most often *assumed* to be picaresque—namely Miguel de Cervantes' 1615 Spanish novel *Don Quixote*—has been interpreted (as will be seen below) as precisely the *opposite* of picaresque by various scholars.

Mark Twain's *Huckleberry Finn*, with its emphasis on constant, complicated travels by a pair of impoverished friends who find themselves getting into all kinds of threatening scrapes and unexpected predicaments, has traits similar to those typically associated with picaresque writing. Is it, however, truly picaresque? Is it even, as some believe, America's *only* true picaresque novel? Or is even this catalog of unpredictable misadventures not quite "picaresque" enough to qualify for admission to that category? As will be seen, answers to all such questions are open to debate.

Ulrich Wicks, perhaps the leading authority on picaresque writing, expresses great and frequent frustration with the alleged looseness with which the term is commonly employed. Indeed, he suggests that picaresque has sometimes been used to describe works, such as *Don Quixote*, that are not "true" picaresque narratives at all. Moreover, he also suggests that so many works have so often been broadly defined as picaresque that the term has sometimes practically lost any genuine meaning. Is it picaresque when Huck himself entertainingly reports, in colloquial language and chronological order, the events he and Jim experienced as they drifted down the Mississippi River? Is it picaresque when they haphazardly encounter one memorable person or group after another? Is it picaresque when they risk and then escape danger, or when they have to steal, or when they often find themselves having to be dishonest with the people they meet? And how does the entrance of the King and the Duke—two of the biggest scoundrels in American literature—affect the status of Twain's book as picaresque? All the features just mentioned are often thought of as picaresque. But do they make Twain's book truly picaresque?

In attempting to answer such questions, the present essay has a number of goals. First, I want to review briefly what Wicks, especially, has had to say about picaresque literature, particularly in his comprehensive 1989 survey *Picaresque Narrative, Picaresque Fictions: A Theory and Research Guide*. This book is important because it extensively surveys an enormous amount of commentary about the subject. Second, I want to report what previous scholars have said about *Huckleberry Finn* as picaresque. Finally, I want to return to Wicks's book and consider more than thirty numbered criteria he associates with picaresque writing and calculate how many of them seem relevant to *Huckleberry Finn*.

## Ulrich Wicks on Picaresque Writing

Wicks's research guide mentions that by the very beginning of the sixteenth century, the term "picaresque" had already begun to have a commonly accepted meaning:

> A work of this kind is, first of all, a *vida* ["life"], and thus narrated by the protagonist; as such, it is true to life in the sense of being empirically valid, as compared to the chivalric romances, which were not and [to] which the emerging picaresque must have dealt a considerable blow. . . . A *vida* is, moreover, chronological in structure. It should be entertaining and well written. Its content is determined by the shady, shifty—even criminal—behavior [of its

main characters]. And, finally, such *vidas* can be read—and indeed written—by everybody. . . . (9)

By this definition, one can certainly see how *Huckleberry Finn* might be classified as picaresque. By the end of the seventeenth century, the new genre had become enormously popular, especially in Spain. By that time, more than thirty works had been produced that have often been classified as picaresque (Wicks 11-12). By the nineteenth century, however, influential writers in English had, according to Wicks, so broadened the idea of picaresque that it had lost much of its original meaning. Wicks argues that Sir Walter Scott and Tobias Smollett

> were responsible for many of the major misconceptions of the picaresque that still haunt theory and criticism in English. The confusion was confounded by the English novelists' love for Cervantes, and in using both *Don Quixote* and [Alaine-René Lesage's] *Gil Blas* as models for their own fiction, the eighteenth-century novelists created a case of literary mistaken identity that continues today in the misapprehension of *Don Quixote* as a picaresque novel even among well-read critics, an error that Hispanists (despite their own lack of unanimity about the nature of the Spanish picaresque genre) would never make. (14)

In other words, Wicks suggests that scholars of Spanish-language works understand, as most English-language readers do not, that *Don Quixote*—which some people consider a great work of picaresque writing—is not, in fact, "picaresque." However that may be, the quotation from Wicks is especially relevant to *Huckleberry Finn* for at least two reasons: First, Twain's well-known hostility toward the works of Walter Scott. Second, Twain's much less well-known suggestion that *Gil Blas* (1715–1735) might have had some influence on the composition of his own greatest novel, a suggestion he later denied (Gribben 1: 407).

Much of the rest of the introductory section of Wicks's book involves his attempt to sort out just how—and how not—to define the genre and which works do—and do not—qualify as picaresque in some coherent, consistent sense of that term. Wicks helpfully surveys numerous scholarly attempts to discuss picaresque fiction but finds fault with many. He also reports the disagreements among the hundreds of scholars who have written about the picaresque, so that by the time one finishes reading his book, one senses, if nothing else, that opinions about "the picaresque" have varied enormously. For example, he cites one important scholar of Spanish literature, Alexander A. Parker, who explicitly rejected the idea that *Huckleberry Finn* is a part of the picaresque genre in any strict sense (Wicks 25). However, Wicks also mentions many other scholars who do regard Twain's novel as picaresque, if only very loosely (203-206). He blames Frank Wadleigh Chandler, one of the earliest and most influential of all scholars of picaresque writing, for "the confusingly loose concept of the picaresque" that allegedly flourished in the twentieth century (27). By reviewing hundreds of individual studies of picaresque writing, Wicks helps one realize just how thoroughly contested the concept of picaresque has been for so many years.

## Earlier Scholars on *Huckleberry Finn* as "Picaresque"

Wicks also surveys what earlier scholars of Mark Twain had to say about the idea that *Huckleberry Finn* is picaresque. He quotes, for example, William Dean Howells, Twain's close friend, as having remarked in *My Mark Twain* (1910) that Twain's novel is one of "the great things in picaresque fiction," although Howells quickly added, "Still, it is more poetic than picaresque, and of a deeper psychology" (204). Wicks also quotes the American scholar Martin Andrew Sharp Hume, who in 1905 called *Huckleberry Finn* "a transparent intention to experiment with an American picaro" (204). Wicks then reports that fifty years later, Lionel Trilling claimed that Twain's book "is based on the simplest of all novel-forms, the so-called picaresque novel, or novel of the road, which strings its incidents on the line of the hero's travels" (204). Trilling, however, also suggested that Twain modified the "linear simplicity of the picaresque novel" because his story has "a clear dramatic organization: it has a beginning, a middle, and an end, and a mounting suspense of interest" (204).

Having surveyed these and various other comments about *Huckleberry Finn* as possibly being picaresque, Wicks comments that his "overview of nearly a century's worth of commentary on the picaresque in America reveals a generic and modal confusion similar to what we find when we look at eighteenth-century English picaresque" (204). He asserts that claims about various American novels, both before and after *Huckleberry Finn*,

> depend on misperceptions about the picaresque. *American literature does not seem to have any more genuine picaresques than do the literatures of other countries* [emphasis added]. . . . [William Dean Howells] perpetuated (however unintentionally) a distorted meaning of a generic term whose ubiquity among subsequent critics and reviewers far exceeds the number of fictions to which it ought accurately to apply. (Wicks 205)

No sooner does Wicks make this pronouncement, however, than he immediately qualifies it, to some extent, when discussing Twain:

> But Howells's statement that *Huckleberry Finn* belongs "with the great things in picaresque fiction" rings true, even if it does not carry the resounding impact of Hemingway's assertion that all of modern American literature comes from this single book by Mark Twain. Whatever else it may be, *Huckleberry Finn* is the exemplary American picaresque, and not only in the limited sense of Trilling's conception of the picaresque. (206)

According to Wicks, then, American literature contains few examples of genuinely picaresque writing, but if there is one work of "exemplary American picaresque" fiction, it is *Huckleberry Finn*.

Other critics have been less equivocal in assessing Twain's novel as picaresque. For example, a 1964 article by Charles R. Metzger is straightforwardly titled "*The Adventures of Huckleberry Finn* as Picaresque." Metzger begins by reporting Twain's comment to Howells that he was thinking of modeling his own new novel on Lesage's *Gil Blas*, and then Metzger remarks that little attention has been paid to *Huckleberry Finn*'s obviously picaresque elements (249). He notes that the

> pícaro [*sic*], in contrast with both the courtly and the folk versions of the romantic hero, is generally not of noble but of humble birth; he does not seek adventure, he tries to survive it; and he generally finds it necessary to conduct life as best he can, usually outside of the established or respectable or legal codes of conduct supported by society. (Metzger 250)

Metzger argues that "the pícaro such as Huck Finn has at best negative status. If accidentally, as in Huck's case, he achieves positive status momentarily, he soon tires of it or loses it." Like most picaros, Huck is of low or ignoble birth. Moreover, Huck, "especially because he is a boy, must like most pícaros rely upon deception, upon stealth, upon flight, i.e., the employment of his wits and his judgment of the odds in any given situation." The typical picaro, like Huck, is a transient, but Huck "is not a transient out looking for trouble (adventure) so much as he is transient [*sic*] trying to avoid it, to get away from it." Huck's deeds often are morally motivated, and while they may not always be "gloriously heroic . . . they are admirable just the same." In addition, Huck's often comic contrivances partly resemble the typical "picaresque prank." Indeed, the prank is "the pícaro's substitute for the hero's physical combat," and Huck is a master of prankish behavior (Metzger 251-252).

Metzger suggests that Huck and Jim constitute a kind of "picaresque team," partly because of their shared low status as boy and slave (252). Metzger is particularly interesting when he notes that unlike

> the romantic hero who lives by a code, who epitomizes all of the military virtues such as strength, courage, unquestioning loyalty, propriety, whose word of honor is inviolable, Huck, as pícaro, is not strong. *He is not particularly courageous or loyal when the situation does not seem to warrant a show either of courage or loyalty* [emphasis added]. Whenever possible Huck avoids a fight. . . . As pícaro, Huck will lie to get out of a jam, but he knows that he is doing

so and is honest enough to admit "stretching the truth." If he deceives others, he does not, at least, deceive himself. (253)

As the italicized phrase shows, Metzger does not romanticize Huck, but he does intriguingly suggest that Huck's heroism is in some ways more impressive than a romantic hero's because it is spontaneous, freely chosen, and not compelled by any formal oath (253). Metzger also suggests that Huck's picaresque flights from corruption constitute implied social satire: "Flight in itself is a severe form of criticism" (253). Finally, he thinks Tom Sawyer "the ideal southern boy, stands in relation to Huck as the ideal romantic hero does to the pícaro" (255). Metzger's discussion of *Huckleberry Finn* as a picaresque novel is not only one of the earliest academic articles devoted to the subject but also one of the best.

Also helpful is Louise K. Barnett's 1979 article "Huck Finn: Picaro as Linguistic Outsider." Barnett emphasizes Huck's distance not only from society but also from the common language and rhetoric of his time, as well as from the "group values and attitudes" such language and rhetoric help sustain (221). "In order to express himself as an individual," Barnett asserts, "Huck must penetrate the deceptive façade of public language and create a speech true to his own feelings and his own view of the world" (222). She also argues that the "reaction of the audience at the first Royal Nonesuch performance is a . . . contest of labels, this time between society and the picaresque rogues, the King and the Duke" (224). Especially interesting is her claim that "Twain extends his presentation of linguistic corruption by challenging *all* speakers of public language, not merely identifiable confidence men" (228). Not until near the very end of her essay, and then only in passing, does Barnett really discuss the picaresque mode explicitly, a fact that makes her article, although interesting for many reasons, less helpful than Metzger's. Metzger had dealt insistently and openly with the idea of the picaresque; this is much less true of Barnett's essay.

Another intriguing discussion of Twain's novel as picaresque appeared in 1979, this time in Alexander Blackburn's book *The Myth of the Picaro*. Blackburn argued that, at first glance, "*Huckleberry*

*Finn* is a novel in which an apparent picaro discovers right uses for his trickery and comes to oppose the confidence men, the symbolic picaros [the King and the Duke], with whom he becomes involved" (178). Indeed, Blackburn asserts that "Huck's relationship to the confidence men is the key to interpretation of Twain's novel as picaresque" (178). Blackburn initially distinguishes between Huck and the typical picaro, whose motives are often selfish: instead, Huck's "tricks serve the causes of justice and brotherhood" (179). Huck is more moral than the standard picaro; he "revolts against a society that threatens to disintegrate into picaresque chaos" (181). Ultimately, however, Blackburn is disappointed with Twain's hero, arguing that the "trouble with Huck Finn's revolt is that it finally lacks intellectual seriousness in spite of the adventurous criticism that it is intended to release" (181). Initially, "Huck, like the picaro, flees an intolerable psychic situation by taking to the road"—or, in his case, the river (183). Huck's behavior seems to grow increasingly moral, but his final cooperation with Tom Sawyer's "evasion" scheme severely disappoints Blackburn, as it has disappointed many other readers:

> In accordance with a quest not for freedom but for pleasure, Huck soon joins forces with Tom to torment poor Jim as if the slave's humanity had never existed. No longer an outcast, Huck has entered into debased civilization [like earlier picaros]—at the price of his soul. . . . What we are [ultimately] loath to admit about Huck is his failed humanity, so we would like to believe that he escapes into freedom even at the sacrifice of love. The truth is that *Huckleberry Finn* has neither real freedom nor lasting love for our comfort. It is almost a nihilistic book. It is certainly a very sad book. (185, 187)

In Blackburn's view, Huck behaves unethically by cooperating with Tom in the "evasion scheme." In a sense, Huck thus becomes, like so many other picaros, a morally compromised figure.

A 1985 article by Stephen Gilman also briefly discusses Twain's novel in relation to the picaresque mode or genre. Gilman begins by noting that Twain's book, like other picaresque writings, presents a single narrator looking back on his life (15), and Gilman abstractly sees the book as structured as "a salvation of time rather than a picaresque loss" (16). Like much of Gilman's essay, this sentence seems less straightforwardly clear than the writing of Metzger, Barnett, and Blackburn. The overall structure and argument of his essay are also harder to follow.

Far more helpful to anyone interested in Huck Finn as picaro is another essay from 1985, this one by Daniel Williams. It is titled "The Heart's Authority: Huckleberry Finn and the Rogue Narrative Tradition." Williams sees Twain's novel as part of a long history of stories that tend to feature a "low-life hero struggling to survive in a hostile world with nothing more than his own wits" (73). This tradition predates picaresque fiction per se and includes Renaissance jest books and so-called "cony-catching" pamphlets (74), which were English works describing the Elizabethan underworld. Williams then discusses the rise of picaresque narratives in the strict sense of the term. Particularly interesting is his suggestion that by exploring "the possibilities of individual freedom, rogues were ideally suited to the New World environment, where ambition meant far more than station" (79). Williams notes that Twain, during the course of his life, especially his early years,

> actually met or read about numerous scoundrels who practiced deception as if it were a fine art. Moreover, he was particularly fascinated with outrageous impostors who pretended to be something they were not. In literature Clemens read and was influenced by several rogue narratives, especially Johnson Hopper's *The Adventures of Captain Simon Suggs* (1845). By the mid-nineteenth century, rogues had become popular characters in American literature, and Clemens, as a printer and as a writer, could not help but follow their activities. (80-81)

Williams then recounts, in some detail, the activities in *Huckleberry Finn* of the King and Duke, the novel's two most obvious rogues. He concludes, however, that the book's "ultimate rogue survivor" is Huck himself, since no other character exemplifies "the same high level of resourcefulness" (Williams 86). In an especially helpful passage, Williams declares that Huck, like so many other literary rogues . . . was launched into this world without the benefits of high birth, wealth, education, or profession. Like the King and the Duke, he soon discovered that survival required deception. As the son of the town drunk, he was a social outcast from the start, viewing society from its ugly underside. The child of chance, he learned how to survive in whatever environment he was thrown into by fate . . . and turned disadvantage into advantage. Deception was practiced, [however] not for profit but to preserve liberty. While other rogues worshipped money, Huck paid homage to his freedom. Throughout the novel he adopted a variety of roles and identities, but whenever a role was thrust upon him for profit . . . he performed miserably. However, whenever he adopted a role or stretched the truth to save either Jim or himself, he was unbeatable. (87)

It would be hard to offer a clearer, more concise assessment of Huck as picaro than this one. Meanwhile, another essay from 1985 by Lyall Powers makes many of the same points already made by Metzger and Williams while also emphasizing the darker view of Twain's book already outlined in 1979 by Blackburn. By the mid-1980s, then, many of the most common views of *Huckleberry Finn* as a work of picaresque fiction had already been outlined by various scholars.

### Huck as Picaro: Thirty-Three Criteria

Ulrich Wicks's *Research Guide* discusses many different attempts to define the characteristics of picaresque fiction. Wicks often faults these attempts, but in the course of doing so, he offers many helpful comments of his own. He argues, for example, that although romance fiction "is picaresque's almost polar opposite on the spectrum" of genres, "the relationship between picaresque and romance is a good deal more complex than a mere antithesis would require" (Wicks 47). Wicks then begins listing various similarities between the two genres.

The numbered listing below presents Wicks's ideas in italics, followed by my own indented comments.

1. *Both picaresque and romance fiction often emphasize small communities of like-minded characters* (47).

One could argue, for example, that for a time, the King, the Duke, and Huck operate as a small community of rogues in *Huckleberry Finn*, although Huck is never a truly willing member of the group.

2. *Both genres often emphasize the so-called "circle of existence," in which a character moves from security to insecurity and then often back again to security* (48).

*Huckleberry Finn* seems to fit this pattern only loosely, especially since Huck ultimately decides to abandon the security he has gained at the end of the book.

3. *Both genres involve an essential quest to find or return to a home of some sort* (48).

*Huckleberry Finn* complicates this pattern by having Huck ultimately reject the home he is taken into.

4. *Both genres often involve a "strong didactic or moral or intellectual impulse"* (48).

*Huckleberry Finn* seems to satisfy all these criteria: It implicitly teaches significant ethical lessons, especially concerning slavery, and it shows Huck pondering many important thoughts and themes, thereby encouraging readers to ponder them as well.

5. *Both genres often involve an "impulse to impose aesthetic and moral order on the chaotic past, which is re-membered now as a structure"* (49).

The possible artistic and ethical orders of Twain's novel have, of course, been discussed in ways too numerous to cover here.

---

6. *Both genres often feature tricksters; "the picaro always finds willing victims and thus gratifies our desires to be tricked, as well as to participate vicariously in the tricking itself"* (49).

Twain's novel is full of tricks and trickery, and part of the pleasure it gives surely derives from watching dupes being tricked, often deservedly so.

In addition to commenting on such similarities between the picaresque and romance genres, Wicks also helpfully outlines numerous traits he considers typical of picaresque writings per se. These are listed as continuations of the list already offered, formatted the same way.

7. *Essential to picaresque writing is "an unheroic protagonist, worse than we, caught up in a chaotic world, worse than ours, in which he is on an eternal journey of encounters that allow him to be alternately both victim of that world and its exploiter"* (54).

Obviously these comments fit *Huckleberry Finn* in many ways, especially if the Duke and King are seen as Twain's essential picaros. Huck, who is heroic in some ways and unheroic in others, is a more ambiguous figure than the two con men with whom he travels for a time.

8. *The "picaresque mode satisfies our impulse for a vicarious journey through chaos and depravity. In picaresque, we participate in the tricks essential to survival in chaos and become victims of the world's tricks"* (54).

Clearly part of the appeal of Twain's novel is the insight it offers into the con men and underworld of Twain's time and perhaps of all times.

9. *The rhythm of picaresque narratives might be called "the Sisyphus rhythm": effort, apparent success, real failure, and then a repetition of that pattern, which involves continual "dis-integration"* (55).

Obviously the episodic nature of *Huckleberry Finn* fits this pattern quite well: the narrative is essentially a compilation of one momentarily successful—but ultimately unsuccessful—scheme after another.

10. *Picaresque narratives almost by definition involve a first-person point of view, but it is important to distinguish between the "remembered 'I'" and the "remembering 'I'"—that is, between the narrator in the present and the ways he appears in his narration of his past* (55).

This idea is obviously relevant to Twain's novel, which offers one of the most memorable first-person narrators in American literature.

11. *Picaresque narratives often open with "provoking, I-dare-you-to-read-me" gestures* (58).

Twain's memorable opening gambits in *Huckleberry Finn*, such as the warning to the reader, clearly seem relevant to this claim.

12. *Readers typically feel one degree of distance or another from the picaro* (58).

Readers of Twain's book are likely to feel most distant from the King, the Duke, and Tom and perhaps least distant from Huck.

13. *Alienation, separation, and aloneness are key themes of picaresque fiction* (58).

All three themes are prominent in Twain's book, especially in connection with Huck and Jim.

14. *Although it is commonly claimed that picaresque narratives simply stop and have no formal conclusions, "a picaresque narrative ends at its beginning point when the picaro decides to narrate his life. This 'end' pervades the entire work and provides the vantage point from which every aspect of the work must be studied"* (59).

This is a claim intriguing for its implications for *Huckleberry Finn:* to what degree, and in what ways, is Huck's account of his experiences colored by his "present" knowledge about his past? Huck knows the outcome of his tale before he begins telling it; how does, or should, this fact influence our reading of his account?

15. *The "panoramic-episodic structure and the Sisyphus rhythm are singularly appropriate to the fictional world rendered in picaresque; form matches subject matter precisely"* (59).

In other words, the episodic form of picaresque fiction is appropriate to the discontinuous, now-this-then-that experiences of picaresque figures, such as the King, the Duke, and Huck.

16. *"The picaro is a pragmatic, unprincipled, resilient, solitary figure who just manages to survive in his chaotic landscape, but who, in the ups and downs, can also put that world very much on the defensive"* (60).

All of this applies to the King and Duke and much of it, arguably, to Huck as well. Huck, however, does seem principled, at least until Tom reenters the novel and concocts the "evasion scheme." It is Huck's willingness to participate in this scheme that troubles many readers.

17. *"The picaro is a protean figure who can not [sic] only serve many masters but play different roles, and his essential character trait is inconstancy (of life roles, of self-identity), his own personality flux [sic] in the face of an inconstant world"* (60).

This comment definitely applies to the King and Duke and, arguably, to Huck as well, although his personality and ethics seem more stable than theirs.

18. *Despite the savvy he soon acquires, part of [the picaro] remains engagingly innocent"* (60).

This comment applies especially to Huck.

19. *There are many more male picaros than female picaras in the picaresque tradition, although picaras are not unknown* (60-61).

No *picaras* appear in *Huckleberry Finn*.

20. *Typically, picaresque narratives involve "a movement from exclusion to attempted inclusion and back to exclusion: outside, inside, outside, resolved finally by a kind of self-exclusion through spiritual, moral, or psychological conversion" in which the picaro rejects the world, as it had rejected him* (61).

This pattern is obviously relevant to Twain's novel, especially since Huck undergoes a kind of moral conversion and also since he finally rejects the idea of being "sivilized."

21. *The picaro is an outsider* (61).

Obviously this is true of the King, the Duke, and Huck.

22. *Picaresque narratives often present a wide diversity of persons and character types—a "cross-section of society both vertically and horizontally"* (61).

Clearly this is true of *Huckleberry Finn*.

23. *In picaresque fiction, what matters is less society itself than the way society is perceived by the picaro* (62).

Part of the interest—and much of the humor—in *Huckleberry Finn* results from Huck's perceptions and misperceptions of society.

24. *Picaresque narratives are highly self-conscious about their own genre and other genres and thus often contain elements of parody, especially parody of "chivalric romances"* (62).

This idea, of course, is clearly relevant to *Huckleberry Finn*, especially when Tom Sawyer appears in the final chapters and concocts his ostensibly chivalric scheme to "free" the already-free Jim.

25. *Picaresque narratives often involve ironic tensions between what is narrated and what is implied* (62).

This idea, explained somewhat abstractly by Wicks, certainly seems to apply to *Huckleberry Finn*, arguably one of the most ironic novels in American literature, especially in its depiction of the "morality" of slavery.

26. *Disillusionment is a main picaresque theme* (62).

Huck clearly is frequently disillusioned throughout his narrative.

27. *Freedom, and sometimes even the sense of being imprisoned in freedom, is a common picaresque theme* (63).

In a sense, Huck's unsettled life gives him more freedom than he really wants, but in another sense, his freedom and Jim's are illusory, since the two characters think of themselves as criminals on the run.

28. *Hunger is another common concern in picaresque narratives* (63).

Huck and Jim's hunger is mentioned a few times early in *Huckleberry Finn*, but hunger otherwise plays little role in the novel.

29. *Picaros often have low or unusual births or childhoods that help render them outsiders almost from the start* (64).

Clearly this is true of Huck.

30. *The tricks played by picaros help emphasize the gullibility of many human beings* (64).

This theme is clearly relevant to *Huckleberry Finn*.

31. *Changes and role-playing help to define picaros: a picaro "is not only the servant of many masters but the master of many masks"* (65).

Huck, the King, and the Duke are all masters of role-playing and identity-switching, as is Tom.

32. *Picaresque fiction often emphasizes one particularly horrible event in order to emphasize the world of chaos* (65-66).

This does not seem especially true of *Huckleberry Finn*, although the several deaths, especially those in the Grangerford-Shepherdson feud, might satisfy this criterion.

33. *Ejection—especially the need to flee—is a common motif of picaresque narratives* (66).

*Huckleberry Finn* is a novel that emphasizes ejection and flight to its very last paragraph.

## Conclusions

Is *Huckleberry Finn* a picaresque novel? Comparing the book to Wicks's thirty-three criteria would suggests, quite definitely, that it is. Indeed, Twain's novel is especially interesting because it features two different *kinds* of picaros: the obviously immoral King and Duke and the much more ethical Huck. The first two figures are obvious con men; Huck, on the other hand, seems anything but. But then Huck, to the disappointment of many readers, cooperates—however reluctantly—with Tom Sawyer's morally repugnant evasion scheme. This scheme is sometimes seen as a major flaw in Twain's novel, as if Twain himself could not resist the impulse to have some final fun at the expense of long-suffering Jim. It can be argued that by bringing Tom Sawyer back into the book, Twain opted to emphasize more lies, trickery, and hair-breadth escapes (in other words, more common features of *picaresque* fiction) before bringing his novel to an end. Twain's reasons for concluding the novel by featuring the evasion scheme have been much debated (see Evans, "Civil Disobedience"), and it is not my intention here to do more than mention the controversy here and simply indicate how it might be relevant to the idea of *Huckleberry Finn* as a picaresque narrative.

However one chooses to address the moral and aesthetic problems raised by Tom's scheme, there seems no denying that in the very last words of his novel, Twain goes out of his way to re-emphasize the book's picaresque dimensions. When we last see Huck, he is contemplating yet another journey, yet more chapters in the ongoing series of his picaresque adventures. His travels have begun again, and perhaps this is one of the reasons Huck and his adventures appealed so strongly to one of America's greatest travel writers and his many readers. Twain was, after all, the author of such splendid travel books as *Innocents Abroad* (1869), *Roughing It* (1872), *A Tramp Abroad* (1880), *Life on the Mississippi* (1883), and *Following the Equator* (1897). Do any of these books offer examples of picaresque writing? An interesting question—but one for which no space remains to answer.

## Works Cited

Barnett, Louise K. "Huck Finn: Picaro as Linguistic Outsider." *College Literature* 6.3 (1979): 221-231.

Blackburn, Alexander. *The Myth of the Picaro: Continuity and Transformation of the Picaresque Novel, 1554–1954*. Chapel Hill, NC: U of North Carolina P, 1979.

Evans, Robert C. "Civil Disobedience and the Ending of Mark Twain's *Adventures of Huckleberry Finn*." *Civil Disobedience*. Ed. Harold Bloom & Blake Hobby. New York: Bloom's Literary Criticism, 2010. 21-29.

Gilman, Stephen. "*Adventures of Huckleberry Finn*: Experience of Samuel Clemens." *One Hundred Years of Huckleberry Finn: The Boy, His Book, and American Culture*. Ed. Robert Sattelmayer, Donald J. Crowley, & John C. Gerber. Columbia: U of Missouri P, 1985. 15-25.

Gribben Alan. *Mark Twain's Library: A Reconstruction*. 2 vols. Boston: G. K. Hall, 1980.

Howells, William Dean. *My Mark Twain: Reminiscences and Criticisms*. New York: Harper & Bros., 1910.

Metzger, Charles R. "*The Adventures of Huckleberry Finn* as Picaresque." *Midwest Quarterly* 5 (1964): 249-256.

Powers, Lyall. "Mark Twain and the Future of Picaresque." *Mark Twain: A Sumptuous Variety*. Ed. Robert Giddings. Totowa, NJ: Barnes & Noble, 1985: 155-175.

Wicks, Ulrich. *Picaresque Narrative, Picaresque Fictions: A Theory and Research Guide*. New York: Greenwood Press, 1989.

Williams, Daniel. "The Heart's Authority: *Huckleberry Finn* and the Rogue Narrative Tradition." *Samuel L. Clemens: A Mysterious Stranger*. Ed. Hans Borchers & Daniel E. Williams. Frankfurt, Germany: Peter Lang, 1986. 71-92.

# Identity Switching in *Huckleberry Finn*⎯⎯⎯⎯

Linda A. Morris

*Adventures of Huckleberry Finn* is a novel rife with characters switching their identities or taking on new, false identities, far more often than one might at first recall. In fact, watching characters switch in and out of identities is one of the ongoing pleasures in reading the novel. We never know when to expect it to happen next, but we do know that the pre-Civil War frontier society that is the setting for the novel offers multiple opportunities for characters to reinvent themselves. For the young protagonist and narrator, Huck Finn, creating a new self in a difficult situation seems to come naturally, but it emerges as a necessity as he and his raft companion, Jim, drift ever farther south into slave territory. For other characters, the frontier society offers nearly unlimited opportunities to defraud naïve folks who live along the Mississippi River—hence the relative success of the two con men known as the King and the Duke. Finally, the ever-innovative and unexpected visitor, Tom Sawyer, freed from the oversight of his Aunt Polly in St. Petersburg and let loose on a frontier plantation, encounters a large stage upon which to enact his elaborate "evasion." It is the same stage, overall, upon which Mark Twain, Tom-Sawyer-like, offers up a tour de force of identities within identities and characters within characters.

Most readers probably agree that the most memorable identity switching comes relatively early, in chapter 10, when Huck dresses as a girl and goes to shore to "find out what was going on." There he meets up with Judith Loftus, who puts him through a series of tests to see if he is "really" a girl. This is but one of the multiple times Huck takes on a new identity in the course of the novel. In almost every other instance, he does so spontaneously with only one real motivation—to get himself (and Jim) out of a tight place. In short, he switches identity when he feels he must do so to maintain their freedom—to survive.

---

Huck is not the only character to switch identities in the course of the action, but he is the only one to do so innocently. In sharp contrast, for example, when the King and Duke take over the raft and the plot for fully twenty-two chapters, it is clear from the beginning that they are practiced impostors, professional con men who impersonate others for their own personal gain. Finally, at the end of the novel, Tom Sawyer enters the action in the guise of his half-brother, Sid. He ostensibly joins Huck in a clever identity switch in order to help free Jim from captivity. But he actually does so in order to mastermind an elaborate and complex plot that takes in everyone, from the Phelps family to Huck and Jim themselves.

This essay will take up these three different forms and motivations of identity switching in the pages that follow, beginning with the relative innocence of Huck's taking on different identities whenever he is in danger, thereby revealing how clever and spontaneous he must be as he rafts down the Mississippi River with the escaped slave Jim. We will then look in some detail at the many times the Duke and King pose as someone they are not in order to defraud gullible folks living along the banks of the river. Finally, we will look at how Tom Sawyer operates as a trickster in the final episodes on the Phelps farm.

## Huck's Multiple Identities

The first instance of Huck's identity switching is, in fact, when he dresses up as a girl and goes ashore from Jackson's Island. As I argued in *Gender Play in Mark Twain: Cross-Dressing and Transgression* (2007), Huck's decision to dress in girl's clothing is a whimsical one that is suggested by Jim. Huck finds that things on the island have become "slow and dull," and he wants to "get a stirring up." Before he can hope to pull off his female impersonation, however, he has to practice, so he receives instruction from Jim in how to walk and act like a girl. This is one of the few times in the novel when he decides ahead of time to take on a different identity rather than do so spontaneously, although he does not think through just *which* girl he is.

**" COME IN."**

Dressed as a girl, Huck introduces himself to Mrs. Loftus as "Sarah
Williams"–a name he forgets a few minutes later.

When Huck enters the house of Judith Loftus in chapter 11, he
gives himself a girl's name in response to Mrs. Loftus's question:
"Sarah Williams." When asked a bit later to repeat his name, he
misremembers and says "Mary Williams":

> Somehow it didn't seem to me that I said it was Mary, before; so
> I didn't look up; seemed to me I said it was Sarah; so I felt sort
> of cornered, and was afeard maybe I was looking it, too. I wished

the woman would say something more; the longer she set still, the uneasier I was. But now she says:

"Honey, I thought you said it was Sarah when you first come in?"

"O yes'm, I did. Sarah Mary Williams. Sarah's my first name. Some calls me Sarah, some calls me Mary."

"O, that's the way of it?"

"Yes'm."

Here Huck means no harm; his self-naming is so spontaneous that he himself forgets what he has named himself. But at the same time he nimbly gets himself out of a tight place, he also raises Judith Loftus's suspicions. She puts him through a series of tests to see if he is really a girl. When he fails, the jig is up. Mrs. Loftus tells him he may as well come clean about who he really is: "So I said it wouldn't be no use to try to play it any longer, and I would just make a clean breast and tell her everything . . ." But, of course, he does no such thing.

In the wink of an eye, Huck reinvents himself yet again, this time as an orphan boy named George Peters, who had been "bound" to a "mean old farmer" who treated him so badly that he stole his daughter's clothes and ran away. What is fascinating here is the mixture of truth and invention—Huck is in fact an orphan, though he does not yet know that Pap is dead, and he had been "bound" to a mean old man, Pap himself, from whom he escaped. What is also fascinating is that for the first time we see just how protean Huck is—how quickly he can invent a new self and a new name (and a new family), which becomes one of the central comic pleasures of the novel. Who is Huck really? Does he have a firm identity of his own? What does it take to keep himself safe and alive, and Jim safe and alive, as he and Jim venture deeper and deeper into slave territory, and farther away from his identity in St. Petersburg?

The ultimate effect of Huck's cross-dressing as Sarah Mary Williams is that he gains valuable information from Judith Loftus, namely that a search party is planning to search Jackson's Island that night to look for Jim. It propels Huck into action and to join his fate with Jim's: "'Git up and hump yourself, Jim! There ain't a minute to lose. They're after *us*" [emphasis added]. And so the long journey down the Mississippi River begins, a journey in which Huck will have to rely on his wits, his quick thinking, and his ability to reinvent himself on the spot to stay alive and to keep Jim free.

The next time Huck takes on a new identity it is not to get himself or Jim out of a tight place, but to attempt to save a gang of robbers and murderers trapped on the wrecked steamboat, the *Walter Scott*. Huck reasons "I begun to think how dreadful it was, even for murderers, to be in such a fix. I says to myself, there ain't no telling but I might come to be a murderer myself, yet, and then how would *I* like it?" (chapter 13). He tells a watchman on a ferryboat that his family is all marooned on the wreck. He not only invents a whole family for himself, but fabricates an entire story and fills it with additional characters—a Miss Hooker, "Miss What-you-may-call her," Bill Whipple, Uncle Hornback, and someone he calls "pap." Once again a "pap" character shows up when Huck creates a new identity for himself, along with a new family. Having escaped from his real Pap, "pap" figures are never far from his imagination—a force that haunts him as he drifts downstream. Ironically, while Huck will not know this until Jim tells him in the final moments of the novel, his "real" Pap was, in fact, in the floating house they had found in chapter 9, and he was already dead. Or as Jim says, "he ain't comin' back no mo'" (chapter 43).

One of Huck's best comic reinventions of himself takes place in a long episode that was omitted from the original printed versions of *Adventures of Huckleberry Finn*, but reinserted in the University of California Press's critical editions after 1985. I refer to the entertaining, energetic "rafting" episode that constitutes most of chapter 16 of that text. The episode takes place on a large raft of the sort that were common on the river in earlier days, peopled with a host of characters who sing ribald songs, who stage a mock fight (and a real fight), characters called "Sudden Death" and "General Desolation," and "The Child of Calamity." There are plenty of yarns spun, too, including a long tale about a dead baby in a barrel—Dick Allbright's baby—that followed a raft from time to time over a three-year period. In the midst of the telling, Huck, who has been hiding, is discovered and hauled out onto the raft proper. When challenged to tell his name, Huck reports "I warn't going to tell my name. I didn't know what to say, so I just says 'Charles William Allbright, sir.'" The raftsmen laugh at such a preposterous possibility—the baby being dead and having been dead for three years—so Huck "admits" he is really "Aleck Hopkins—Aleck James Hopkins" who lives on a trading scow with Pap, and who has come onto the raft for an adventure. With that admission, he is released overboard to swim to shore, where he rejoins Jim.

There are two more incidents in which Huck takes on new identities before the final episode on the Phelps farm (not including his time with the Duke and the King). One comes almost immediately after the raft incident, in the same chapter, this time with Huck in a canoe attempting to discover if he and Jim have yet passed Cairo, where the Ohio River joins the Mississippi. Further, because his "conscience" has begun bothering him, he determines to reveal that he has a runaway slave with him on his raft. On the way, he encounters two men on a skiff who are searching for five escaped slaves; when pushed by them to tell if the man on his raft is black or white, Huck finally says "white." When they threaten to go see for themselves, Huck begins a clever deception, saying that he hopes they will go see because his Pap is sick (and his mother and sister, too), and no one will help them. Huck carefully leads the men on until they conclude that Pap "has the small pox," which they guess is why people won't go near the raft. They begin to back away, tell Huck to go on downstream twenty miles, and as an afterthought, each give him a twenty dollar gold piece, passed carefully to him on a paddle, because they don't want to come near him and because they feel sorry for him. Huck never gives himself a name in this episode, but once again, he gives himself a pap and a mother and sister. His deception is clever and totally spontaneous, a yarn and identity invented on the spot to save himself and to save Jim, in spite of his original intention at this point to turn Jim in. It is a close call, but his wit and his protean ability to switch identities save the day.

Huck's next self-invention comes about a third of the way through the novel, when the raft is smashed to pieces by a steamboat, and Huck and Jim are separated in the dark. Huck hauls out of the river and is immediately surrounded by barking and howling dogs, "and I knowed better than to move another peg." (chapter 16) When confronted by a voice from inside the house, demanding to know who he is, Huck immediately responds, "It's me—George Jackson, sir." For two chapters, and for an extended stay on shore with the Grangerford family, Huck *is* George Jackson. When asked to tell his story, he invents, as ever, Pap, as well as a whole family—a sister, three brothers, and a mother. In the same sentence in which he introduces his family, however, they all die off, except Pap. But before the sentence finishes, Pap, too, is dead; once more Huck/George goes forward as an orphan. One chapter later, the Grangerford men themselves are all dead, killed in a deadly feud with the Shepherdsons, and Huck is rather miraculously reunited with Jim, who has been in hiding throughout the whole episode.

## Sinister Identity Switching: The Duke and the King

Shortly after the Grangerford chapters, two scoundrels, the Duke and King, take over the raft and the plot for nearly half the chapters in the book. These are the chief impostors of the novel, and they move in an out of various identities for one reason only: to defraud a host of gullible citizens living along the banks of the Mississippi River. They are cheats, they are frauds, they are con men, they are scoundrels, and they are "low-down humbugs." Nevertheless, they provide a long series of seriocomic interludes and pages of entertainment for the reader.

From the moment we meet them, the scoundrels are each running to escape from a group of local men and their dogs, who are hell bent on capturing them. Clearly they have been perpetrating some form of fraud and have to jump on Huck and Jim's raft to escape the men pursuing them. Strangers to each other until this point, they proceed to introduce themselves to each other in the most grandiose terms. The younger one declares himself to be the Duke of Bridgewater, while the older one, not to be outdone, claims to be "the late Dauphin," or Louis XVII, "rightful" king of France. They do this to lay claim to some kind of special treatment by impressing the other with their credentials and would-be identities. As a matter of fact, we never do know who they "really" are, for their self-naming sticks throughout the many escapades they orchestrate, referred to in the narrative as simply "the Duke" or "the King" and occasionally addressed by Huck as "your Majesty." It doesn't take Huck and Jim long to figure out they are frauds, but as long as Huck and Jim are in their power, they have no choice but to go along with them. Or as Huck says, "If I never learnt nothing else out of pap, I learnt that the best way to get along with his kind of people is to let them have their own way." (chapter 19)

Huck, for his part, also takes on a false identity before the two impostors. He tells the Duke and King that he is from Pike County, Missouri, and invents another entire family for himself, with the whole family dying, except Pa and brother Ike, and their slave, Jim. According to Huck's story, he, Pa, and Ike, plus Jim, were headed down to New Orleans on a raft when they were run over by a steamboat. Pa, a drunk, and Ike, only four years old, were killed in the accident, and Huck and Jim were left on their own. (chapter 20) As he will do so often, Huck fashions a new identity for himself (this time with no name attached) and weaves into his tall tale, which he creates on the spur of the moment, bits and pieces of his real story. Apparently the mixture of truth and falsehood gives him maximum room to create a new identity when circumstances call for it.

As the story unfolds, the two impostors, the Duke and the King, take on a variety of other identities, all created to defraud the locals along the way for their personal gain. They claim to be variously a printer; a salesman; a mesmerizer; a fortune teller; a doctor; a preacher; a pirate; Romeo and Juliet; the Shakespearean actors David Garrick the Younger and Edmund Kean the Elder; and, most prominently (and most perniciously), Harvey and William Wilks, supposed brothers to a recently deceased farmer, Peter Wilks, father of three unmarried daughters. Most often, Huck (and to some extent,

Jim) are mere witnesses to the various frauds the King and Duke perpetrate, such as the King frolicking naked on the stage, painted in stripes and colors, in "The King's Camelopard," or "The Royal Nonesuch." Huck describes the King's performance from the point of view of a spectator to the action on the stage and simultaneously as one observing the crowd:

> and at last when he'd got everybody's expectations up high enough, he rolled up the curtain, and the next minute the King come a-prancing out on all fours, naked; and he was painted, all over, ring-streaked-and-striped, all sorts of colors, as splendid as a rain-bow. And—but never mind the rest of his outfit, it was just wild, but it was awful funny. The people most killed themselves laughing; and when the King got done capering, and capered off behind the scenes, they roared and clapped and stormed and haw-hawed till he come back and done it over again; and after that, they made him do it another time. Well, it would a made a cow laugh, to see the shines that old idiot cut. (chapter 23)

At crucial times in the text, the Duke and King also force Huck and Jim to take on false identities, all to further their own ends. For instance, in order to "work the towns" without having to keep Jim tied up on the raft all day (if he weren't tied up people might think he is an escaped slave, they reason) the Duke decides to dress Jim up "in King Lear's outfit":

> it was a long curtain-calico gown, and a white horse-hair wig and whiskers; and then he took his theatre-paint and painted Jim's face and hands and ears and neck all over a dead dull solid blue, like a man's that been drownded nine days. Blamed if he warn't the horriblest looking outrage I ever see. Then the duke took and wrote out a sign on a shingle, so—*"Sick Arab—but harmless when not out of his head."* (chapter 24).

Dressed up in new store-bought clothes and heading out to see what adventure he might stir up, the King renames Huck "Adolphus," his servant, and for a brief time renames himself "Elexander Blodgett—*Reverend* Elexander Blodgett . . . one of the Lord's poor servants." In this guise, he pumps information out of a "young country jake" that leads him to reinvent himself once again, this time as Harvey Wilks. Thus the King launches his longest and most complex defrauding scheme. There are layers of identities at work in this episode. We see the unnamed scoundrel, masquerading as the late French king, assuming the identity of the Reverend Blodgett, remaking himself into Harvey Wilks, the long-absent brother of the newly deceased farmer Peter Wilks. Meanwhile, the unnamed Duke will become, in this long episode, William Wilks, the deaf-mute younger brother of Peter Wilks. Huck will continue in his public role as their servant, while Jim, in the meantime, is confined to the raft dressed as King Lear, the Sick Arab, and absent from any of the drama at the Wilks farm.

Huck's disgust with the King and Duke throughout the Wilks episode is explicit. He is forced to bear witness to all their fraudulent emotions (sorrow over the death of their "brother"), the Duke's blubbering and hand-waving as a supposed deaf-mute, their fake piety as they kneel before their "brother's" coffin. Huck's narration during this section, presented in indirect discourse, is forceful and disparaging:

> Well, by and by the king he gets up and comes forward a little, and works himself up and slobbers out a speech, all full of tears and flapdoodle about its being a sore trial for him and his poor brother to lose the diseased, and to miss seeing diseased alive, after the long journey of four thousand miles, but it's a trial that's sweetened and sanctified to us by this dear sympathy and these holy tears, and so he thanks them out of his heart and out of his brother's heart, because out of their mouths they can't, words being too weak, and cold, and all that kind of rot and slush, till it was just sickening; and then blubbers out a pious goody-goody Amen, and turns himself loose and goes to crying fit to bust. (chapter 25)

The King and Duke's deception is ultimately exposed, first by a doctor friend of the late Peter Wilks, who laughs at the King's fake English accent, declaring the King to be "the thinnest kind of imposter." The doctor's view does not prevail, and the King, in his greed, sells off all the slaves, separating children from their parents and all the slaves from the Wilks family. Meanwhile, Huck has taken an extraordinary risk and tells the oldest daughter, Mary Jane, the truth about the fake brothers. "Well, I says to myself, at last, I'm agoing to chance it; I'll up and tell the truth this time, though it does seem most like setting down on a kag of powder and touching it off, just to see where you'll go to." (chapter 27) He persuades Mary Jane to leave town for a brief few hours, assuring her that the slaves will all be returned and the families reunited. The King holds a formal auction, two days after the funeral for Peter Wilks, and sells everything that can be sold, even a grave lot. Two minutes later, the "real" brothers get off a steamboat and are escorted into town, where they immediately challenge the King and Duke to prove they are Peter's brothers. The King refuses to back down, and for a few pages, there are two sets of brothers claiming to be the rightful heirs to the estate. In the dust-up that ensues, Huck breaks away from the grip of the doctor and makes it back to the raft and to Jim, only to be followed by the Duke and King who also run away from the crowd and retake the raft.

### Enter Trickster Tom Sawyer

Huck escapes from the clutches of the Duke and King only when the Duke "sells" Jim to an Arkansas farmer, Silas Phelps, for a promised $200 reward. This action, in turn, launches the final episodes in the novel consisting of Huck, Tom, and Jim's adventures on the Phelps's farm. When Huck learns from the Duke what has happened to Jim, he immediately heads for the Phelps farm where, much to his surprise, he is greeted warmly by Aunt Sally Phelps:

"It's *you*, at last!—*ain't* it?"

I out with a "Yes'm," before I thought.

She grabbed me and hugged me tight; and then gripped me by both hands, and shook and shook, and the tears come in her eyes, and run down over; and she couldn't seem to hug and shake enough, and kept saying, "You don't look as much like your mother as I reckoned you

would, but law sakes, I don't care for that, I'm so glad to see you."
(chapter 32)

Expecting a visit from her nephew, Tom Sawyer, Aunt Sally is sure Huck *is* Tom and introduces him as such to Uncle Silas, who is as glad to see him as Sally is. If Sally and Silas are overjoyed that "Tom" has arrived, "it warn't nothing to what I was; for it was like being born again, I was so glad to find out who I was."

With these words, a new chapter opens out in the novel in the section often referred to as "The Evasion." Tom Sawyer, when he inevitably arrives, and after having been briefed by Huck, first tells the Phelpses that his name is William Thompson, a stranger from Hicksville, Ohio. In that guise he provocatively leans over and kisses Aunt Sally on the mouth, which sets her ready temper flying: "You owdacious puppy." Then he declares himself to be Sid Sawyer, his half-brother, and says he persuaded Aunt Polly to let him come along, eleven hundred miles down the Mississippi River, with "Tom." For the rest of the novel, the two boys are known to the family as Tom and Sid. With the "real" Tom guiding every part of the plot, they proceed to inflict no end of mischief on Aunt Sally and enact Tom's elaborate scheme to free Jim.

Jim, meanwhile, is also present under a false identity, albeit one forced upon him by circumstance. He has ostensibly been captured as an escaped slave (which he actually is) but an escaped slave invented by the Duke via a "wanted" poster describing Jim and saying there is a $200 reward for his capture by his owner at St. Jacques plantation below New Orleans. So like both Huck and Tom, Jim is represented in an identity that is not his own, and all will remain so until the final pages of the novel. What differs about his switched identity, here and earlier, is that it is forced upon him by others.

While the switched identities of Huck and Tom (and Jim) hold until the final pages of the book, there are still more identity switching to take place as part of Tom's wildly imaginative plot to rescue Jim. In the final moments of the escape plan, Huck masquerades as a serving girl, dressed in a girl's dress that they "snitched" off the clothes line that belonged to "that yaller girl." In short, he is a white boy masquerading for a brief few moments as a slave girl. Tom's script has him taking on the role of Jim's mother for the escape, a plot supposedly based on the French king Louis XVI's escape from "The Tooleries" (Tuileries). Tom steals one of Aunt Sally's gowns in order to pass for Jim's mother. But as Huck points out, if he takes Jim's place in the guise of Jim's mother, he will have to stay behind when they escape, so instead, he stuffs Jim's clothes full of straw and leaves them on the bed, and he dresses *Jim* in Aunt Sally's gown. In that disguise, Jim escapes dressed (as it were) as his own mother. In these invented identities the three flee from the Phelps's place, chased by a posse of neighbors with guns and by a pack of dogs. Tom is shot in the leg, Huck returns to the town, and Jim comes out of hiding on an island, still dressed in Aunt Sally's dress, to help a doctor tend to Tom. Shortly after they are all once again back at the Phelps's place, still carrying their alternate identities.

Unraveling all the assumed identities only happens when Tom's Aunt Polly unexpectedly arrives from St. Petersburg and reveals that "Sid" is really Tom, and "Tom" is really Huck Finn. Tom then proudly retells the whole story of "the Evasion," which he has masterminded. Only then does he reveal that he has known from the beginning that Jim has been freed by his former owner, Miss Watson, back in St. Petersburg, and that he has masterminded an elaborate plot to free a man who is already free. He is the ultimate trickster, in part by withholding crucial information from his friend Huck about Jim and in part by putting everyone through weeks of pranks and high jinks.

In the end, as the story is wrapped up, we as readers may feel a bit like Uncle Silas when all is revealed to him:

Aunt Sally she was one of the mixed-upest looking persons I ever see; except one, and that was Uncle Silas, when he come in, and they told it all to him. It kind of made him drunk, as you may say, and he didn't know nothing at all the rest of the day, and preached a prayer meeting sermon that night that give him a rattling reputation, because the oldest man in the world couldn't a understood it. So Tom's Aunt Polly she told all about who I was, and what, and I had to up and tell how I was in such a tight place that when Mrs. Phelps took me for Tom Sawyer—she chipped in and says, "O, go one and call me Aunt Sally, I'm used to it, now, and 't ain't no need to change"—that when Aunt Sally took me for Tom Sawyer, I had to stand it—there warn't no other way, and I knowed he wouldn't mind, because it would be nuts for him, being a mystery, and he'd make an adventure out of it, and be pretty satisfied. And so it turned out, and he let on to be Sid, and made things as soft as he could for me. (chapter 42)

In terms of the whole subject of switched identities and invented selves, one of the most satisfying lines in the whole novel is Huck's statement that "Tom's Aunt Polly, she told all about who I was, and what . . ." At last it would seem that Huck's identity is fixed for once and for all, but we know, through all these adventures, that Huck's "real" identity is fluid, protean, imaginative. Back in the fold of Tom and Aunt Polly and the freed Jim's St. Petersburg world, Huck's identity may be firm and solid, but when he cuts loose again and heads out to the territories "ahead of the rest," well, he'll just have to trust to Providence to "put the right words in my mouth when the time come . . ." (chapter 32) and to tell him who he is.

# "Pow-wows of cussing": Profanity and Euphemistic Variants in *Huckleberry Finn*——————

Sarah Fredericks

The world along the Mississippi River, as Huck tells us in *Adventures of Huckleberry Finn*, is filled with cussing. Examples are numerous. He mentions "a pow-wow of cussing" on a steamboat in chapter 16. Town men in chapter 18 cavort, "cussing and yelling." Huck hears "talking and cussing and laughing" on rafts in chapter 19. Country folks talk "lazy and drawly, and [use] considerable many cuss words" in chapter 21. The scoundrel known as the King even cusses himself in chapter 27. Even folks on the pious Phelps farm cuss the captive Jim "considerable," and when the doctor in their town defends Jim, "every one of them [promises], right out and hearty, that they wouldn't cuss him no more" (chapter 42). No one in the novel, however, seems more proficient at cussing than Huck's own Pap:

> Then the old man got to cussing, and cussed everything and everybody he could think of, and then cussed them all over again to make sure he hadn't skipped any, and after that he polished off with a kind of a general cuss all round, including a considerable parcel of people which he didn't know the names of, and so called them What's-his-name, when he got to them, and went right along with his cussing (chapter 6).

At least nineteen times, Huck mentions someone swearing. Yet, despite the large volume of "cussing" throughout the novel, explicit curse words are nearly absent from the novel.

Profanity was one of Sam Clemens's favorite vices, matched only by his smoking. Most of his works push the boundaries of nineteenth-century standards of propriety, cleverly incorporating explicit words or expressions in such a way as not to offend delicate sensibilities irreparably. In *Huckleberry Finn*, however, he is uncharacteristically circumspect in his avoidance of explicit curse words. Instead he uses a variety of non-explicit variants that function connotatively, replicating the act of cussing without using the explicit words. Because of the near absence of explicit profanity throughout the novel, Huck and Jim's passionate, almost-profane expressions at pivotal moments in their character development become stronger. The non-explicit profanity in the novel also contributes to the book's characterizations and extends its satire's nuances.

## Defining "Dirty Words"

Any discussion of "dirty words" necessitates clarification of what constitutes foul language, the nomenclature used to distinguish among its different forms, and the complex factors involved in its offensiveness. Dirty words can be classified by the taboos or social proscriptions they violate. "High taboos," for example, are prohibitions regarding the sacred and include profanity, blasphemy, cursing, and oaths. "Low taboos" often refer to the human body, its functions, and effluvia and include insults, vulgarity, and obscenity. "Obscenity" is often reserved for the most highly charged and caustic words in a given community. In modern America, racial slurs—particularly the word "nigger"—are some of the most vitriolic appellations and are considered by many unspeakable, hence the circumlocution "n-word" for "nigger." The fact that the word appears more than two hundred times in *Huckleberry Finn* has led many schools and libraries to consider dropping the novel. In 2011, NewSouth Books published controversial altered editions of *Tom Sawyer* and *Huckleberry Finn* in which the word "slave" replaces "nigger" and "Indian" replaces "Injun." Modern taboos regarding racial slurs make it impossible for readers to overlook the word, whereas most nineteenth-century readers did not consider it as objectionable.

In addition to the individual taboos violated, the offensiveness of a word or phrase is tightly bound to its rhetorical situation. Perceptions of a word's offensiveness are influenced by the dynamics of its context, the demographic characteristics of and personal relationships between speakers and listeners, the exigency of the situation, and intervening moral and social constraints. Language that is highly offensive in one context may actually reinforce a positive social connection in another. Boundaries demarcating what constitutes swearing can also blur. Foul language comprises both the words themselves and the intentions and functions of speech acts— what Ruth Wajnryb calls their "domains of achievement," namely, "catharsis, aggression, and social connection" in *Expletive Deleted: A Good Look at Bad Language* (25). Words can be classified as explicit or non-explicit and still function connotatively as foul language. Conversely, words that might be explicit in one context may not be in another, depending on their domains of achievement.

## Patterns of Profanity in Twain's Works

Early in his writing career, Mark Twain boldly defended his use of "shocking words." In an 1864 article about the Nevada legislature for the *Territorial Enterprise*, he addressed the prudish practice of censoring potentially offensive language:

> When I spell "devil" in my usual frank and open manner, [a compositor] puts it "d——l"! Now, Lord love his conceited and accommodating soul, if I choose to use the language of the vulgar, the low-flung and the sinful, and such as will shock the ears of the highly civilized, I don't want him to appoint himself an editorial critic and proceed to tone me down and save me from the consequences of my conduct; that is, unless I pay him for it, which I won't. I expect I could spell "devil" before that fastidious cuss was born (Twain, *Mark Twain of the Enterprise* 139)

This audaciousness was later tempered by his deeply felt desire for recognition by respectable writers, creating a tension between warring impulses of subversive rebellion and submission to propriety. More often than not, in his use of profanity, Twain adopts the role of the good bad boy whose scampish revolt against domestication secretly delights his mother.

Whereas Twain reveled in low taboo subject matter, he most consistently employs high taboo explicit language, especially curses and profanity. In the nineteenth century, even the mildest vulgarities

---

were heavily suppressed due to Victorian sensibilities regarding low taboo words. For example, "limb" often replaced "leg," and "sweat" was considered unconscionably vulgar. Consequently, low taboo language largely disappeared from published discourse. With high taboo profanity, Twain could use stronger expressions and shades of variants. For example, he uses "damn" at least once in nearly every major published work except *Huckleberry Finn* and *The Prince and the Pauper* (1881) and the variants in those—"blame" and "confounded"—are non-explicit substitutes for "damn." At the time, "damn" was one of the strongest swear words allowed in works intended for broad readership, and thus it was one Mark Twain repeatedly used. Subjectivity over standards of decency, however, meant that "damn" was frequently censored with dashes, appearing as "d——n," "d——," or even "——."

Profanity could also be variously censored within a single work to reflect nuances in respectability and decorum of the speaker, for a profane word uttered by a laborer or backcountry rustic was decidedly less shocking than one spoken by the educated or genteel. In *Life on the Mississippi* (1883), a number of speakers use "damn" or "damned," ranging from steamboat pilots and mates to a pet parrot. In chapter 53, an old man in Hannibal uses the word, telling the narrator, "if you send a damned fool to St. Louis, and you don't tell them he's a damned fool they'll never find it out." This same profane expression, however, is censored in a yarn narrated in chapter 36 by a college professor recalling a gambler shouting, "Four kings, you d——d fool!" As the narrator of *Life on the Mississippi*, Twain himself uses "damn" ambiguously. For instance, in chapter 25 he describes the profane Uncle Mumford who makes vain oaths and "goes gravely damning around." By redefining "damning" as the act of using the word "damn," Twain invokes the profane word without actually using it.

Throughout his works, Twain exploits norms dictating from whom profanity is considered least distasteful, often softening its offensiveness by constructing a frame narrative. The frame permits him to introduce all manner of crass, profane, or vernacular speech to audiences by forcing ostensibly refined narrators (and the readers by extension) to be humorously "trapped" into listening to tales by voluble and foul-mouthed rustics who might realistically be expected to use foul language. From the garrulous Simon Wheeler of the jumping frog story to the imaginary traveling companion Mr. Brown of some of Twain's travel narratives, colorful rustics allowed Twain to distance his narrators from rough language or vulgar expressions. In *A Tramp Abroad* (1880), for example, Twain uses the frame to create a double insulation. Chapters 2 and 3 recall a conversation with a prospector named Jim Baker, whose interpolated yarn recounts a blue jay's expert ability to swear. Frustrated in his attempts to fill a house with acorns, the bird says, "I'm d——d if I *don't* fill you, if it takes a hundred years!" By using a frame construction, the profanity is twice removed from Twain's narrator, and its offensiveness diminished further by the guise of local color and tall tales.

Another common technique for including profanity is the creation of puns around profane words, playing on ambiguities between offensive and inoffensive meanings. For example, in an 1869 editorial for the *Buffalo Express*, Mark Twain explained how visitors to Niagara Falls were astonished by the astronomical prices for hacks (taxicabs), saying that before they were regulated, "hack fares were so much higher than the Falls that the Falls appeared insignificant." "It became apparent," he added, "that either the Falls had to be discontinued or the hackmen had to subside. They could not dam the Falls, and so they damned the hackmen." The pun plays on two levels: *dam* for "restrict" and *damn* for "condemn," as well as *damn* for "condemn" and *damn* as an explicit curse. Similarly, in chapter 15 of *A Connecticut Yankee* (1889), Twain compares the usefulness of the donkey to that of an aristocrat: "Take a jackass, for instance: a jackass has that kind of strength, and puts it to a useful purpose, and is valuable to this world because he is a jackass; but a nobleman is not valuable because he is a jackass." Here the pun plays between *jackass* for "donkey" and *jackass* as a non-explicit epithet for a stubborn person versus *jackass* as an explicit epithet for a stupid person. Despite his stated antipathy for puns, Twain used the form on a number of occasions.

Twain frequently gives readers a taste of the profane without replicating the full crime, creating the suggestion of swearing while leaving the exact words up to readers' imaginations. One way he achieves this effect is by including only a few swear words and then dashing out more offensive words, explaining to readers, as he does in chapter 20 of *A Tramp Abroad*, that the omitted material is "not Sunday school words," so he is "obliged to put blanks where they occur." That same book relates an encounter in Germany with a young American man studying abroad. When asked if he is homesick, the youth enthusiastically responds, "Oh, hell yes!" He continues:

> Yes indeedy! If *I* ain't an American there *ain't* any Americans, that's all. And when I heard you fellows gassing away in the good old American language, I'm —— if it wasn't all I could do to keep from hugging you! My tongue's all warped with trying to curl it around these —— —— —— forsaken wind-galled nine-jointed German words here.

Twain's use of dashes here is playfully irreverent. Although they seem at first to be merely polite self-censoring, they ironically shift the offense of profanity to the book's readers, forcing them to supply the missing offensive words themselves.

Twain occasionally indulges in a more pervasive style of profanity, repeating the same offense throughout a work. In "'Party Cries' in Ireland," a sketch he first published in *Sketches New & Old* in 1875, Mark Twain wrote about a town so deeply and painfully divided between religious factions that its government outlawed party cries such as "To hell with the Pope!" and "To hell with the Protestants!" Offenders were subject to steep fines. When a drunkard shouted "to *hell* with" over and over, a policeman, smelling a fine, tries to get the drunk to complete his thought by asking him, "To hell with *who*? To hell with *what*?" The forty-shilling fine, unfortunately, is "too expinsive" for the drunk, so he asks the policeman to finish the line himself. Mark Twain's excessive repetition of "to hell with" loosens the phrase from its denotative offense.

In other situations, Twain uses non-explicit substitutes that maintain the rhythm, energy, color, and (sometimes) sound of profane expressions while tempering their offensiveness. These variants give the impression of swearing and allow for shades of nuance in tone, style, and voice. For example, his variants for "damn" include *beaten, blame, blazes, bother, cuss, dam, dern, durn, deuce, drat, dum, hang, plague, (dead) rat,* and *thundering*; for "damned," he uses *blamed, blasted, blessed, confounded, cussed, dashed,* and *ding-busted*; and for "damnation," he uses *nation, dumnation,* and *perdition.* His variants for "Lord" include *land, lan, law, laws,* and *lawsy*; for "Jesus," he uses *geeminy, geewhillikins,* and *Jackson*; for "God" he uses *dad-, goodness, (by) George, (by) Jackson, (great) guns,* and *(great) Scott*; and for "hell" he uses *blazes, dingnation, Halifax, Jericho, Sam Hill, thunder,* and *yell.* One of the few low taboo variants, "shit" becomes *shucks.* Twain uses these colloquialisms and dialectical variants throughout his works to supplement and supplant explicitly profane words.

## Profanity in Huckleberry Finn

Given Twain's penchant for profanity, the absence of foul language in *Huckleberry Finn* is surprising. The only explicitly profane remark occurs in chapter 21 when a minor character, Boggs, cries, "O Lord, don't shoot!" While explicitly foul language is scarce, non-explicit variants appear more than 160 times in the novel. In some cases, Twain's palettes of variants for his characters more realistically render their dialect, capturing the music, vitality, and sensation in their speech while authentically representing their regional and racial voices. For instance, Jim's variants *dern, ding-,* and especially *dad-* were non-explicit profanities prevalent in the South and South Midland regions, and *dad-fetch* and *dog my cats* were widely used in southern African American vernacular English.

In other instances, variants help indicate differences in education and class. The King, for example, uses three times as many kinds of variants as the Duke does, and he uses non-explicit profanity twice as often. Twain also creates different palettes of profanity for men and women. His male characters primarily use variants for "damn" and "damned," and his female characters use variants for "Lord" and "God." Between men and women, he positions the children—Tom, Buck, and Huck—whose usages illustrate both the sphere in which they reside as well as their attempts to build credibility outside that sphere by utilizing stronger, more masculine profanity.

One might ask if the lack of profanity in *Huckleberry Finn* is simply the result of Twain's intention for the novel's audience to include children and young adults. By nineteenth-century standards, explicit profanity would have certainly been considered inappropriate given that context. Mark Twain himself maintained that some language was not fit for women and children—despite the fact that he pushed such boundaries within his own home. If he considered *Huckleberry Finn* a boys' book like *Tom Sawyer*, then one might expect the same aversion to profanity in the latter as he expressed about the former.

Mark Twain initially did not intend *Tom Sawyer* for children. Writing to his friend and literary confidant William Dean Howells in July of 1875, he said, "It is *not* a boy's book, at all. It will only be read by adults. It is only written for adults" *(Mark Twain-Howells Letters* 1:91). However, both his wife, Olivia, and Howells urged him to reconsider his position. He capitulated, and marketing *Tom Sawyer* for children caused him to reconsider the profanity in the manuscript, particularly in chapter 35, in which he had Huck bemoan the widow's domestic fastidiousness by saying, "they comb me all to hell."

Twain sent the manuscript proofs for *Tom Sawyer* to Howells for feedback, and after Howells edited the manuscript, he was surprised to find that Howells had not struck out the word "hell." He immediately wrote to Howells, asking whether the word should be altered. Concerned about his newly intended younger audience, he was uneasy about that small bit of profanity, even though his wife and the genteel audiences he had tried it out on had made no objection to it. In his January 18, 1876 letter to Howells, he explained, "I tamed the various obscenities until I judged that [they] no longer carried offense." He added, "when I saw that you, too, had let it go without protest, I was glad, & afraid, too—afraid you hadn't observed it. Did you? And did you question the propriety of it? Since the book is now professedly & confessedly a boy's & girl's book, that dern word bothers me some, nights, but it never did until I had ceased to regard the volume as being for adults. (*Mark Twain's Letters*)

Howells replied, "I'd have that swearing out in an instant . . . it won't do for the children" (*Mark Twain-Howells Letters* 124). In the secretarial copy of *Tom Sawyer*, Twain immediately changed the "hell" to "thunder," but when he went back to the original manuscript, either out of carelessness in the emendation or some subconscious desire to retain the profanity, he struck through the word "hell" and later wrote above it "hell" (Gerber et al. 453). Despite this ambiguous alteration, the first American edition used "thunder" instead of "hell."

For all the ruckus about "hell," however, other profanity remained in *Tom Sawyer*. In chapter 9, after stabbing the doctor, "Injun Joe" mutters "*That* score is settled—damn you," and Muff asks upon awakening, "Lord, how is this, Joe?" In chapter 29, Huck follows two men toward the house of the Widow Douglas and overhears Injun Joe curse, "Damn her, maybe she's got company." When Joe's partner learns of his plans to mutilate the widow, he responds "by God, that's—" before Joe silences him. As outcasts from society, Joe and his partner are given a surprising freedom of expression. Perhaps a bit more surprising are the instances when Huck and Tom irreverently use "Lord" and its variants as mild profanity. In the graveyard, Huck gets spooked, saying "Lord, Tom, they're coming!" and "Lordy, Tom, we're goners!" (chapter 9). In chapter 10, Tom says, "Oh, lordy, I'm thankful," and Huck ups the stakes with a triple doozy: "Oh, *lordy*, lordy, lordy, I wisht I only had half your chance." All told, the expletives "Lord" and "lordy" appear more than a dozen times in *Tom Sawyer*. Considering Twain's stated concern about profanity in a children's book, revisions to edit out such language thus seem rather lax.

When he began composing *Huckleberry Finn* in 1876, Mark Twain considered the book a companion to *Tom Sawyer*. From the opening line of the novel, *Huckleberry Finn* is positioned in relation to *Tom Sawyer*. The two novels share settings and characters, and Twain's notes about possible plot points suggest he had adolescent readers in mind for *Huckleberry Finn*, especially when writing the first few chapters. However, *Huckleberry Finn* provided an opportunity to do something he could not do with Tom, to take a boy up through and out of childhood. Certainly by the completion of the second part of the novel, its standing in his own mind as a children's book was dubious.

To dismiss *Huckleberry Finn*'s lack of profanity solely as the result of the novel's being seen as a children's work is to overlook the ways in which the boundaries between adolescence and maturity become permeable. Moreover, the absence of foul language intensifies significant turning points within the novel, and the use of non-explicit variants extends his satire. Ultimately, Huck's avoidance of profanity as a narrator characterizes him as a boy on the cusp of maturity. Although he faces adult choices and consequences in his journey along the river, his language is not yet fully that of a man.

## Euphemisms, Denotative Meanings, and Turning Points

Just as repetition can dull an utterance, intentionally withholding it further sharpens its bite when it finally appears. It becomes anticipated. Huck avoids the profanity "hell" throughout the novel, using variants instead. In chapter 37, he tells readers, "I wished I was in Jeruslem [*sic*] or somewheres." In chapter 39, he says of Aunt Sally, "you could hear her whoop to Jericho." Huck's non-profane expressions replicate connotative usage and non-literal meaning of the profanity "hell." However, Huck also avoids denotative meanings of the word "hell." He uses various conceptual euphemisms for the theological idea of hell, each progressively more concrete and connotative. By avoiding the word "hell" and creating a progression of conceptualizations of the place, Twain heightens the impact when Huck finally speaks the word at Huck's crisis of conscious.

At the beginning of the novel, Huck, as narrator, demonstrates a reluctance even to use the word "hell." In chapter 1, he relates Miss

---

Watson's comically childish circumlocutions for both heaven and hell: "Then she told me all about the bad place, and I said I wished I was there. . . . She said it was wicked to say what I said; she was going to live so as to go to the good place." Such connotatively weak euphemisms as "the bad place" and "the good place" are so far removed from the precision and power of the words "hell" and "heaven" as to be almost bereft of meaning. Both Miss Watson's exaggerated piety and Huck's non-literal desire to go to "the bad place" diminish the religious concept and associated system of morality to the point of abstraction.

As the novel progresses, Huck struggles with the conflict between his affection and sympathy for Jim, for whom he gradually feels responsible as a fellow human being, and antebellum morality, which dictated that helping Jim escape constitutes an act of theft. In chapter 31, Huck's divided conscience forces him to assess his system of morality in frank terms, and his euphemistic language becomes more concrete:

> Well, I tried the best I could to kinder soften it up somehow for myself . . . but something inside of me kept saying, "There was the Sunday school, you could a gone to it; and if you'd a done it they'd a learnt you, there, that people that acts as I'd been acting about that nigger goes to everlasting fire."

Huck's language no longer depicts hell as an ambiguous and abstract "bad place," but as a literal place of eternal torment and pain. Though perhaps a cliché to modern readers, the euphemism "everlasting fire" conjures for Huck a definitive consequence for his actions. Hell becomes real.

As the novel builds to its pivotal point, Huck finally drops substitutions and unequivocally calls the bad place "hell." He admits to himself how close he is "to being lost and going to hell" (chapter 31). Moved by recollections of his relationship with Jim, Huck determines to defy the law of both God and man as he understands them, casting off all euphemism: "All right, then," he asserts, "I'll *go* to hell" (chapter 31). By rejecting softening substitutions, Huck lays bare the naked truth of his self-damnation. His assertion is not profanity in the technical sense because his reference to hell is neither flippant nor contemptuous. The lack of exclamation point helps distinguish it from a merely superficial emphatic response. Nevertheless, his phrasing so closely mirrors the curse "go to hell!" as to have the shocking bite of profanity and thus adds weight and energy to Huck's crucial declaration. Huck is both literally and figuratively damning himself. Had Huck used "hell" freely throughout the novel, his declaration would be less resonant.

With Jim, Twain creates a tension between competing emotional discharges of progressively more earnest invocations of "Lord" and profane variants *laws*, *lawsy*, and *lan'*, alternating between connotative and denotative domains of achievement as he builds to a pivotal point in humanizing Jim. Stranded on the wrecked steamboat *Walter Scott* in chapter 12, Jim laments, "Oh, my lordy, lordy! raf'? Dey ain' no raf' no mo'; she done broke loose en gone I—en here we is!" "Lordy," a variant for "Lord," connotatively expresses surprise or dismay. As a nonliteral expletive, "lordy" makes the sentence more forceful and emotionally expressive. Jim is neither calling upon God nor conceptualizing him in a theological manner with the expression. In chapter 16, he uses a similarly connotative expletive, praising Huck for his clever deception: "But lawsy, how you did fool 'em, Huck!"

Later, in chapter 18 Jim's use of variants becomes more denotative and emotionally forceful. Reuniting with Huck after the Grangerford-Shepherdson feud erupts, Jim says to Huck, "Good lan'! is dat you, honey? . . . Laws bless you, chile, I 'uz right down sho' you's dead agin . . . .Lawsy, I's mighty glad to git you back again, honey." Jim's variants "lawsy" and "lan'" both function as expletives; that is to say, their syntactical importance resides in their emphatic emotional expression (their domain of achievement) rather than in their literal meaning. The use of "laws" for "Lord," however, is denotative. The phrase "Laws bless you" also has semantic meaning, functioning either connotatively as a mildly profane expression of gratefulness or denotatively as an earnest benediction.

In the final scene of chapter 23, a crucial moment in Huck's relationship with Jim and Jim's characterization in the novel, Jim finally uses the word "Lord." Huck awakens to find a melancholic Jim mourning the family he has left behind. Jim confesses to Huck an incident in which he struck his beloved four-year-old daughter for ignoring his spoken request to close a door, to learn afterward that she had been rendered deaf and dumb from scarlet fever. Concluding his poignant reminiscence, Jim professes, "de Lord God Amighty fogive po' ole Jim, kaze he never gwyne to fogive hisself as long's he live!" Huck's realization of Jim's abiding love for his family is a watershed in his relationship with Huck. Jim undergoes, as Jocelyn A. Chadwick asserts, a "racial awakening" (*The Jim Dilemma* 107), and Jim's confession of fallibility confirms for Huck Jim's ultimate humanity.

It is at this point that Jim invokes the strongest nomenclature for God that appears in the novel, and the earnestness of his self-condemnation is heightened by his explicit and formal address for God. Twain was adamant that this phrasing, which sensitive readers might misinterpret for strong profanity, remain untouched by editors, writing in the manuscript's margin, "This expression shall not be changed" (Doyno, *Writing "Huck Finn"* 122). As with Huck's declaration about going to hell, Jim's language is not technically profane. Although his invocation may not be a literal request for God's forgiveness because its linguistic flexibility creates room for ambiguity, his expression solemnly uses religious language to reaffirm his full responsibility for his actions. Both emotionally and stylistically, a variant would have irreparably weakened Jim's declaration, shifting the tone altogether. After this climax, Jim never uses the word "Lord" or any of its variants again. It is no coincidence that the only two instances of near-profanity in the novel occur at moments of critical formation or revelation.

### Variants, Characterization, and Satire

Throughout his writings, Twain frequently targets self-righteous Christians who fastidiously uphold the letter of God's law while blatantly violating its spirit. Twain particularly criticized Christians who professed values such as compassion, mercy, and kindness while treating others viciously and lacking basic human empathy, especially concerning slaves. In *Huckleberry Finn*, he adds another dimension to the satire of religious hypocrisy that he has begun with Miss Watson by targeting the intemperate Aunt Sally. Nowhere is this criticism more evident than in her blatant disregard for the slave who is killed in Huck's fabricated story about a steamboat accident in chapter 32. Her religiosity also allows her to be easily misled by Huck, as illustrated by the incident with the missing spoon in chapter 37.

Aunt Sally's use of non-explicit profanity contributes to Twain's satire, for more than three-quarters of her mildly profane expressions address, invoke, or name the Lord. She uses expressions such as *mercy sakes*, *law sakes*, *for the land's sake*, and *goodness sakes* (all variants for "for the Lord's sake"); *laws-a-me* and *lawsamercy* (variants for "Lord help me" or "have mercy on me"); and *my land* and *good land* (variants for "my Lord" or "good Lord"). She also says *I declare to gracious* and *I declare to goodness*. Her two expressions that fall outside this pattern, *hang the troublesome rubbage* and *plague take the things*, are both euphemisms for "damn." Aunt Sally's frequent use of variants for profane expressions that use "Lord" is ironic, since the third law of the Ten Commandments in the Bible prohibits taking the Lord's name in vain (Exodus 20:7). As a Christian, Aunt Sally lives up to the letter of God's law by refraining from actually saying the word "Lord" disrespectfully; however, she violates its spirit by unthinkingly and irreverently using expressions that replicate profanity's disregard for that which is sacred.

Non-explicit variants also deepen the satire of the ferryman occurring in chapter 13. In that chapter, Huck climbs aboard a double-hull ferry boat in order to find someone to rescue the thieves and would-be murderers stranded on the *Walter Scott*. He encounters a sleeping man and, rousting him, inquires whether he is the watchman. Both clarifying his identity and confusing it, the man tells Huck, "I'm the captain and the owner and the mate and the pilot and watchman and head deck-hand; and sometimes I'm the freight and passengers" (chapter 13). This humorous catalogue of identities gives him a compound-identity; that is, he performs multiple roles and simultaneously embodies their competing social positions and their conventional values. He becomes an everyman. Not only does he do the jobs of many people, but he also uses various forms of profanity associated with different kinds of people.

The sheer variety of the ferryman's non-explicit profanity reinforces his everyman characterization. Within his short exchange with Huck, he uses more than a dozen mild, non-explicit profanities: *blame it, dang it, blame', derned,* and *beatenest* (variants for "damn," "damned," and "damndest"); *how in the nation* and *dingnation* (variants for "damnation" or "hell"); and *good land, gracious sakes, great goodness, great guns, my George,* and *by Jackson* (variants for "Lord," "God," and "Jesus"). The ferryman's expressions include variants for nearly every explicit high taboo profanity with the exception of "goddamn" and "Christ." His speech features the greatest proportional variety of non-explicit profanity spoken by any character in the novel and includes expressions typical of both men and women as well as men of a variety of social stations and education levels. Essentially, he curses as though he were many different people.

In his depiction of the ferryman, Twain particularly satirizes the self-serving "Good Samaritan" who is only interested in helping someone in need if the Samaritan can benefit from it. Knowing that the ferryman would not waste his time and energy rescuing criminals, Huck concocts a lie about his family and Miss Hooker being stranded on the *Walter Scott.* Even then, however, the ferryman, though sympathetic to their plight, thinks primarily of pecuniary remuneration: "I'd like to [help], and, blame it, I don't know but I will; but who in the dingnation's a-going' to pay for it? Do you reckon your pap—" (chapter 13). When Huck interrupts to inform him that Miss Hooker's affluent Uncle Hornback will foot the bill, the watchman immediately leaps into action, desperate for the opportunity to do a service for the wealthy man and earn his favor as well as his money. By paralleling the ferryman's multiple identities with his multiple uses of non-explicit profanity and thereby reinforcing his characterization as an everyman, Twain extends his satire beyond one isolated instance to all people who do good only when there is profit in it.

In chapter 6 of *Tom Sawyer*, the anonymous narrator claims that Huck "could swear wonderfully," and in chapter 6 of *Huckleberry Finn*, Huck himself confesses, "I had stopped cussing, because the widow didn't like it; but now I took to it again because pap hadn't no objections." Despite these assertions of Huck's proficiency with profanity, his narrative and speech in *Huckleberry Finn* lack explicitly profane language. This avoidance of profanity seems more than just the result of Twain's unwillingness to include profanity in a children's book—there was swearing in *Tom Sawyer*, after all—or his concerns about nineteenth-century literary standards of propriety, for profanity frequently appears in his other works. Rather, it suggests Huck's level of maturity and how Twain might have wanted his readers to conceive of his narrator and protagonist. Huck easily replicates a variety of syntactical structures associated with profanity, demonstrating his intimate familiarity with both its cadences and rhetorical utility. Nevertheless, he refuses to fully accept profanity's mark of maturity. Even as he confronts adult problems and responsibilities in his journey along the river, a childish innocence remains in his language. He lies, steals, and runs away, but he isn't quite "bad," and he isn't quite an adult. Even as he escapes the widow's attempts to "sivilize" him and imagines lighting out for the Territory, his language resolutely remains that of a boy not yet ready to grow up.

## Works Cited

Chadwick-Joshua, Jocelyn. *The Jim Dilemma: Reading Race in "Huckleberry Finn"*. Jackson: UP of Mississippi, 1998.

Doyno, Victor A. *Writing "Huck Finn": Mark Twain's Creative Process*. Philadelphia: U of Pennsylvania P, 1991.

Gerber, John C., Paul Baender, & Terry Firkins, eds. *The Adventures of Tom Sawyer.* Berkeley: U of California P, 1980.

Twain, Mark. *Adventures of Huckleberry Finn*. Ed. Victor Fischer & Lin Salamo. Berkeley: U of California P, 2001.

_____. *The Adventures of Tom Sawyer.* Ed. John C. Gerber, Paul Baender, & Terry Firkins. Berkeley: U of California P, 1980.

_____. *Mark Twain at the Buffalo Express: Articles and Sketches by America's Favorite Humorist.* Ed. Joseph McCullough & Janice McIntire-Strasburg. DeKalb, IL: Northern Illinois UP, 1999.

_____. *Mark Twain-Howells Letters.* Ed. Henry Nash Smith & William M. Gibson. 2 vols. Cambridge, MA: Harvard UP, 1960.

_____. *Mark Twain of the Enterprise: Newspaper Articles and Other Documents 1862–1864.* Ed. Henry Nash Smith. Berkeley: U California P, 1957.

_____. *Mark Twain's Letters. Mark Twain Project Online.* The Mark Twain Papers, U of California Berkeley, 2016. Web. <http://www.marktwainproject.org/>.

Wajnryb, Ruth. *Expletive Deleted: A Good Look at Bad Language.* New York: Free Press, 2005.

# Why Huck Finn Can't Stand Being Sivilized____

Philip Bader

*Adventures of Huckleberry Finn* (1885) is a book about many things; one thematic element that tends to be neglected is civilization. Its protagonist, Huck, is a child of low birth and indifferent education. Residing on the fringe of polite society, he serves as a guide to readers in navigating the antebellum South of the mid-nineteenth century. The world he reveals includes well-meaning widows intent on civilizing the backward, violent fathers disdainful of the high-born, creative and resilient frauds with little regard for the people they cheat, random corpses, aristocratic murderers, and the implicit brutality of slave culture. Huck does not dwell on these issues or draw conclusions about them. He merely describes them and leaves readers to determine their deeper significance.

What ultimately emerges in *Huckleberry Finn* is an essentially hypocritical and violent society that espouses ideals it does not practice, the chronic oppression and manipulation of the weak by the strong, and a young boy's alternating desire for connection to that society and his growing awareness of the emptiness at its core. As Huck moves through the violent landscape of the novel, what seems natural to him contradicts the values of the individuals and communities with whom he interacts. In the final chapter, he ends up essentially where he began at the opening of his narrative—on the outside of a society that bewilders and, in some instances, terrifies him.

## "Sivilization" and Its Discontents
Huck Finn is a child of the tanyards, a victim of sustained and violent abuse at the hands of a drunken father who has made his way in the world on his own terms. The good citizens of St. Petersburg view him with a mixture of disdain and fear. In chapter 6 of *The Adventures of Tom Sawyer* (1876)—the prequel to *Huckleberry Finn*—Huck is introduced as a "juvenile pariah" who is "idle and lawless and vulgar

and bad." Worse, those same qualities make Huck the envy of every other young boy, and that fact poses a threat to the stability of the community. This shabby misfit, however, proves his worth when he saves Widow Douglas from the villainous Injun Joe in chapter 29 of *Tom Sawyer*. At that novel's end, he has earned respect, wealth, and the interest of the widow, a prominent citizen who wants to usher him into the ranks of the civilized. As chapter 35 of *Tom Sawyer* illustrates, respectable society has not so much invited Huck as it has "dragged him" into civilization, and his discomfort is acute. For a boy accustomed to sleeping in a tanyard hogshead and following the dictates of his own will, life with the Widow Douglas and her pious sister, Miss Watson, threatens to smother him with uncomfortable clothes, frustrating table manners, the monotony of polite speech, and the tedium of a schoolroom and a church pew. In short, it creates an environment wherein "the bars and shackles of civilization shut him in and bound him hand and foot" (*Tom Sawyer*, chapter 35).

*Huckleberry Finn* opens as Huck makes an uneasy truce with respectability. His friend Tom Sawyer has lured him back into civilized bondage with the promise of extravagant adventures in his band of "respectable" robbers. It seems hardly coincidental that what persuades Huck to return to the smothering atmosphere of civilization is membership in an organization whose bloody oath of initiation and stated objectives are to rob and butcher respectable citizens. Equally telling is Huck's disenchantment with the gang when he realizes that Tom's devotion to adventure is little more than bookish make-believe. In chapter 3, Tom says he has secret news of a large group of Spanish merchants and rich Arabs, complete with a retinue of elephants, mules, and camels bearing priceless jewels. In reality, the caravan is merely a children's Sunday-school picnic. The gang drives the children off and seizes a few doughnuts and other trifles, only to be routed by the Sunday-school teacher and driven into a humiliating retreat. Tom explains the misadventure by citing *Don Quixote* and blaming the meddling of enchanters, whom he says are conjured by rubbing old tin lamps. Huck tests the hypothesis on a lamp and concludes that the whole adventure is "only just one of Tom Sawyer's lies."

Huck's rejection of Tom's fictional reality closely parallels his evaluation of the competing versions of religion presented by Miss Watson and Widow Douglas. While he formulates his opinion about Tom and the gang in chapter 3, Huck also comments on the efforts of the two women working so hard to civilize him. Miss Watson tells him that whatever he prays for would come to him, a promise he tests with only limited success. Widow Douglas emphasizes service to others, but Huck can find no benefit in that for himself. He does, however, recognize that the deity described by Widow Douglas has certain advantages.

> I judged I could see that there was two Providences, and a poor chap would stand considerable show with the widow's Providence, but if Miss Watson's got him there warn't no help for him any more.

These contradictory perspectives on God, one of the most essential civilizing influences society offers, present two versions of reality that appear equally beyond Huck's acceptance. One can imagine from Huck's depictions of each that the widow's god emphasizes the benefits and rewards of service, while that of Miss Watson stresses the harsh consequences of disobedience, an outcome he would keenly understand as the son of a violent father. While Huck prefers the widow's Providence, he concludes that his disposition, being "so ignorant and so kind of low-down and ornery," would pose an insurmountable obstacle (chapter 3).

## A Liberating "Death"

Huck's dalliance with respectability in the early chapters gets more complicated in chapter 4 when he discovers signs that his father, who has been absent from St. Petersburg for more than a year, has returned. Despite the smothering effects of life with the Widow Douglas, including a curb on both impolite language and the soothing benefits of tobacco, Huck has struck a balance. He learns the basics of reading and writing, and he even begins to enjoy schooling. He also enjoys occasional forays into delinquency, and he says the hidings he gets as a consequence "done me good and

---

cheered me up." But a harsher parental authority reasserts itself with the arrival of Pap Finn, who has no regard for Huck beyond what he would feel for any other personal possession. Huck belongs to him, and so does the fortune that he has heard spoken of in town. Pap Finn, with his greasy hair, toad-belly skin, and destructive addiction to alcohol represents the fate that society aims to deny to Huck. Despite the efforts of Judge Thatcher and the Widow Douglas, who petition for guardianship of Huck, the court sides with Pap Finn. This mechanism of justice concludes that it "mustn't interfere and separate families if they could help it" (chapter 5). Much like many slaves in Missouri, Huck belongs to a violent and dangerous owner.

After exhausting all his options to secure his son's fortune, including the pretense of reforming his ways under a judge's supervision, Pap Finn kidnaps Huck in chapter 6 and whisks him off to a remote log cabin several miles up the Mississippi River. Huck quickly falls back into the familiar rhythm of his former life until, in a whiskey-fueled rage, his father tries to kill him. Huck has been cut off from the civilizing influence of the Widow Douglas, and his father has crossed the line from physical abuse to attempted murder. His family, such as it is, and a well-meaning society seeking to reform him have both failed Huck. When a rising river brings him a derelict canoe, he conceives a plan that would liberate him from all his present troubles. He does not think of escaping back to St. Petersburg, where his father will continue to present an imminent threat. Instead, he stages his own death in an elaborately conceived scene of brutal violence that will allow him to strike out on his own, free of social and familial obligations.

### A Peaceful Pilgrim in a Violent World
In his essay "Presentations of Violence in *Adventures of Huckleberry Finn*," Victor Doyno proposes a thought experiment. He asks readers to imagine what it would be like to talk to a young teen who has wandered the country in extreme poverty and homelessness.

Imagine that this child—who will tell us about American society— has, within the last fourteen to eighteen months, seen three people die, had her or his own life threatened four times, and has been in the company of at least five dead bodies. (Doyno, "Presentations" 75-76)

One might reasonably expect that a child from a broken and violent home who witnesses the worst that society has to offer would exhibit signs of significant trauma or a propensity for violence. However, despite experiencing what Doyno describes, Huck at no point in the novel shows any inclination to violent action. That fact belies his reputation as a vulgar and bad boy. Rather, he proves a valuable witness to the ways in which residents of so-called civilized society cheat and kill one another, and the contradictory assumptions that underlie civilization itself. Huck's journey downriver with the runaway slave Jim provides a glimpse of civilization writ large and adds to the stock of information he has of its claims about reality and its faithfulness to the ideals it promotes.

Huck's experiences on the river also provide a useful contrast to the imaginary violence of his adventures with Tom in the early chapters of the novel. In chapter 2, Tom's gang can discuss the nuances of slaughtering wayward members of the group with a levity that underlies Twain's humorous intent. But when Huck and Jim later, in chapter 12, confront a real band of murderers seriously contemplating killing one of their group on the wreck of the steamboat *Walter Scott*, the imminent violence is palpable and terrifying. Violence is no longer a creative pastime carried out among friends in an isolated but safe location. Similarly, Huck can take pride in his attention to the small details of faking his own murder in chapter 7, even wishing that Tom was there to "throw in the fancy touches." But when he returns to town and visits the home of Mrs. Loftus, he discovers that Jim is suspected of having really killed him, so he and Jim are no longer safe on Jackson's Island. The drowned and disfigured body found in the river in chapter 3 and another corpse (later revealed to be that of Pap Finn) that Huck and Jim discover inside the floating house during the river's flood in chapter 9 offers an important reminder. Random violence remains an imminent threat for a young boy and an escaped slave adrift and at the mercy of both the river and the communities through which it passes.

Huck's unvarying pacifism has its roots, Doyno further suggests, in his turbulent upbringing, which has instilled in him an innate fear of violence. A child faced with the unpredictability of an alcoholic and quick-tempered father, Doyno argues, "may carry extreme fears about violence; he may develop a great social ability to placate, or to seem to agree, along with his great wish to keep some semblance of peace." This quality might explain Huck's passive reaction to the arrival of the King and Duke in chapter 19. This invasion of spurious nobility fundamentally alters the peaceful atmosphere on the raft and reduces its two inhabitants to little more than servants. Huck quickly identifies the newcomers as "low-down hum-bugs and frauds," and yet he and Jim defer to their every whim. Despite the increasing indignities that Huck and Jim endure as the King and Duke begin to dictate their every move, they make no objections. As Huck explains it, "I hadn't no objections, 'long as it would keep peace in the family." It is worth noting that Huck's deference has its limits. When directly confronted with the suffering of others, as he is with Mary Jane Wilks in chapter 26, and as he was in chapter 29 of *Tom Sawyer* when Injun Joe plotted his revenge on the Widow Douglas, Huck takes significant risks to intervene.

Huck's uncivilized upbringing has endowed him not only with an essentially peaceful disposition but also an uncharacteristically empathetic approach to others. Nothing in his background in the novel clearly accounts for this quality. He has every reason to feel bitterness over his past and a desire for revenge against those who have mistreated him. In *Mark Twain and Huck Finn* (1960), Walter Blair argues that Huck "is a youth who has been educated while shifting for himself in a rough world. He has acquired a knowledge of human frailty and, even more impressive, tolerance toward it" (103).

Two episodes in particular highlight Huck's facility for empathy. When Huck and Jim flee the band of murderers aboard the *Walter Scott* by stealing their paddle boat in chapter 13, Huck begins to worry about the fate of the murderers, who now have no means of escaping the teetering wreck. "I says to myself, there ain't no telling but I might come to be a murderer myself, yet, and then how would I like it?" He enlists the help of a ferryboatman and even paddles out to the wreck after it becomes unmoored and starts to sink. By then, however, the men have presumably drowned. Later in chapter 33, Huck sees the King and Duke, tarred and feathered, being ridden out of the Phelpses' town on a rail. He and Jim have been bullied and threatened from the moment they accepted the pair onto their raft. The two fake nobles are also responsible for imperiling Jim's life by selling him to the Phelpses. However, the pathetic image of the two rogues suffering at the hands of a mob strikes a compassionate chord in Huck.

> Well, it made me sick to see it; and I was sorry for them poor pitiful rascals. it seemed like I couldn't ever feel any hardness against them any more in the world. It was a dreadful thing to see. Human beings can be awful cruel to one another.

Huck takes no pleasure in the suffering of others, even if those who suffer might deserve to be punished. He identifies with rogues because he sees himself as closer to them in character than he does more civilized members of society.

## Slavery and Huck's War on Conscience

Mark Twain makes almost no reference to slavery in *Tom Sawyer*. In *Huckleberry Finn*, the story is more firmly rooted in the antebellum South and described through the language and understanding of a young boy who has accepted the assumptions and obligations of that slave-holding culture without question. Huck's decision to help Jim escape in chapter 8 violates a fundamental tenant of slave culture. It drives him further beyond the confines of acceptable society, puts his life in danger, and even threatens his fate in the hereafter. "People would call me a low down Ablitionist and despise me for keeping mum—but that don't make no difference. I ain't agoing to tell, and I ain't agoing back there anyways." At this early stage in the novel, Huck seems to have turned his back on respectable society. In *Searching for Jim* (2003), a study of slavery in Twain's boyhood home of Hannibal, Missouri, Terrell Dempsey describes slave culture at the time in which *Huckleberry Finn* is set. Slaves were bought and sold, and newspapers regularly reported on the value of human flesh like the fluctuating stock market prices found in modern newspapers. Slaves were, however, more than mere economic commodities: "In short, they were human livestock. But slavery was far more—it formed the very heart of the society and touched every aspect of community life" (Dempsey 9-10).

Huck is a product of that slave-holding society, which has shaped his view of slavery and affected the conscience that nags him throughout the novel. In chapter 16, he begins to feel the weight of his loyalty to the escaping slave Jim. When Jim thinks their raft is nearing Cairo, Illinois, Huck realizes how close Jim is to being free, and that he is to blame. "It hadn't ever come home to me before, what this thing was that I was doing," he says to himself, adding that he could have run ashore and turned him in. He fears that he has done Jim's legal owner, Miss Watson, wrong by depriving her of her rightful property. Huck's conscience attacks him more savagely in chapter 31 when he feels the pull to inform Miss Watson of Jim's whereabouts so she can get him back. He feels the hand of Providence "slapping me in the face and letting me know my wickedness." He acknowledges that he could have gone to Sunday school, where he would have learned "that people that acts as I'd been doing about that nigger goes to everlasting fire."

In an 1895 notebook entry, Mark Twain described *Huckleberry Finn* as "a book of mine where a sound heart & a deformed conscience come into collision & conscience suffers defeat" (qtd. in Doyno, *Writing "Huck Finn"* 167). Ironically, civilization has deformed that conscience by making Huck feel shame for recognizing Jim's fundamental humanity. He writes a letter to Miss Watson but cannot bring himself to send it. Society is against him, and God will consign him to eternal torment. Having betrayed society up to this point, Huck finally accepts the ultimate permanent exile by declaring, "All right, then, I'll go to hell," as he tears up the letter.

## Aristocracy and Civilized Barbarism

When Huck arrives on the doorstep of the Grangerford house in chapter 17, he confronts for the first time a family of extravagant wealth and respectability. They are members of the South's aristocratic class whose affluence outstrips anything Huck might have seen in St. Petersburg. The Grangerfords stand at the apex of social hierarchy, as do the neighboring Shepherdsons and other local plantation owners, most of whom are extended family members of one clan or another. "Colonel" Grangerford presides over a household that possesses more than one hundred slaves. He has vast land holdings and regularly hosts his neighbors at lavish parties. This aristocratic class embodies the highest aspirations of respectable southern society. "It is they who set the standard, who stamp their values on society with the visible presence of their 'style,'" writes Harold Beaver in his critical study, *Huckleberry Finn* (65). After Huck weaves an elaborate lie about his origins, the family offers him a place in their home for as long as he wants to stay, and he quickly falls under their spell. He also strikes up a fast friendship with the youngest son, Buck, who seems to share his dislike for fine clothes.

Huck's description of the Grangerford house in chapter 17 unintentionally reveals that appearances might not be what they seem. He notes that it "was so nice and had so much style," but his close examination of the interior reveals a household more concerned with appearances than authenticity. An elaborate clock does not work, two "outlandish" parrots are made of chalk, a cat and dog are ceramic, and the beautiful fruit in a basket are artificial. The walls of the home are decorated with maudlin portraits drawn by Emmeline Grangerford, whose death at the age of fifteen was occasioned—so the family claims—by her failure to conceive an appropriate rhyme for one of her many obituary poems. The portraits all convey a sense of loss and mourning. One depicts a woman leaning against a tombstone; another shows a young woman with a dead bird in her hand. The most unusual, however, displays a woman with six "spidery" arms and hangs above Emmeline's bed like a religious icon in a room that has been preserved just as it was at the time of her death. On her birthday, the family adorns the unfinished portrait—the last she had drawn—with flowers. Huck notes that the imagery is dark and not particularly to his liking and even suggests, with unusual levity under the circumstances, that given her disposition, Emmeline "was having a better time in the graveyard." Despite all these macabre signs, Huck does not see the darkness at the heart of the family. Instead, he sees a comfortable home, and the chapter ends with his appreciation for the quality and quantity of the food it offers.

The physical appearance of Colonel Grangerford seems to cement Huck's opinion of the family. Dressed from head to foot in white linen, the patriarch is a "gentleman all over" by virtue of his well-bred origins, and he presides over a family whose respectability could not conceivably be challenged. Family members salute the colonel each morning at breakfast and pledge their duty to him. Not until a few days later, when Buck makes an unsuccessful attempt to kill Harney Shepherdson, does Huck have any cause to question what he sees (chapter 18). The two boys flee back home, and Huck inquires about the nature of the feud. "There was trouble 'bout something and then a lawsuit to settle it; and the suit went agin one of the men, and so he up and shot the man that won the suit—which he would naturally do, of course. Anybody would," Buck says. This kind of extralegal violence comes naturally to the Grangerfords. Huck follows up with a series of reasonable questions and finds that Buck can neither explain how long the feud has been running nor which family started it. When Huck learns of the death of Buck's cousin Bud, he innocently asks if the Shepherdson who shot him was a coward. "There ain't a coward amongst them Shepherdsons— not a one." Like Colonel Sherburn's shooting of Boggs in chapter 21, killing an unarmed man in cold blood does not reflect poorly on a man's character but confirms an assumed nobility and privilege.

In similar fashion, the church service in chapter 18 further indicates that the Grangerfords and Shepherdsons live by their own code. They arrive at the service heavily armed. With the families' long history of unrestrained violence, the tension in the church must be palpable as the feuding families listen together to a sermon about the virtue of brotherly love and the divine qualities of "faith, and good works, and free grace"—qualities that each family gratuitously betrays at every opportunity. Ironically, the church also serves as a potential mediator between the two families because it is where young Sophia Grangerford and Harney Shepherdson plot their elopement. This institution of peace and civilization could have been the site where the first seeds of redemption for both families might have sprouted, but hatred ultimately wins out.

At Sophia's request, Huck gallantly retrieves the Testament she has left at the church. It contains a note from Harney with instructions on where to meet. Harney's note will unintentionally spark events causing the feud violently to erupt, with the result that the Grangerford family will be destroyed and the respectable home to which Huck has become attached will fall. As appearances fall away, Huck sees the family for what it is. "Beneath displays of civilization," Walter Blair notes in *Mark Twain and Huck Finn*, "is a savagery which erupts above the surface when the feud breaks out" (234).

That savagery plays out quickly the next morning when the family discovers the elopement. By the time Huck wakes and becomes aware of the fighting, Colonel Grangerford and his eldest sons are dead, and Sophia and Harney have escaped to safety across the river. From a perch in a cottonwood tree, Huck watches as Buck and his cousin Joe are attacked by a band of Shepherdsons that outflank their position. The boys try to escape to the river, but their attackers follow from the riverbank and fire at them, screaming "Kill them, kill them." More than any other violent confrontation he has witnessed or experienced in the novel, this terrible scene leaves Huck shaken. He warns readers early on that he does not want to be explicit about what he saw and that his description will be short. He concludes on a dire note. "I ain't ever going to get shut of them— lots of times I dream about them."

After pulling Buck and Joe's bodies from the river and covering their faces, Huck goes in search of Jim. Earlier in the chapter he had learned that the raft survived its collision with a steamboat and that Jim has patiently repaired and restocked it. When they get a few miles downriver, Huck meditates on the day's events and concludes that no matter how nice civilization might appear, there is no home like a raft. "You feel mighty free and easy and comfortable on a raft" (chapter 18).

## Frontier Justice and Cowardly Mobs

The killing of Boggs by Colonel Sherburn in chapter 21 follows chronologically and thematically the mayhem of the Grangerford-Shepherdson slaughter. The King and the Duke enter an unidentified but typical "one-horse town" in a bend of the river on the Arkansas side. The houses and commercial buildings show unmistakable signs of neglect, and the storefronts are occupied by "loafers roosting on them all day long" and who are "a mighty ornery lot." Towards noon, activity in the town picks up. Whiskey begins to flow and a few fights break out. Boggs, the town drunk, barrels into town screaming threats at the prosperous merchant Colonel Sherburn, whom he claims has swindled him. Boggs is a harmless drunk, by the accounts that Huck hears among the townspeople, but Sherburn takes offense. He says he will allow Boggs to vilify him until one o'clock, after which he will come for him. As the deadline approaches, other townspeople try unsuccessfully to restrain Boggs. As he continues to hurl insults at Sherburn, a call is made to summon Boggs's daughter in a last effort to calm him. Then, when Sherburn's patience has run out, he calmly fires two shots into Boggs while the latter's daughter looks on. Sherburn then drops his gun in the street and walks away. Boggs ultimately expires on the floor of a drug store with a heavy Bible pressing down on his chest as spectators crowd to see his body through the shop windows. The scene—which duplicates an incident Mark Twain had witnessed as a boy—takes on the quality of a circus, with a clown-like old man re-enacting the shooting for the benefit of those who might not have seen it in real time.

A call to lynch Sherburn soon follows. In chapter 22 a mob gathers outside Sherburn's house, breaking down his fence and confronting the man, who comes out on his porch roof carrying a shotgun. Under his withering gaze, the crowd's energy fades. After excoriating them for daring to think they could lay hands on a true man, he dismisses them as cowards. "If any real lynching's going to be done, it will be done in the dark, southern fashion; and when they come they'll bring their masks, and fetch a man along." The mob quickly disperses in humiliation.

Sherburn's reprimand of the lynch mob represents a compelling indictment of frontier justice. For modern readers, the description of masked men arriving at night with a rope to perpetrate an extrajudicial hanging cannot fail to conjure images of the Ku Klux Klan and the long history of American racial violence before and after slavery. For all his talk of manhood, however, Sherburn is guilty of the senseless gunning down of a harmless and unarmed drunk in front of his daughter. Sherburn may well consider himself a man because he possesses the fortitude to kill Boggs, but his actions are more in line with those of a bully who sees his fellow townspeople as inferior to him. Like the Grangerfords and Shepherdsons, Sherburn cloaks himself in the mantle of a southern gentleman who lives by his own code of conduct; is disdainful of the poor masses; is accountable to no one; and yet remains, despite his violent actions, firmly ensconced within civilized society.

## Back to the Beginning
Writing to his friend Joseph Twichell about the South African War in January 1900, Mark Twain summed up his thoughts about "civilization" in language that might well apply to how he depicted civilization in *Huckleberry Finn*:

> My idea of our civilization is that it is a shabby poor thing and full of cruelties, vanities, arrogancies, meannesses, and hypocrisies. As for the word, I hate the sound of it, for it conveys a lie; and as for the thing itself, I wish it was in hell, where it belongs. (Twain 2: 695)

The river journey at the heart of Huck Finn's narrative offers Huck clear examples of the violence and cruelty that lies near the surface of society, respectable or otherwise, as well as contradictions that prove too difficult for him to unravel. What makes Huck a social outcast when he first appears in chapter 6 of *Tom Sawyer* is his ambivalence to societal norms and the coveted circumstances that allow him to escape the torments of formal education. He is, for all intents and purposes, an orphan who fends for himself and does what he likes when he likes, thereby making himself the envy of other children and the scourge of their mothers. By that novel's end, Huck Finn has made good. Made wealthy by the discovery of a treasure, he has a stable home at the widow's. All this is, more or less, where Huck stands at the end of *Huckleberry Finn,* when it is revealed that Miss Watson has been dead for two months and had freed Jim in her will. Jim, in turn, tells Huck that he has nothing more to fear from his father, whose dead body was the corpse they discovered in the floating house in chapter 9. Even Tom, fully recovered from his gunshot wound and proudly wearing the bullet around his neck, is eager for a new set of adventures with Huck and Jim "amongst the Injuns" in the Territory. Huck is again faced with the proposition of choosing between civilization and the uncertain prospect of Tom's unpredictable schemes.

Huck's world contains largely flawed moral guides. His father is an abusive and violent drunkard. The Widow Douglas and Miss Watson mean well in their efforts to educate him, but their competing moral codes confuse rather than enlighten, and their social beliefs prohibit things that give Huck pleasure. Characters whom Huck encounters along the Mississippi River are a mixture of loafers, gamblers, thieves, murderers, and charlatans of various sorts who bring disaster or death to those who fall under their influence. Even his comrade Tom Sawyer proves to be a flawed and frustrating companion, but at least a manageable one.

What motivates much of Huck's behavior in the novel is a desire for freedom. He makes a tenuous peace with the "smothery" respectability of life with the Widow Douglas because it allows a measure of personal liberty to play hooky from school, sneak a pipe full of tobacco or join Tom Sawyer in occasional adventures. The return of his father and the claims of parental authority drive him to the freedom of life on the river. Though Huck is periodically charmed by individuals in the communities he encounters down the river, their underlying contradictions similarly convince him that personal liberty cannot be found within respectable society.

Harold Beaver suggests in *Huckleberry Finn* that Mark Twain uses Huck's moral and physical journey in the novel as a way of prioritizing the values of the individual over the communal and that in writing the novel, Twain "came to recognize that the highest form of freedom was not dependent on communal sanctions, but . . . on each man's and woman's consciousness of what is right" (196). Huck repeatedly falls back on what he determines to be the best course of action in the novel when confronted with a difficult choice, regardless of the consequences. His initial rejection of civilized society has more to do with a desire to live unfettered by outside obligations and curbs on the activities that gave him the most pleasure.

In the end, Huck's moral perceptions deepen, and the only true civilizing anchor for Huck is a runaway slave who stands similarly outside of society. His relationship with Jim is the healthiest in the novel. The "society" they create on the raft stands well above that of the so-called civilized society from which they flee. In the final chapter of the novel, Huck has come full circle. Instead of the Widow Douglas, it is Sally Phelps who offers to adopt Huck and resume the agenda to sivilize him. Perhaps it is no surprise that he decides to strike out early for the Territory ahead of Tom and Jim. He has had enough of civilization.

## Works Cited

Beaver, Harold. *Huckleberry Finn.* London: Unwin Hyman, 1988.

Blair, Walter. *Mark Twain and Huck Finn.* Berkeley: U of California P, 1960.

Dempsey, Terrell. *Searching for Jim: Slavery in Sam Clemens's World.* Columbia: U of Missouri P, 2003.

Doyno, Victor A. "Presentations of Violence in *Adventures of Huckleberry Finn.*" *Mark Twain Journal* 42.2 (Fall 2004):75-76.

_____. *Writing "Huck Finn": Mark Twain's Creative Process.* Philadelphia: U of Pennsylvania P, 1991.

Twain, Mark. *Mark Twain's Letters.* Ed. Albert Bigelow Paine. 2 vols. New York: Harper & Brothers, 1917.

# "Huck Finn, He Hain't Got No Family": Home, Family, and Parenting in *Huckleberry Finn*_____

John Bird

"We are a very happy family," thirteen-year-old Susy Clemens wrote as she began a biography of her father in 1885. As she wrote those words, Mark Twain's latest novel, *Adventures of Huckleberry Finn*, was being read by its first audience. The Clemens family of three daughters and two loving and doting parents was indeed "very happy," enjoying life and togetherness in their sumptuous Hartford, Connecticut, mansion and in their summers at Quarry Farm in Elmira, New York, where Mark Twain had labored for more than seven years on what was to become his greatest work. By contrast, *Huckleberry Finn* presents us with the very opposite of a happy family. The novel's main plot focuses on a journey down the Mississippi River, but it can also be read as a journey from house to house. In one sense, Huck Finn is searching for freedom, both for himself and for his companion, the runaway slave Jim, but in another sense, he is searching for a home, for a family, for a mother and father, all central to a young person's sense of well-being, and all denied him in his young life. Huck is about Susy Clemens's age when he "writes" his story, a very different story than hers. Huck is a creation of Mark Twain's memory and imagination, just as this happy family was his and his wife's and his children's creation. Reading *Huckleberry Finn* as a search for home, for family, and for parents reveals important thematic and psychological aspects of the novel, as well as insights into Mark Twain's (or Samuel Clemens's) domestic life, since his family was as central to his own identity and sense of well-being as were his work and his public image.

## Finding Home

The first chapter of the novel focuses on houses. At the end of *The Adventures of Tom Sawyer*, Huck has gone to live with the Widow Douglas, who, Huck tells us as he begins his story, "took me for her son, and allowed she would sivilize me," but he finds it "rough living in the house all the time, considering how dismal and regular and decent the widow was in all her ways" (chapter 1). Huck resumes his former clothes, his "old rags," and goes back to live in a large cask, which he clearly sees as his home: "my sugar-hogshead," he calls it. He returns to the widow's at his friend Tom Sawyer's urging. On the opening page, then, Twain sets up a contrast between family and individual freedom, between home and homelessness.

The widow's house is one of the best in town, but hers is already a broken family: her husband is dead and there is no mention of children. Recently arrived to live with her is her sister, Miss Watson, and Huck emphasizes her age and childlessness in his description of her: "a tolerable slim old maid, with goggles." These two women attempt to become Huck's surrogate parents, giving him rules to abide by, manners to adhere to, proper but uncomfortable clothes to wear, lessons to learn, and a religion to follow. Miss Watson is stern and strict, the Widow Douglas more loving and nurturing, with the traditional parenting roles of father and mother split between them.

But there are other members of Huck's new family: slaves. Huck does not say how many, but Miss Watson has at least one— Jim—and the widow has several more. As his first night in his new home ends, Huck says, "By-and-by they fetched the niggers in and had prayers, and then everybody was off to bed." Like other homes in the novel, this one has the semblance of being a happy family, but its religious hypocrisy and inhumanity are highlighted.

Huck sneaks off in the night with Tom Sawyer, and after Tom plays a gratuitous trick on Jim, they join a few other boys and go to Tom's secret hiding place in the cave, where Huck is to be initiated into another family: Tom Sawyer's Gang. The oath involves "killing" anyone who tells the group's secrets, then killing their families. Putting Huck's status in sharp focus, Ben Rogers asks, "'Here's Huck Finn, he hain't got no family—what you going to do about him?'" (chapter 2). Tom answers, "'Well, hain't he got a father?'" Ben's reply gives us our first real glimpse at Huck's squalid family background: "'Yes, he's got a father, but you can't never find him, these days. He used to lay drunk with the hogs in the tanyard, but he hain't been seen in these parts for a year or more.'" The boys talk it over and decide it will not be fair for Huck to join if he does not have a family. Huck says, "I was most ready to cry." We think of Huck as tough, pragmatic, and street-smart beyond his years, but he is also very sensitive, which he rarely reveals. This moment when he is near tears shows us just how much he yearns to belong to a group, to a family, even if it is a pretend one. But he has a solution: "all at once, I thought of a way, so I offered them Miss Watson— they could kill her." He does not offer the widow, suggesting that his attachment to her is stronger than he is willing to let on.

The return to his new home further underscores the parenting split between Huck's two surrogate parents: "I got a good going-over in the morning, from old Miss Watson, on account of my clothes; but the widow she didn't scold, but only cleaned off the grease and clay and looked so sorry that I thought I would behave a while if I could" (chapter 3). Another way Miss Watson and the Widow differ is in their religious instruction. Miss Watson believes in a stern, judging Old Testament God, while the widow believes in a more loving and forgiving New Testament God: "Sometimes the widow would take me one side and talk about Providence in a way to make a body's mouth water; but maybe next day old Miss Watson would take hold and knock it all down again" (chapter 3). Confused by this contradiction, Huck decides there must be "two Providences," and he decides to belong to the widow's, "if he wanted me." Huck continues to wrestle with this confusing theology at various times in the narrative, as he searches for a home, an earthly one and, at times, a heavenly one.

By the end of the chapter, Huck has seen through the pretense of Tom Sawyer's Gang, abandoning that attempted family, and Tom's presence begins to fade in the narrative. Huck even begins to tolerate school and to get used to life at the widow's: "I liked the old ways best, but I was getting so I liked the new ones, too, a little bit" (chapter 4). Huck is indeed becoming "sivilized," and we can even see signs of affection growing for his surrogate mother: "The widow said I was coming along slow but sure, and doing very satisfactory." But that emerging family feeling is interrupted when Huck sees evidence that his father has returned to St. Petersburg. Significantly, he goes not to his friend Tom Sawyer for counsel, or to Judge Thatcher, who could give him legal advice and protection, but to Jim, who interprets a prophecy from the hair-ball. That night, Huck returns to what he now calls "my room" to encounter his wayward father. This first scene with Pap Finn is extremely important in our understanding of Huck's past, his heritage, his upbringing, his present situation, and his outlook and hopes for the future.

## Encountering Father

Huck tells us that he "used to be scared of him [Pap] all the time, he tanned me so much" (chapter 5). He is scared now, too, at first, but he is not very convincing when he says, "I seed I warn't scared of him worth bothering about." Huck is actually terrified of his father, his only living relative, and rightly so. His description of his father highlights that terror:

> He was most fifty, and he looked it. His hair was long and tangled and greasy, and hung down, and you could see his eyes shining through like he was behind vines. It was all black, no gray; so was his long, mixed-up whiskers. There warn't no color in his face, but a white to make a body sick, a white to make a body's flesh crawl—a tree-toad white, a fish-belly white. (chapter 5)

One of Twain's brilliant moves is his portrayal of Pap Finn, who occupies only a few pages of the novel, but who casts a large shadow over the whole narrative. Twain only gives us hints about Huck's upbringing, at Pap's "parenting," leaving the reader to fill in the gaps and imagine what must have been a horrible past. Pap is ignorant and illiterate and proud of both. He is a virulent racist and a violent alcoholic, lashing out in rage at the whole world, but landing blows only on his son. We know only two facts about Huck's mother: that she is dead and that she, like Pap, could not read or write. Did she die in childbirth, and Huck never knew his mother? Or did Huck know her? Did she give him affection? (Huck's good nature surely came from her, not from his father.) Was she also a victim of Pap's abuse, both verbal and physical? Her absence shows us the depths

---

214

of Huck's empty family life: he is an abandoned child, homeless, the son of an alcoholic, with the coping skills such children must develop to survive—defensiveness, outward toughness, inner strength, and a capacity for smoothing over disagreements. For bad but also for good, his situation forms his character and explains his deep need for and longing for a real family, a deep need he never explicitly expresses, but which runs as an undercurrent throughout his narrative.

That first confrontation with Pap, father and son staring each other down, in Huck's nice new room, reveals the changes Huck has undergone in his new home, his new life. Pap assails Huck over his "starchy clothes," his ability to read and write, his education, even saying, "'First thing you know you'll get religion too'" (chapter 5)—a total inversion of the way society thinks a parent should act. Pap angrily tears up "a little blue and yaller picture of some cows and a boy," which was given to Huck "for learning my lessons good," a picture that this new Huck clearly prizes. "'I never see such a son,'" Pap says twice in his tirade. We have never seen such a father, surely one of the most depraved fathers in all of literature.

The conflict between the new Huck and the old Huck comes with a new home: Pap kidnaps his son and virtually imprisons him in an old log hut. At first, Huck is content to revert to his old carefree and lazy ways, saying, "I didn't see how I'd ever got to like it so well at the widow's, where you had to wash, and eat on a plate, and comb up, and go to bed and get up regular, and be forever bothering over a book an have old Miss Watson picking at you all the time. I didn't want to go back no more" (chapter 6). That contentment changes, however: "But by-and-by, Pap got too handy with his hick'ry, and I couldn't stand it." Again, Huck understates the horror, which his next line reveals: "I was all over welts." "Too handy with his hick'ry" actually means beatings severe enough to leave painful marks all over Huck's body. A climactic scene in Huck's prison of a home builds, with Pap going on a drunken racist tirade against "govment" and "a free nigger . . . from Ohio; a mulatter, most as white as a white man" (chapter 6). Pap drinks himself into a stupor, experiences the nightmare of delirium tremens, finally chasing his son around the cabin, wielding a knife, calling Huck "the Angel of Death." After Pap passes out, Huck sits watch, training a gun on his sleeping father, contemplating patricide in self-defense. Huck has rejected his new home at the widow's, and now he must reject this return to an old home, by elaborately staging his own murder and "lighting out."

## Finding a New Home, Learning About Jim

His escape to Jackson's Island is an attempt at freedom, but after he finds Jim, a new chapter in Huck's search for home and family begins. Jim has run off, too, afraid of being sold by Miss Watson and having his family broken up. The two runaways set up home on the island, a cave, reminiscent of Tom's make-believe gang, but now home to a very real gang of two. During their stay, they encounter another house, floating in the spring rise, a house that contains "old greasy cards," "old whisky bottles," "a couple of masks made out of black cloth," charcoal markings on the walls with "the ignorantest kind of words and pictures," and dirty calico dresses and women's underclothes, suggesting a combination gambling house and house of ill repute. It also contains a dead man, shot in the back, and in a moment of both parental concern for Huck and self-preservation, Jim covers the body and warns Huck not to look: "'It's too gashly'" (chapter 9). Even though what seems like a friendship, and more, is beginning, Huck still carries the influence of his friend Tom and the value system he imbibed from Pap—he disrupts their free life together by playing a trick on Jim that ends with Jim being bitten by a rattlesnake. Huck never takes responsibility for his action, either to Jim or to the reader.

In order to understand their situation, Huck takes on a new identity, dressing as a girl, coached by Jim on how to act like a girl, and visits another house, the home of Judith Loftus. Part of Huck's disguise is his lie about his family, a pattern that will be repeated several more times. Significantly, even his pretend families are broken: he tells Mrs. Loftus, "'My mother's down sick, and out of money and everything'" (chapter 11). Later when Mrs. Loftus sees through his disguise, he tells her he will "make a clean breast and tell her everything," but his lie is again about a broken family, with a dead mother and father, and with Huck apprenticed to a "mean old farmer" who mistreats him. Huck is partly working on her sympathy, but these lies reveal the way his imagination works and, even more deeply, his conception of family: given his past, family means broken homes, dead parents, poverty, and mistreatment. Even in his lies, he reveals to us something about his inner psychology.

Huck learns that his "murder" has been blamed on Jim, and when he gets back to the cave, he says, significantly, "'Git up and hump yourself, Jim! There ain't a moment to lose. They're after us!'" The searchers are after Jim, not "us," but Huck has begun to identify his situation closely with Jim's. That "after *us*" is followed by several chapters in which he and Jim grow closer as friends, setting up a home on the raft, sharing their food, sharing companionship, sharing conversation, creating a semblance of family life. But Huck still retains his attitudes of superiority over blacks that he has learned from Tom, Pap, the widow, and his whole white society: their idyllic home is disrupted when they are separated by fog, and Huck plays yet another trick on his friend, convincing Jim that he has merely dreamed the whole episode. But the leaves and rubbish on the raft show that the fog was indeed real. In one of the most poignant scenes in the novel, Jim educates Huck, then shames him, saying how happy he was to find Huck again, but "'all you wuz thinkin 'bout wuz how you could make a fool of old Jim wid a lie. Dat truck dah is *trash*, en trash is what people is dat puts dirt on de head er dey fren's and makes 'em ashamed'" (chapter 15). Huck's response and the time it takes for him to respond show just how firmly his prejudice has been formed by Pap and by the otherwise respectable people he wants to join: "It was fifteen minutes before I could work myself up to go and humble myself to a nigger—but I done it, and I warn't ever sorry for it afterwards, neither. I didn't do him no more mean tricks, and I wouldn't done that one if I'd a knowed it would make him feel that way." His last comment is very important: up to this point, Huck is oblivious to the fact that Jim, and other blacks, have the same feelings as whites. This moment would seem to mark a significant change in Huck's attitude and in his relationship with Jim.

But Mark Twain continues to highlight the conflict that is raging within Huck, a conflict Huck blames on his conscience, seemingly internal to him, but actually formed by his society and his upbringing. The very next night after Huck's realization of Jim's humanity, Jim begins talking about his freedom when they reach Cairo, and they both feel "trembly and feverish": Jim to be so close to freedom, Huck because he is letting that happen. "It hadn't come home to me before, what this thing was that I was doing," Huck says, "home" being a key word (chapter 16). His mind is on the home he has just left; his conscience says to him, "'What had poor Miss Watson done to you, that you could see her nigger go off right under your eyes and never say one single word?'" Huck forgets how much she tormented him, now seeing her parenting of him as positive:

> "What did that poor old woman do to you, that you could treat her so mean? Why, she tried to learn you your book, she tried to learn you your manners, she tried to be good to you, every way she knowed how. *That's* what she done."

Jim makes things worse for Huck by making plans to save all his money in the free state so he can buy his wife, then they would both work to buy their children—" and if their master wouldn't sell them, they'd get an Ab'litionist and steal them." This first mention of Jim's fractured family could have resonated with Huck's situation if Huck were more sympathetic, but he is in the full throes of his inner conflict: "It most froze me to hear such talk." Huck decides to turn Jim in, but when he encounters two men hunting for five runaway slaves, he lies, protecting Jim, telling the men his companion on the raft is white. Then he continues to lie to keep them from checking, conjuring up another imaginary family, and again, a family in distress: his imaginary father, mother, and sister all sick with smallpox. Huck realizes he would have felt bad if he had turned Jim in, and he would have felt bad if he had not. So he just puts the conflict out of his mind. The way is clear for him to join his new family of two.

## Joining a New Family

Instead, Twain has Huck visit another house and join another family. When a steamboat hits the raft, Huck and Jim are separated again. Huck swims ashore and finds a house. In words that nearly echo Susy Clemens's, Huck says, "It was a mighty nice family, and a mighty nice house, too" (chapter 17). Huck describes the house and its contents in detail, the fullest description of a house in the entire novel. Huck gets taken in by this family, the Grangerfords. They give him some of their youngest son's dry clothes, they feed him, and they listen to his story about his "family," another imagined broken family: sister Mary has run off to get married, brother Bill leaves to hunt for her, then brothers Tom and Mort die, leaving "just me and pap," who also dies. An orphan in both his reality and his imagination, he has now found the nicest family he has seen: Saul and Rachel Grangerford, their two older sons, Bob and Tom, their two beautiful daughters, Miss Charlotte and Miss Sophia, and Buck, who is Huck's age, "thirteen or fourteen or along there." Immediately, Buck says, "You got to stay always," and then the parents "said I could have a home there as long as I wanted it." So Huck, at long last, has found a family, a home. But this seemingly perfect family has two dark problems: they own over a hundred slaves, and they are engaged in a blood feud with the area's other aristocratic family, the Shepherdsons.

Huck becomes a full member of the family, seated at the table for meals, and like all the others, with his own personal slave. After a few weeks, Huck begins to refer to "our house" and "our folks" (chapter 18). In a marker of just how much Huck wants a home, a family, he makes no mention of Jim, not saying that he even thinks about him or wonders where he is. Huck's slave finally leads Huck to the swamp where Jim has been hiding, mending the raft, the home Huck has so quickly abandoned.

Huck's newfound family is shattered by the violence of the feud the next day, a scene of carnage so bloody that Huck says he doesn't want to talk about it. In an echo of *Romeo and Juliet*, Sophia Grangerford elopes with Harney Shepherdson, and the fighting that breaks out sees Colonel Grangerford and his two older sons shot down. Then Huck witnesses the murder of his new "brother," Buck. "I cried a little when I was covering up Buck's face," Huck says (chapter 18). We can feel Huck's disillusionment over what he thought was the ideal home, family, and parents. He has seen the widow's genteel aristocracy meet Pap's wanton violence. He thought he had found home, but he has just found another House of Death.

## Returning to the Raft, But Home Invaded

Huck and Jim's return to the raft brings relief, but even more, a renewed sense of home and family. As Huck tells us, "We said there warn't no home like a raft, after all. Other places do seem so cramped up and smothery, but a raft don't. You feel mighty free and easy and comfortable on a raft" (chapter 18). The long elegiac passage that follows—"Two or three days and nights went by; I might say they swum by, they slid along so quiet and smooth and lovely" (chapter 19)—underscores Huck and Jim's contentment, as does Huck's description of their conversation and their lazy, naked drifting down a river that they feel they have to themselves. These days and nights are the happiest moments of the whole narrative, but they last only a few days: the tranquility of the raft is ended by the arrival of the King and Duke.

The two con men make what amounts to a home invasion. They take Huck and Jim's beds in the wigwam, leaving them out in the elements. Even worse, when they go into towns along the river to work their schemes, they leave Jim tied up in the wigwam in case anyone sees an unattended slave on the raft. To make things "easier" for Jim, they dress him in women's clothes, paint him blue, and make a sign that says, "Sick Arab—but harmless when not out of his head" (chapter 24). The fragile home and family Huck and Jim establish on the raft have been destroyed.

Even so, in their brief moments alone, Huck and Jim continue to develop their brotherhood. In another poignant scene, Jim has again taken Huck's watch rather than waking him, showing not only friendship but also a growing sense of parental concern. Jim has his head between his knees, "moaning and mourning to himself"

---

(chapter 23). Huck knows Jim is thinking about his wife and children, then Jim says his children's names aloud, Elizabeth and Johnny. Huck's comment shows how much he is learning about Jim in particular and about blacks in general, but also revealing the depth of his racist upbringing: "I do believe he cared just as much for his people as white folks does for their'n. It don't seem natural, but I reckon it's so." Twain's irony is palpable: Jim cares *much* more for his children than Huck's white father ever has for Huck. Jim, of course, has become a better and truer father to Huck than Pap Finn.

The next victim of the King and Duke's con games is another family, the Wilks girls, once again in a broken home, three motherless girls who have now lost their father. In his time there as the King's valet, Huck grows so accustomed to being part of a family that he calls their home "our house," as he did during his stay with the Grangerfords. The King and Duke plot to sell the slaves, separating families, which is the breaking point for Huck: he does what he can to foil the plot, recognizing the value of family.

### Losing Jim, Finding His Heart

Back with Jim on the raft, Huck is so elated "to be free again and all by ourselves on the big river and nobody to bother us" (chapter 29) that he skips and jumps and cracks his heels—but the King and Duke invade their home again. "It was all I could do to keep from crying," Huck says. He will cry again soon, in deeper despair, when he learns that they have sold Jim, "for forty dirty dollars" (chapter 31). Huck's crisis of conscience as he decides what to do next is the climax of the novel, bringing to a head the conflict Huck feels between his upbringing and his newfound connection with Jim. As he did in chapter 16 with the slave traders, he decides to turn Jim in, rationalizing that "it would be a thousand times better for Jim to be a slave at home where his family was, if he'd *got* to be a slave" (chapter 31). Significantly, he goes back to the raft and sits in the the wigwam—the home he and Jim have set up providing him with a place for his deepest inner meditation in the novel. His racist upbringing first predominates, but his memories of Jim and their time come back to him: "I see Jim before me, all the time, in the day, and in the night-time, sometimes moonlight, sometimes storms, and we a floating along talking, and singing, and laughing." He remembers Jim taking Huck's watch and letting him sleep, Jim's joy at their reunion when they were separated in the fog and at the Grangerfords, and how "he would always call me honey, and pet me, and do everything he could think of for me, and how good he always was." Huck here is describing the most loving parenting he has ever received, and when he tears up the letter he has written that would enslave Jim again and says to himself, "'All right, then, I'll *go* to hell,'" he chooses Jim, his new family. Much has been written about Jim as a father figure to Huck, but Jim also takes on the nurturing roles of a mother, as well as the companion and confidant role of a brother. Despite the separation of race, Huck and Jim are a family of two. In his attempt to rescue Jim, Huck encounters the story's final home, its final family, one that brings him back nearly full circle.

### Finding Home at Last

When Huck arrives at Phelps farm, where he knows Jim is being held captive, he first encounters a slave family, "a nigger woman . . . with a rolling pin in her hand" and "a little nigger girl and two little nigger boys," hiding behind their mother's gown (chapter 32). Then "the white woman . . . about forty-five or fifty year old" comes running out with "her little white children, acting the same way the little niggers was doing." His emphasis on black and white focuses our attention on slavery and the intimate family relations and race relations on a "one-horse cotton plantation." When Aunt Sally mistakes Huck for her nephew Tom Sawyer, Huck tells us, "It was like being born again, I was so glad to find out who I was." Instantly, Huck has a family, an aunt and uncle and cousins. When Tom arrives, Huck becomes a member of Tom Sawyer's Gang again, but this time with the real mission of freeing Jim.

In many ways, this home and family are the most stable in the novel: an intact family, with a mother and father and children, something Huck has only seen at the ill-fated Grangerfords. They are good Christians; in addition to being a farmer, Uncle Silas is also a preacher. But they are also slaveowners, the curse on white southerners and on America in the nineteenth century. Racism is so much a part of their being that they are totally unconscious of its stain. When Huck lies to Aunt Sally about why he was delayed, saying the steamboat "blowed out a cylinder-head," Aunt Sally shows her Christian good nature by asking, "'Good gracious! Anybody hurt?'" Huck replies, "'No'm,' then adds, gratuitously, "'Killed a nigger.'" This good Christian woman reveals the depths of her racism when she immediately replies, "'Well, it's lucky, because sometimes people do get hurt'" (chapter 32).

Readers and critics focus so much on Tom's "Evasion" that we might not realize Huck stays in this house longer than any on the journey, his most stable home since his time at the widow's. Two revelations come at the end: Jim has been free for months, for the bulk of the journey, since Miss Watson's death, and is now free to return and reunite with his family, and Huck has been free of Pap since the very start of the journey, secrets that Tom and Jim respectively conceal until this point. In the end, Huck is offered a home and family at last. Despite Huck's protests that he has "got to light out for the Territory ahead of the rest, because Aunt Sally, she's going to adopt me and sivilize me and I can't stand it. I been there before" (Chapter the Last), it may be that Huck really does find his home as a member of the Phelps family rather than lighting out again, as most readers assume. One offhand and somewhat buried comment from Huck, earlier in his stay, supports the idea that this becomes his new home. Speaking of Uncle Silas, Huck says, "He was a mighty nice man," then adds, "And always is" (chapter 37), suggesting perhaps a permanent stay—which means of course discounting the novel's sequels, in which Huck does not live with Uncle Silas and Aunt Sally, but staying strictly within the narrative of *Huckleberry Finn*, his words do suggest that possibility. Despite his protests, Huck yearns for a family, for a home, for stable parents, even for the discipline, education, manners, and religious training he had begun to experience in his time with the Widow Douglas. Reading *Huckleberry Finn* this way focuses not on the adventures, but on Huck's desire to go home to a place he has never had.

## Coming Full Circle

In an interesting way, this novel reveals just how deeply Mark Twain loved his family, loved his wife and children, loved the home he and Olivia Clemens had created, a family at the height of its happiness in 1885 when *Huckleberry Finn* was published. Like Huck, Samuel Clemens was a wanderer, raised by a stern, distant father who died when Sam was eleven. Like Tom Sawyer, he had a strong, loving mother who often struggled with her son's rambunctious ways. Samuel Clemens set off on a journey when he was not much older than Huck, wandering the world, in a sense homeless, to find his future wife in the form of a miniature carried by her brother. He too was "sivilized" by his wife and her family (somewhat), and while he sometimes chafed at domesticity the way Huck did, he also embraced it and came to recognize this family, even more than his work and his fame, as the center of his life. It is comforting to imagine the same happening to Huckleberry Finn.

# "It's *Tom Sawyer!*" (No it ain't . . . it's Huck Finn!)

Hugh H. Davis

Huckleberry Finn and Tom Sawyer are iconic characters in American literature, and readers often feel they know Samuel Clemens's boy protagonists well. Arguably Mark Twain's most famous creations, the pair are linked through their joint appearances in literature and in a variety of spinoff materials, including stage, film, and television adaptations as well as advertisements, toys, memorabilia, and illustrations. They are associated with Mark Twain's literary output as well as with perceptions of American culture, and Tom and Huck are contrastingly perceived both as opposing examples of American boyhood, polar opposites in how they are accepted and understood, and as inextricably linked characters, tied together through readers' associations of the youthful protagonists as narrative partners and eternal companions. Readers' perceptions of these characters dominate and drive the legacy for both. However, contrary to many of these readers' popular perceptions, which often mistake one character for the other, Tom and Huck are very different kinds of characters. Despite their literary origins and existences as distinct figures, readers have long merged and mixed them as though they were interchangeable and not the unique literary creations they truly are.

Perceptions of Tom Sawyer and Huckleberry Finn often precede readers actually picking up either *The Adventures of Tom Sawyer* (1876) or *Adventures of Huckleberry Finn* (1885) to meet the characters themselves. Since these characters first debuted in Clemens's novels, they have appeared and reappeared over and over again in a variety of forms and formats, shaping audience perceptions and, in turn, being shaped by those further perceptions. At the climax of chapter 32 of *Huckleberry Finn*, Aunt Sally Phelps asks, when she is greeted by a young boy, "Who do you reckon 't is?," as she and Silas Phelps are confused by the appearance of their young visitor. They leap to the conclusion that "It's *Tom Sawyer!*" After all, he is the young man they expect to encounter, but readers of *Huckleberry Finn* know the Phelpses are wrong, and they are, instead, looking at Tom's friend Huckleberry Finn. While those reading the books know that it is Huck Finn whom Sally and Silas Phelps see, the confusion between Huck and Tom persists through a variety of depictions of the characters. The confusion of misreads of the novels and jumbled beliefs about the characters lead to a blurring of the distinctions between the two. Adaptation theory suggests that readers come to an oft-adapted work and read not only it but also the history and legacy of that text's adaptations. Readers do the same with popular characters, so prior presentations of Huck and Tom inform their understandings and expectations for future and further encounters. Each encounter with Tom and Huck is a commentary upon and contribution to the characters' histories, legacies, and perceptions. While Aunt Sally might be meeting Huck for the first time and insisting he is Tom, readers meet the characters again and again; however, readers' understandings of both Tom and Huck have been shaped and molded with each iteration they encounter of these iconic figures.

Tom and Huck have long histories and legacies as literary characters and icons, but their histories are also partly shaped by ways readers limit them and strip them of their multi-dimensionality. This tendency to oversimplify the characters renders them one-dimensional and ignores the depth of Clemens's characterizations. Obviously, the original literary appearances present the pair as children, as do the vast majority of adaptations, but the result is that the pair are often turned into nineteenth-century versions of the Little Rascals—boys who play hooky from school, get involved in silly scrapes, and impishly misbehave, only to find that everything turns out all right at the end of their adventures, typically a result of their ingenuity, charm, or luck. When the two boys are made distinct from each other (and not presented as two sides of the same nostalgic and rustic coin, lumped together as just a pair of boys out for adventure), Tom is often turned into a too-smart-for-his-own-good child who has a habit of misbehaving but who really, deep down, is a good boy. Huck, meanwhile, is presented as the more rustic and more backward youth, a barefoot country kid (if not young bumpkin) who comes from the "wrong side of town" and has the deck stacked against him in terms of society.

HUCKLEBERRY FINN.

True Williams's first illustrations of Tom and Huck in
*The Adventures of Tom Sawyer.*

## Huck and Tom Among the Illustrators

Long-standing perceptions for these characters begin with the novels themselves, aided, in part, by the books' illustrations. True Williams, the original illustrator for *Tom Sawyer*, significantly contributed to the perceptions of the characters. As Beverly R. David relates in chapter 5 of *Mark Twain and His Illustrators*, Williams's fastidiousness as an artist created highly accurate depictions of children from the time. Consequently, his original depictions of Tom and Huck match both Clemens's textual descriptions and authentic 1850s attire for children. *Tom Sawyer*'s original frontispiece features mischievous

Tom, wearing his Sunday best but remaining barefoot to symbolize his rebellion from minor rules and expectations—while still keeping that challenge within clear bounds. David suggests that initial image of Tom might seem too "precious" for modern readers, but there is no denying that it sets the tone and launches Tom's story. He is drawn barefoot throughout the rest of the novel but is otherwise clad in very typical dress for a boy of the era, including regularly being hatted. Tom is shown wearing a rounded version of a felt hat with a narrow brim, which David reports was especially popular among boys of the time, a trend seen in many illustrations of the character since.

Meanwhile, Williams depicted Huck with textual accuracy, placing him in an over-sized coat, matching Huck's initial description as "always dressed in the cast-off clothes of full-grown men" with "a vast ruin" of a hat. Although Edward W. Kemble's illustrations for *Adventures of Huckleberry Finn* provide more enduring and persistent images of Huck, Williams's original *Tom Sawyer* illustrations offer a noteworthy and influential introduction to the character. Williams distinguishes Tom and Huck from each other through their clothes and by making Huck appear slightly older than Tom. Although the text suggests the boys are the same age—though without specifying either's age—Williams's art suggests that the harder-living Huck is Tom's slight senior, further distinguishing the boys. This move by Williams in the earliest artistic depiction of the boys created a trend revisited both on Hollywood soundstages and on future illustrators' drawing tables, presenting Huck as the older boy.

Despite distinctions made with age and wardrobe, the boys are still treated as very typical nineteenth-century youths, offered as representatives of polar ends of the young male spectrum. True Williams lifted and modified images he had already drawn for Mark Twain's *Sketches, New & Old* (1875) in *Tom Sawyer*. For example, his engraving for the opening of the novel's fourth chapter, showing Tom climbing a tree, is clearly adapted from his depiction of Jim in "The Story of the Bad Little Boy." Williams also adapted the image of Jacob Blevins he drew for "The Story of a Good Little Boy" in *Sketches* to create the image of "Huck Transformed" that opens chapter 35 of *Tom Sawyer*.

This division of Huck and Tom along behavioral lines, with one "bad" and the other "good," has long been associated with them, as they have come to represent opposite examples of young boys. Tom is shown as the misbehaving, but good, little boy, and Huck is depicted as the bad influence and delinquent child. Later renderings and adaptations have continued to promote this dichotomous view, and the idea that the two boys should be seen as opposites or contrasts of boyhood has persisted. Illustrators since Williams have taken his lead in promoting this broad view of the two. The original art produced by Williams, which repurposed earlier illustrations of youth, reveals that the artist saw the children as matching broad ideas and general perceptions of young boys. Tom and Huck serve as sort of literary "everyboys," representing the wide array of children who might read the novels.

## Huck and Tom as Nostalgic Americana

The idea that Huck and Tom appeal to audiences young and young-at-heart can be seen in the continuing and extended lives of these characters throughout retellings and adaptations. For example, Ric Averill's play *Tom Sawyer* (2008) is an adaptation of the first two-thirds of *The Adventures of Tom Sawyer*, stopping with the courthouse sequence and emphasizing a "boys will be boys" view of the adventures for both Huck and Tom. Director Jeffrey Emmerich's note for the College of the Albemarle's 2016 production of this play asks, "What little boy doesn't have a bit of Tom Sawyer in him?" Emmerich further relates that he grew up thinking of Tom as his best friend and idol and that "I'm guessing [Mark Twain] WAS Tom Sawyer." He tells the audience, "Everyone is going to relate to one character or another in today's play." While the idea that at least one character in the entire play might spark a connection for any and every audience member is an oversimplification of the text's appeal, the suggestion that each child represents some piece of Mark Twain's characters within himself or herself does emphasize the long-standing view that Tom and Huck serve as ersatz representatives of all children and of American childhood. Tom and Huck become symbols for a nostalgic view of childhood and of earlier American life.

The projection of Mark Twain's most visible fictional characters as representative for all children occurs among both youth and adult readers. As Robert McParland notes in *Mark Twain's Audience* (2014), many adults read novels like *Huckleberry Finn* and are encouraged to recall their own childhoods while following Huck and Jim down the Mississippi, imagining themselves in Huck's bare footsteps. Both *Tom Sawyer* and *Huckleberry Finn* elicit childhood associations for their readers, creating nostalgic views not only of their own childhoods but of American culture in general. McParland cites ads from such newspapers as the *New York Tribune* from the early decades of the twentieth century that looked back on the novels and their characters as emblems of boyhood and innocence. The dark and grisly aspects of the books and of their characters' lives gave way to a sanitized vision of the two boys as symbols of youthful fun and simpler, rustic life. Huck and Tom eventually both come to be presented as cheery boys whose idyllic existence comes from a nostalgia for an America of the imagination. McParland points out that many twentieth-century immigrants to America cited that their images of America were informed through their reading of both *Huckleberry Finn* and *Roughing It* (1872). These works provided the immigrants with a literary construction of the nineteenth-century United States, one that shaped and defined their impressions and expectations for America.

The use of Clemens's fiction to shape an oversimplified and fictionalized version of American culture, one in which Huck and Tom sit front and center, normally by a fence needing white-washing or on a raft, has permeated popular culture both directly tied to Clemens's work and through elements that are only tangentially connected. Visitors to Disneyland, Walt Disney World, and Tokyo Disneyland can explore attractions called "Tom Sawyer Island," artificial landmasses surrounded by the man-made "Rivers of America" at these related theme parks. First opened in 1956 at Disneyland in California, the attraction contains caves and structures, such as

"Tom & Huck's Treehouse," that reference the famous characters without requiring or imparting knowledge of the literary texts. They instead offer diversions tied obliquely to the books but more fully to a vision of America as part of an "Adventureland." In 2007, the original California Disneyland attraction merged Tom and Huck with the *Pirates of the Caribbean* franchise and became "Pirate's Lair on Tom Sawyer Island," further separating the characters from the novels but reinforcing their importance as icons both of Americana and family-friendly adventure.

In 1980, Kenner Toy Company released the first male doll in its *Strawberry Shortcake* line, "Huckleberry Pie." Dressed in patched denim clothes and wearing a straw hat that evoked E. W. Kemble's original illustrations of the literary character, this toy-line character was presented as easygoing and laid back (with a southern drawl when presented in cartoon form), spending his leisure time fishing. This nod to Huck Finn provided many children, particularly of Generation X, their first pseudo-introduction to Twain's protagonist; however, the toymakers made a point of stating that their character was not mischievous, showing an assumption about Huck as simply a rambunctious child.

The next presentation of these famous characters in toy form took a more direct connection to the source material while still revealing the perception of these characters as belonging to the nation. In 1983, the Effanbee toy company premiered the "Mark Twain Collection" of dolls as part of a "Great Moments in Literature" series. Effanbee had produced dolls of Howdy Doody, Charlie McCarthy, and many Disney characters over its history, but by the 1970s was primarily creating realistically proportioned collectors' dolls of famous figures. These included luminaries and icons of Old Hollywood, such as John Wayne, Groucho Marx, and Humphrey Bogart, and American presidents, such as Abraham Lincoln and Teddy Roosevelt. Into this mix of celebrities and historical figures, Effanbee launched a new line, with dolls produced over three years of Mark Twain, Huck Finn, Tom Sawyer, and Becky Thatcher. While the Mark Twain doll presented the famous image of the author in his white suit, the dolls based on the three fictional characters evoked the most famous illustrations, with Tom and Becky recalling True Williams's work and Huck giving three dimensions to Kemble's art. Although the move to "Great Moments in Literature" would suggest a shift to fictional subjects for the company, Effanbee's catalog continued its primary focus on real-life examples of Americana and icons of American popular culture, except for this trio from Mark Twain's literary output. By placing and casting the characters alongside their creator, the doll makers reinforce the notions that Tom, Becky, and Huck represent American culture and serve as icons alongside the author. These dolls, then, further promote the notion that the novels can be read as pseudo-autobiography by Clemens, with an association of him as "America's author" and his most famed creations as archetypal examples of American youth.

## Huck, Tom, and Imbedded Biography

The original preface for *Tom Sawyer* states, "Most of the adventures recorded in this book really occurred." This statement inspires the ongoing idea that Mark Twain's own youth is imbedded in the fictional childhoods for Tom, Becky, and Huck. Some readers then presume that Mark Twain's actual youthful experiences are retold as part of the fictional lives of his creations. That presumption has, in turn, been expanded upon significantly over the years, with a variety of examples where lines between the author's personal history and his literary art blur. The (auto)biographical view of Clemens's works as having all grown from his personal experiences and the idea Huck and Tom represent America merge in Hannibal, Missouri, the author's hometown and the basis for St. Petersburg in the books. Billing Hannibal as "America's Hometown," the city's tourism industry is driven by notions that Tom and Huck are examples of traditional American children and that they grew out of Clemens's own childhood. The idea that the author's childhood is simply transferred into the texts of *Tom Sawyer* and *Huckleberry Finn* is presented directly through the tourist offerings of historic buildings that reveal what connections can be, might be, and have been determined. The reinforcement of these connections is underscored by many businesses in the town, "Pudd' N Head's Antiques" and

"Becky's Old Fashioned Ice Cream Parlor," along with the "Mark Twain Dinette" and "Mark Twain Brewing Company," all of which seek to link Mark Twain, his creations, and American nostalgia. The presentation of Hannibal exemplifies the desire to place Tom Sawyer, Huckleberry Finn, and Samuel Clemens as a trio of friends, as fiction and nonfiction merge.

The desire to see imbedded biography, and the blending of fiction and nonfiction, in Mark Twain's works runs throughout the popular culture iterations of the author. For example, the final scene of the 1944 biopic *The Adventures of Mark Twain* features the aged Mark Twain disappearing over the horizon with his most famous creations. Will Vinton's Claymation film *The Adventures of Mark Twain* (1985) shows the author and his famed trio of child protagonists teaming up in an aerial adventure. As Clyde V. Haupt points out in *Huckleberry Finn on Film* (1994), many adaptations of that novel project onto the protagonist an abolitionist philosophy. An episode of *Fantasy Island*, "The Angel's Triangle/Natchez Bound" (1982), features a young Sam Clemens on a steamboat meeting a stowaway boy named Huck Finn helping a runaway slave named Jim. Clemens is then inspired to write future works and to take part in a life of abolitionism based on his encounters with the young boy. The budding author sees in the orphan a seeming reflection of his own idealism.

## Huck and Tom Among the Readers

Readers have long seen apparent reflections of their own ideals and thoughts in these famous characters. McParland's review of letters and oral commentaries from the nineteenth century reveals, not surprisingly, that boys in particular enjoyed reading the adventures for both Tom and Huck, with them often seeing their own images in Twain's characters. However, McParland also notes where readers separated the two characters, placing them in two categories. While Tom was seen as a familiar character who resisted social controls and conventions, the recalcitrant Huck was seen as a practitioner of social rebellion. While Tom pushes against boundaries, he stays within societal expectations, but his friend challenges social norms and the boundaries of civilization. Tom functions and misbehaves within society, while Huck is the pariah fighting constrictions from a society that does not accept him.

The quintessential Tom Sawyer of readers' memories appears in Clemens's original novel, *The Adventures of Tom Sawyer*, introduced and presented by an anonymous third-person narrator. The Tom of the sequel stories, including *Huckleberry Finn*, which are all narrated by Huck, shifts as a character. In the initial volume, Tom fulfills the tradition in nineteenth-century American fiction of being a "good bad boy," seen also in such books as Thomas Hughes's *Tom Brown's School Days* (1857). Tom pulls pranks (albeit minor ones, without serious consequences) and skips school; outsmarts other children; and, in general, exasperates adults. However, Tom's misbehavior is often tied to noble acts, such as lying in order to save Becky from punishment.

In contrast, Huckleberry Finn is also a "bad boy," but one whose origins as son of the town drunk mark him as an outcast who literally lives outside the town and metaphorically lives outside society and its norms. Tom, meanwhile, rests comfortably within these norms. While Huck is read, perhaps especially by the prudish middle class, as the "bad apple" who will ruin the other children, Tom is simply a "bad kid," seen as naughty and perhaps cheeky but returning to and supporting the norm in the long run. However, as presented through Huck's eyes, Tom becomes emblematic of the stagnancy of those norms in society. He is only willing to help Huck rescue Jim from captivity because he knows Jim is already lawfully free, and, in turn, he makes both Huck and Jim into pawns in his series of imaginative, but cruel, games. Huck, in contrast, is willing to risk being caught breaking the law and in committing, in his understanding, a damnable sin by helping Jim escape from captivity.

Mark Twain demonstrates for Tom Sawyer what Judith Yaross Lee has called a "wandering affection," with the original character, the version beloved by so many readers, giving way to a "self-centered tyrant" whose elaborate and structured play marks him as a clear member of the St. Petersburg society. The Tom Sawyer presented in the sequel novels—seen and presented by Huck—is a child of the town who remains part of that town's system. That Tom Sawyer in particular is a clear part of the world and its conventions, accepting of society's ills as established guidelines and further rules to follow ("Sawyer, Tom" 656-657). As Everett Carter noted, compared to Tom, Huckleberry Finn is seen as a sort of patron saint for nineteenth-century counterculture ("Finn, Huckleberry" 288-289). Huck rejects societal expectations. Even though his understanding of consequences is incorrect, he knows he is challenging the norms and values of middle-class American society.

Within the first novel, Tom remains a model for children as the fun child who might stray slightly but who is proven the hero in the end. In the later stories, however, he is more controlling and pedantic. Huck, on the other hand, becomes the model for a slightly older audience and adult readers, in particular, as he develops and demonstrates his conscience and reveals himself to be an independent thinker, free of society's constraints. While critics have a temptation to contrast, or at least balance, Huck's pragmatism with Tom's romanticism, those qualities primarily are highlighted because of oversimplified or limited takes on the characters, particularly those formed by only remembering the pair from each of their original novels. The more appropriate contrast, should such a division be necessary, would be to counter Tom's conventionality and restraint with Huck's idealism and independence. Where Tom narrows within the system, Huck breaks free of it.

## Huck and Tom and Tom and Edward

The seeming duality for Huck and Tom can be seen in other works by Clemens as well. Many of the author's works feature doubles or pairs, with Tom and Huck his most famous duo. Even within *Huckleberry Finn*, the reader encounters the noteworthy scoundrels known as the Duke and the King (or Dauphin), with Huck and Jim serving as the primary narrative duo, while the re-entry of Tom Sawyer in the novel's final third reestablishes Tom and Huck as Twain's primary pair of characters. Besides Tom and Huck, the most noteworthy literary pair in the Mark Twain canon are probably the titular protagonists of *The Prince and the Pauper* (1881), the author's noted novel about two sixteenth-century English boys, written and published between *Tom Sawyer* and *Huckleberry Finn*. Prince Edward Tudor and the pauper Tom Canty represent many of the qualities seen in Tom and Huck. The two Toms, Sawyer and Canty, are both resourceful and clever, escaping the world's difficulties through reading and surviving through their reliance on their wits. Both Tom Canty and Huckleberry Finn have abusive fathers. Both Edward Tudor and Tom Sawyer are youthful representatives of society. Once away from the castle, Edward is forced to navigate a world unknown to him with the help of just one supportive adult (Miles Hendon). Edward's immediate and required independence, as well as his loss of his biological father while then finding a father-figure to journey alongside him, anticipates Huck's journey, both narratively and metaphorically, in the later novel.

Just as *Tom Sawyer* shows its protagonist moving towards maturity, *Prince and the Pauper* and *Huckleberry Finn* detail paths for youthful characters to mature. All three novels place children at their centers and show them mature through trials and tribulations as they inhabit worlds in which seemingly few adults are available to help them. Clemens uses his young lead characters to provide a commentary on their worlds and the world of the reader. *Prince and the Pauper*, like *Huckleberry Finn*, is a novel that sounds a call for social justice and makes that call through its young heroes. However, while it and *Tom Sawyer* also share a third-person, omniscient narrator, *Huckleberry Finn* famously tells its story in Huck's distinctive first-person voice. The result of the first-person narration is a strong connection between readers and their storyteller. Where Tom Sawyer, Tom Canty, and Edward Tudor all demonstrate maturation, and where the newly crowned King Edward does bring elements of social change to England through his throne at the conclusion of *Prince and the Pauper*, these characters are observed by readers through the distance of the third-person narrative structure. The effect of having Huck narrate his novel creates a bond from fictional character to real-life reader. Huck's struggles with his conscience make him a complex and multifaceted figure; where Edward is able to bring change through royal decree,

Huck, the societal outcast and a boy, does not have any power. He cannot bring any change other than to his own mindset. The sense that, though he lacks power, he acts anyway resonates with readers.

## Conclusion

In R. Kent Rasmussen's *Dear Mark Twain: Letters From His Readers*, Mark Twain's contemporary readers confirm that the fully realized character of Huck had strong appeal. In 1888, a thirteen-year-old boy, Herbert Philbrick, wrote directly to Huck Finn, having been so enchanted by the character that he felt him real. He praised Huck (as well as Jim and Tom), showing how well he connected to him. Mark Twain also had correspondence affirm how easily readers could connect with the young Huck. Enid Snipe, another young fan of Clemens's books, wrote to the author in the last decade of his life, saying, "Huck is the best—Huck was more human." Huck's complexity and multidimensionality create a perception of the protagonist as being more human than other characters in the work and in the different Tom and Huck stories, as he appeals to characters precisely because he brings out the challenges of humanity.

The history of the two novels and the ways they have been presented have contributed to reader perceptions of both Huck and Tom. Both novels might be read first by children who later rediscover the books as adults. However, as McParland notes in *Mark Twain's Audience*, from very early on, *Tom Sawyer* was presented as a children's book far more often than *Huckleberry Finn*, with the latter novel given canonical status in all of American literature. While the first book is treated as a classic of children's literature, it is not named as often as an adult work. With the books divided for their supposed/assumed audiences, the protagonists, in turn, are split among readers. The perception of Tom—as a child who might misbehave but who is, in general, good—becomes linked to readers' nostalgic memories of the book, read in their own childhoods. The perception of Huck—as a social rebel who follows his conscience more than society's expectations—is linked then to readers' associations of reading the novel as they themselves mature, and they thus connect Huck with their own perceptions of their personal self-discovery and maturation.

The misreading of Huck as some sort of flipside to Tom comes from an over-reliance on seeing the characters as limited to the perceived world of *Tom Sawyer*. While Clemens does feature a more gentle tone in the final published Tom and Huck stories, *Tom Sawyer Abroad* (1894) and *Tom Sawyer, Detective* (1896), than in *Huckleberry Finn*, the idea that the first literary appearance of the pair is to be seen as a kind and even mild story ignores the work's darker elements, such as the horrific fate of Injun Joe, and provides a sanitized, and in many ways blurred, view of the characters. For one thing, it ignores the fact that each novel has its own tone. However, that blurred take on the characters is, in many ways, the prevalent one. Tom is often interpreted as simply the "sivilized" Huck, serving as the model not merely for any archetypal boy but for specifically the refined version of Huck after Aunt Sally got through with him following the events of *Huckleberry Finn*. That type of misreading, often prevalent in juvenile approaches to the character, particularly in adaptations, stems from efforts to offer a *Huckleberry Finn* that is in a child-friendly—and thus sanitized—form. Two Disney cinematic offerings in the 1990s offer big-screen takes on the blurring: *The Adventures of Huck Finn* (1993), which erases Tom Sawyer from the narrative while grafting elements of Tom onto the film's Huck, and *Tom and Huck* (1995), an adaptation of *Tom Sawyer* that highlights the rambunctious side of the children and elevates the two into equal narrative status. The interpretations by filmmakers reveal persistent and habitual efforts to place Tom and Huck into convenient slots as characters, often limiting potentially more complex interpretations.

In American education, when the books are taught, *The Adventures of Tom Sawyer* is traditionally taught in upper elementary grades (to fourth or fifth graders), while *Huckleberry Finn* is traditionally taught to upper secondary students (most commonly in the eleventh grade). The placement of *Huckleberry Finn* with late adolescent readers causes those who encounter the book as an educational rite of passage to associate the character with lessons on independence and American culture. The book has a long history of being taught as a didactic novel, encouraging the need for social justice, and Huck as a character is interwoven into readings that promote *Huckleberry Finn* as a novel being read as a call for social rebellion and societal change. Text and protagonist are read as one and the same, and Huckleberry Finn exists for those who truly read the novel in a school setting as the rebellious youth.

Although those who read the novel are clearly producing and maintaining powerful perceptions of Huck as an agent of social rebellion, the popular culture perceptions of the characters—ones that reset to the *Tom Sawyer* view of rascals on adventures—persist overall. One surprising example of this legacy was found with the 1968–1969 television series *The New Adventures of Huckleberry Finn*, a prime-time children's series that combined live actors playing Huck (Michael Shea), Tom (Kevin Schultz), and Becky (Lu Ann Haslam) with animated figures as the trio fled from the villainous Injun Joe. The trio are presented as having been chased into caves outside of Hannibal—not St. Petersburg, as Mark Twain's novels renamed Clemens's hometown—and, in their running, having fallen through a magical portal, so that they visit a new place each episode as they seek to return to their hometown in Missouri. Each episode, then, is a crossover from the world of Mark Twain to some adventurous and often fantastic landscape, with Huck and Tom encountering leprechauns, mummies, pirates, cursed Incan and Aztec ruins, and mad scientists. Stories blend elements from *The Arabian Nights* and mythology, as well as linking the heroes with Aladdin, Hercules, and Don Quixote. The series continued the adventures of Tom, Becky, and Huck while also prolonging perceptions of the characters as icons of childhood adventure. Tom and Huck are not just interchangeable, but they are also taking the place of Jason against the Gorgon and Gulliver among the Lilliputians. The characters could go any place to find a good adventure, and Twain's characters are seen as the starting point for those adventures; even when the characters are presented with limited depth, they inspire further connections to other literary and fictional worlds.

In *Dear Mark Twain*, a letter from Orion Clemens to his brother Samuel from 1885 features Orion relaying to his sibling the views an Iowa resident, John H. Craig, had of *Huckleberry Finn*. Craig reported that both Jim and Huck "are real characters" for him as a reader, and he especially praised the development of Huck, finding him "as distinctly a created character as Falstaff." Huck stands out as a real character who can exist alongside the most noteworthy of Shakespeare's creations. Although presentations of the character through art and adaptations suggest a limited understanding of the character, to the point that he is confused with his literary comrade Tom, and although some presentations leave readers/viewers having to determine who they reckon it is, Huckleberry Finn stands up throughout as a unique and individual character, the literary embodiment of an American idealistic spirit.

## Works Cited

David, Beverly R. *Mark Twain and His Illustrators: 1869–1875*. Troy, NY: Whitston Publishing Company, 1986.

"Finn, Huck." *Mark Twain Encyclopedia*. Ed. J. R. LeMaster & James Wilson. New York: Garland, 1993. 288-289.

McParland, Robert. *Mark Twain's Audience: A Critical Analysis of Reader Responses to the Writings of Mark Twain*. Lanham, MD: Lexington Books, 2014.

Rasmussen, R. Kent, ed. *Dear Mark Twain: Letters from His Readers*. Berkeley: U of California P, 2013.

"Sawyer, Tom." *Mark Twain Encyclopedia*. Ed. J. R. LeMaster & James Wilson. New York: Garland, 1993. 656-657.

# RESOURCES

# Chronology of Mark Twain's Life and Legacy____

*Mark Twain is the subject of each entry, except as otherwise stated.*

| | |
|---|---|
| Nov. 30, 1835 | Samuel Langhorne Clemens—later better known as Mark Twain—is born in the northeastern Missouri village of Florida. The sixth of seven children of John Marshall and Jane Lampton Clemens, he will outlive all his siblings, his wife, and three of his own four children. |
| 1839–1853 | Lives in Missouri's Mississippi River town of Hannibal, on which he will later model the fictional St. Petersburg of *Tom Sawyer* and *Huckleberry Finn*. After leaving school at eleven, he does printing work for local newspapers, including his brother Orion's papers, and writes occasional sketches and essays. |
| Mar. 24, 1847 | John Marshall Clemens's death leaves his family impoverished. |
| 1853–1856 | Sam Clemens leaves Missouri to work as a printer in St. Louis, Philadelphia, and New York; after returning to the Midwest, he does similar work for Orion in southern Iowa. |
| May 1857-Apr. 1861 | Spends two years training as a steamboat pilot on the Lower Mississippi—mostly under Horace Bixby—and two more years as a licensed pilot. |
| June 13, 1858 | Steamboat *Pennsylvania* blows up south of Memphis, severely injuring his younger brother, Henry, who dies eight days later. |
| Apr. 12, 1861 | Civil War begins when Confederates fire on Fort Sumter in Charleston, South Carolina. Clemens, who is |

in New Orleans, will soon end his piloting career when war stops steamboat traffic on the Lower Mississippi.

| | |
|---|---|
| **June 1861** | Clemens drills for about two weeks with a Missouri militia unit called up by the state's pro-Confederate governor. |
| **July 1861** | Crosses the plains with his brother Orion, who has been appointed secretary to the government of the newly created Nevada Territory. |
| **July 1861-Sept. 1862** | Prospects and collects mining claims in western Nevada. |
| **Sept. 1862-May 1864** | Works as a reporter for the *Virginia City Territorial Enterprise*. |
| **Feb. 3, 1863** | Uses the pen name "Mark Twain" for the first time in a report written in Carson City for the *Enterprise*. |
| **June. 1864-Dec. 1866** | After relocating to California, briefly reports for the *San Francisco Morning Call*, does some prospecting in the depleted gold fields of Tuolumne and Calaveras counties, and writes for a variety of publications. |
| **Nov. 18, 1865** | Publication of his jumping frog story in New York's *Saturday Press* helps build his national reputation. |
| **Mar.–Aug. 1866** | Visits the Hawaiian (Sandwich) Islands as a correspondent for the *Sacramento Union*. After returning to San Francisco, he launches what will become a long and successful lecturing career by speaking on the islands in Northern California and western Nevada. |

| May 14, 1867 | Publishes his first book, *The Celebrated Jumping Frog of Calaveras County and Other Sketches.* |
| :--- | :--- |
| June–Nov. 1867 | Tours Mediterranean Europe and the Holy Land with the *Quaker City* excursion; his travel letters to San Francisco and New York newspapers are widely reprinted, expanding his reputation. After he returns, Elisha Bliss of the American Publishing Co. (APC) of Hartford, Connecticut, invites him to write the book about his travels that will become *The Innocents Abroad.* |
| Mar-July 1868 | Visits California for the last time to secure the rights to his *Quaker City* letters from the *San Francisco Alta California*; while there, he finishes writing his book with the help of Bret Harte. |
| July 20, 1869 | APC publishes *The Innocents Abroad, Or, The New Pilgrims' Progress*, the first of Clemens's five travel books, which will be his best-selling book throughout his lifetime and the best-selling American travel book of the 19th century. |
| Aug. 1869 | Clemens buys an interest in the *Buffalo Express* and becomes one of the newspaper's editors. After settling in Buffalo, New York, he begins the first of several major eastern lecture tours. |
| Feb. 2, 1870 | Marries Olivia (Livy) Langdon, the daughter of a wealthy Elmira, New York, coal magnate. The newlyweds settle in a Buffalo house given to them by Livy's father. |
| Nov. 7, 1870 | The couple's first child, a son named Langdon, is born; he will live only twenty-two months. |

| | |
|---|---|
| Feb. 1871 | Isaac Sheldon publishes *Mark Twain's Burlesque Autobiography and First Romance*, the first part of which is essentially a farce about imaginary ancestors that Clemens would later regret having published. |
| Mar. 1871 | After a year of family misfortunes, Clemens sells his Buffalo house and interest in the *Express* and relocates to Elmira, where his family stays on the Quarry Farm of Livy's sister, Susan Crane. Over the next two decades, his family will spend most of their summers on the farm, where Clemens will do much of his most important writing. |
| Oct. 1871 | His family settles in Hartford, Connecticut, before he starts another long lecture tour. His first daughter, Susy, is born the following March. In September 1874, the family will move into a magnificent new house that will be their home until 1891. |
| Feb. 29, 1872 | APC publishes *Roughing It*, an embellished account of Clemens's years in the Far West and Hawaii. |
| Aug.–Nov. 1872 | Clemens makes his first visit to England, to which he will soon return with his family. |
| Dec.1873 | APC publishes *The Gilded Age*, a novel by Clemens and his Hartford neighbor Charles Dudley Warner. Clemens's portions of the novel revolve around events modeled on his own family's history. |
| June 1874 | Clemens begins writing *Tom Sawyer* in earnest during the same month his second daughter, Clara, is born. |
| Jan.–Aug. 1875 | Publishes "Old Times on the Mississippi," his first extended work about steamboating, in a seven-part series in *The Atlantic Monthly*. |

| | |
|---|---|
| July 5, 1875 | Tells William Dean Howells he has finished writing *Tom Sawyer* and turns to dramatizing the story. |
| July 21, 1875 | APC publishes *Mark Twain's Sketches New & Old*. |
| Nov. 5, 1875 | Delivers manuscript of *Tom Sawyer* to APC. |
| June. 9, 1876 | *The Adventures of Tom Sawyer* is published first in England, as American publication is delayed. |
| June. 28, 1876 | Belford Brothers in Canada publishes a pirated edition of *Tom Sawyer* that soon floods American markets. |
| Dec. 8, 1876 | APC publishes the first American edition of *Tom Sawyer*. |
| Dec. 17, 1877 | Clemens delivers burlesque speech at a Boston birthday banquet for poet John Greenleaf Whittier that afterward causes him great embarrassment. |
| Apr. 1878- Aug. 1879 | Travels in western Europe with his family. |
| Nov. 12, 1879 | Delivers triumphant speech honoring Gen. Ulysses S. Grant at a Union army reunion in Chicago. |
| Mar. 13, 1880 | APC publishes *A Tramp Abroad*, a fictionalized account of episodes from Clemens's recent European travels. |
| Dec. 12, 1881 | James Osgood of Boston publishes *The Prince and the Pauper*, Clemens's novel about boys switching places during sixteenth-century England. |
| Apr.–May 1882 | Clemens travels by steamboat from St. Louis, Missouri, to New Orleans, and then upriver to St. Paul, |

Minnesota, to gather material for the book to called *Life on the Mississippi*.

| | |
|---|---|
| **May 17, 1883** | Osgood publishes *Life on the Mississippi*, which expands Clemens's 1875 "Old Times on the Mississippi" articles and adds new material from his 1882 return to the river. |
| **May 1, 1884** | Clemens founds his own publishing house, Charles L. Webster & Co., with Webster, his nephew by marriage, as company president. |
| **July 1884** | Begins writing unfinished sequel to *Huckleberry Finn* that will be first published in the December 20, 1968 *Life* magazine as "Huck Finn & Tom Sawyer Among the Indians." |
| **Dec. 10, 1884** | *Adventures of Huckleberry Finn* sees its first publication in England by Chatto & Windus, which will become Clemens's only authorized English publisher. |
| **Feb. 18 1885** | *Huckleberry Finn* is belatedly released in America by Webster. |
| **Dec. 10, 1889** | Webster publishes *A Connecticut Yankee in King Arthur's Court*, Clemens's novel about a contemporary American thrust back to sixth-century England. |
| **Oct. 27, 1890** | Jane Lampton Clemens, Clemens's mother, dies at the age of eighty-seven. |
| **June 1891-May 1895** | Clemens family closes down the Hartford house—to which they will never return—and goes to Europe to live to cut down living expenses. As they move around in western Europe, Clemens makes numerous |

quick trips to the United States to look after his failing business interests.

| | |
|---|---|
| **May 1892** | Webster publishes *The American Claimant*, Clemens's novel about an American who claims to be heir to an English earldom. |
| **1893–1894** | Clemens publishes *Tom Sawyer Abroad*, first as a serial in *St. Nicholas Magazine*, then as the last book issued by his firm Webster & Co., which goes into bankruptcy in April 1894. |
| **Nov. 28, 1894** | APC publishes *Pudd'nhead Wilson*, Clemens's novel about slavery and miscegenation set in another fictional Missouri town modeled on Hannibal. |
| **Apr. 1895-Apr. 1896** | *Harper's Magazine* serializes Clemens's novel *The Personal Recollections of Joan of Arc*, which afterward is issued in book form by Harper and Brothers, Clemens's new authorized American publisher. Harper will soon begin reissuing all his books in uniform editions. |
| **May 1895-July 1896** | Leaves England with his family, beginning a round-the-world lecturing trip. After summering at Elmira, he, Livy, and daughter Clara travel cross-country to British Columbia, whence they cross the Pacific to Hawaii, Fiji, Australia, and New Zealand and then cross the Indian Ocean to Ceylon, India, and South Africa before returning to England. Meanwhile, daughters Susy and Jean remain behind in Elmira. Profits from the lecturing tour will pay off debts from his publishing firm's bankruptcy, and he returns to America hailed as a triumphant hero. |

| | |
|---|---|
| Aug. 18, 1896 | Daughter Susy dies of spinal meningitis while Clemens is in England. |
| July 1896–<br>Oct 1990 | After being rejoined by daughter Jean, the family remains in Europe four more years. |
| Aug.–<br>Sept. 1896 | Publishes *Tom Sawyer, Detective* as a serial in *Harper's New Monthly Magazine.* |
| Nov. 13, 1897 | Harper and APC publish Clemens's fifth travel book, *Following the Equator*, a relatively sober account of his round-the-world trip. |
| Dec. 11, 1897 | Orion Clemens dies. |
| Oct. 15, 1900 | After an unbroken absence of five years, Clemens returns to the United States with his family and rents a house in New York City. |
| Apr. 10, 1902 | Harper publishes Clemens's *A Double-Barrelled Detective Story*, a novella that includes Sherlock Holmes as a bumbling detective. |
| May 1902 | Clemens pays his last visit to Hannibal and the Mississippi River during a trip to Columbia to accept an honorary degree from the University of Missouri. |
| Nov. 1903–<br>June 1904 | Takes his family to Florence, Italy, hoping the mild climate will help his wife Livy's failing health. |
| Jan. 14, 1904 | Begins dictating his autobiography to his family secretary, Isabel Lyon. |

| | |
|---|---|
| June 5, 1904 | Livy dies in Florence; the rest of the family soon returns to the United States. |
| Aug. 31, 1904 | Pamela Clemens Moffett, Clemens's last surviving sibling, dies. |
| Sept. 1904–June 1908 | Clemens takes up residence on Fifth Avenue in New York City, where he is lionized as a public speaker and banquet guest. |
| Dec. 5, 1905 | Col. George Harvey, president of Harper and Brothers and editor of *Harper's Weekly*, hosts a grand seventieth birthday banquet for Clemens at New York's Delmonico's restaurant. |
| Jan. 1906 | Albert Bigelow Paine moves into Clemens's home to begin work as Clemens's authorized biographer. |
| June–July 1907 | Clemens makes last trans-Atlantic voyage to accept an honorary degree at Oxford University in England. |
| June 18, 1908 | Clemens moves into his last home, a newly built house outside Redding, Connecticut. |
| Apr 8, 1909 | Publishes *Is Shakespeare Dead?* |
| Dec 24, 1909 | His youngest daughter, Jean, dies of a heart attack suffered during a seizure. |
| Jan.–Apr. 1910 | Visits Bermuda on his last trip outside the United States. When his health seriously declines, Paine goes to Bermuda to bring him home. |
| Apr. 21, 1910 | Samuel Langhorne Clemens dies of heart failure in his Stormfield home at the age of seventy-four. Three days |

| | |
|---|---|
| | later, he is buried in Elmira's Woodlawn Cemetery, where all members of his family will eventually be interred. |
| Aug. 18, 1910 | His only grandchild, Nina Clemens Gabrilowitsch, is born at Stormfield. |
| Sept. 1910 | William Dean Howells publishes *My Mark Twain*, a personal tribute to his close friend. |
| Aug. 1912 | Now Clemens's literary executor, Paine publishes his three-volume *Mark Twain: A Biography*. Over the next quarter-century, he will edit and publish numerous collections of Clemens's previously unpublished writings. |
| 1917–1918 | Silent film adaptation of *Tom Sawyer* is released in two parts: *Tom Sawyer* and *Huck and Tom; Or, The Further Adventures of Tom Sawyer*. Jack Pickford, Mary Pickford's brother, plays Tom, and Robert Gordon plays Huck. |
| Feb. 1920 | Silent film adaptation of *Huckleberry Finn* is released. |
| Dec. 1930 | First sound film adaptation of *Tom Sawyer* is released, with Jackie Coogan as Tom and Junior Durkin as Huck Finn. |
| Aug. 1931 | First sound film adaptation of *Huckleberry Finn* is released, with the same leads as the previous year's *Tom Sawyer*. |
| Dec. 1931 | American copyright of *Tom Sawyer* expires; many unauthorized editions soon follow. |
| Apr. 9, 1937 | Paine dies in New Smyrna, Florida; Bernard DeVoto succeeds him as editor of the Mark Twain Papers. |

| | |
|---|---|
| Feb. 1938 | David O. Selznick releases first color film adaptation of *Tom Sawyer*, with Tommy Kelly as Tom. |
| Mar. 1939 | MGM releases *The Adventures of Huckleberry Finn* with Mickey Rooney as Huck and Rex Ingram as Jim. |
| 1940 | American copyright of *Huckleberry Finn* expires and authorized new editions begin appearing. |
| Jan. 1946 | DeVoto resigns as editor of Mark Twain Papers. His successor, Dixon Wecter, will move the collection to the University of California at Berkeley three years later. |
| 1960 | MGM releases first color film adaptation of *Huckleberry Finn* as *The Adventures of Huckleberry Finn*, with Eddie Hodges as Huck and boxer Archie Moore as Jim. |
| Nov. 19, 1962 | Clara Clemens Samossoud, Clemens's longest-surviving child, dies in San Diego, California. |
| Jan. 16, 1966 | Nina Clemens Gabrilowitsch, Clemens's only grandchild and last direct descendant, dies in Los Angeles. |
| 1970 | Scholar John Seelye publishes *The True Adventures of Huckleberry Finn*; he will issue a revised version in 1987. |
| Oct. 13, 1972 | US Post Office issues eight-cent "Tom Sawyer" stamp using an illustration painted by Norman Rockwell. |
| Apr. 1973 | *Reader's Digest* releases musical film adaptation of *Tom Sawyer*, with Johnny Whitaker as Tom, Jeff East as Huck Finn, and Jodie Foster as Becky Thatcher. |

| Apr. 1974 | *Reader's Digest* and United Artists release musical film adaptation of *Huckleberry Finn*, with Jeff East returning as Huck, Paul Winfield as Jim, Harvey Korman as the King, and David Wayne as the Duke. |
| --- | --- |
| Mar. 1975 | Twenty-one-year-old Ron Howard plays Huck in television production of *Huckleberry Finn*, with Antonio Fargas as Jim. |
| 1980 | University of California Press publishes first corrected edition of *Tom Sawyer* based directly on original manuscript material, prepared by the editors of the Mark Twain Papers. |
| July 1981 | Kurt Ida plays Huck in new television adaptation of *Huckleberry Finn*, with Brock Peters as Jim. |
| 1982 | Georgetown University Library publishes two-volume facsimile edition of original handwritten manuscript of *Tom Sawyer.* |
| Feb. 1984 | *Big River*, a Tony Award-winning musical adaptation of *Huckleberry Finn*, opens on Broadway. |
| 1985 | University of California Press publishes the first critical edition of *Huckleberry Finn* corrected by the editors of the Mark Twain Papers. |
| Feb.–Mar. 1986 | Public Broadcasting System broadcasts four-hour adaptation *The Adventures of Huckleberry Finn* over four weeks, with Patrick Day as Huck, Samm-Art Williams as Jim, and Lillian Gish as Mrs. Loftus. |
| Oct. 1990 | The long-missing first half of the original manuscript of *Huckleberry Finn* is found in Los Angeles. After it is authenticated, it is announced to the world in Feb. 1991. |

| | |
|---|---|
| Apr. 1993 | Disney production of *The Adventures of Huck Finn* stars future Hobbit Elijah Wood as Huck and Courtney B. Vance as Jim. |
| Oct. 13, 1993 | US Postal Service issues *Huckleberry Finn* stamp in its "Youth Classics" series. |
| 1995 | New film adaptation of *Tom Sawyer*, *Tom and Huck*, stars Jonathan Taylor Thomas as Tom and Brad Renfro as Huck. |
| Apr. 1996 | Random House publishes first edition of *Huckleberry Finn*, incorporating material from manuscript rediscovered in 1991. |
| 2001 | University of California Press publishes the first new edition of *Huckleberry Finn*, fully integrating material from the manuscript found in 1991, in is Mark Twain Library series; a scholarly edition will follow two years later. |
| 2007 | Jon Clinch publishes *Finn*, a novel about Huck Finn's father. |
| 2010 | University of California Press publishes the first of three projected volumes of *Autobiography of Mark Twain*, edited by Harriet Elinor Smith and other editors of the Mark Twain Papers. The book will spend many weeks on the *New York Times* list of best-selling nonfiction. |
| 2011 | NewSouth Books in Alabama publishes editions of *Tom Sawyer* and *Huckleberry Finn* that substitute less objectionable terms for "nigger" and a few other words. |

**June 25, 2011**   US Postal Service issues a new Mark Twain first-class stamp depicting Mark Twain with steamboat in the background.
2015 University of California Press completes publication of the three-volume *Autobiography of Mark Twain*.


(adapted from R. Kent Rasmussen's chronology in the 2014 Penguin Classics edition of *Adventures of Huckleberry Finn*; reprinted with permission)

# Bibliography

*For a fuller list of editions of* Adventures of Huckleberry Finn, *see pages 45-46 at the end of Victor Fischer's essay.*

Arac, Jonathan. *"Huckleberry Finn" as Idol and Target: The Functions of Criticism in Our Time.* Madison: U of Wisconsin P, 1997.

_____. "Revisiting Huck Finn: Idol and Target." *Mark Twain Annual* 3 (2005): 9-12.

Beaver, Harold. *Huckleberry Finn.* London: Unwin Hyman, 1988.

Berkove, Lawrence I. & Joseph Csicsila. *"Adventures of Huckleberry Finn*: The Hoax of Freedom." *Heretical Fictions: Religion in the Literature of Mark Twain.* Iowa City: U of Iowa P, 2010. 81-109.

Bird, John. "'And Then Think of Me!': *Huckleberry Finn* and Cognitive Dissonance." *Mark Twain Annual* 14 (2016): 138-149.

Blair, Walter. *Mark Twain and Huck Finn.* Berkeley: U of California P, 1960.

Branch, Edgar Marquess & Robert H. Hirst. *The Grangerford-Shepherdson Feud by Mark Twain.* Berkeley, CA: Friends of the Bancroft Library, 1985.

Budd, Louis J., ed. *New Essays on "Adventures of Huckleberry Finn."* Cambridge, UK: Cambridge UP, 1985.

Camfield, Gregg. *The Oxford Companion to Mark Twain.* New York: Oxford UP, 2003.

Chadwick, Jocelyn. "Huck Finn: Icon or Idol—Yet a Necessary Read." *Mark Twain Annual* 3 (2005): 37-42.

Chadwick-Joshua, Jocelyn. *The Jim Dilemma: Reading Race in "Huckleberry Finn."* Jackson: UP of Mississippi, 1998.

Champion, Laurie, ed. *The Critical Response to Mark Twain's "Huckleberry Finn."* Westport, CT: Greenwood P, 1991.

Clinch, Jon, *Finn: A Novel.* New York: Random House, 2007.

Cooley, Thomas, ed. *Adventures of Huckleberry Finn.* By Mark Twain. New York: W. W. Norton, 1999.

Davis, Hugh H. "On Teaching *Huckleberry Finn.*" *Mark Twain Journal* 54.2 (Fall 2016): 60-70.

De Koster, Katie, ed. *Readings on "The Adventures of Huckleberry Finn."* San Diego, CA: Greenhaven P, 1998.

Dempsey, Terrell. *Searching for Jim: Slavery in Sam Clemens's World.* Columbia: U of Missouri P, 2003.

Donoghue, Denis. *"Adventures of Huckleberry Finn." The American Classics: A Personal Essay.* New Haven, CT: Yale UP, 2005. 217-250.

Doyno, Victor A. *Writing "Huck Finn": Mark Twain's Creative Process.* Philadelphia: U of Pennsylvania P, 1991.

_____. "Huck's and Jim's Dynamic Interactions: Dialogues, Ethics, Empathy, Respect." *Mark Twain Annual* 1 (2003): 19-30.

_____. "Presentations of Violence in *Adventures of Huckleberry Finn." Mark Twain Annual* 2 (2004): 75-93.

Evans, Robert C. "Civil Disobedience and the Ending of Mark Twain's *Adventures of Huckleberry Finn." Civil Disobedience.* Ed. Harold Bloom & Blake Hobby. New York: Bloom's Literary Criticism, 2010. 21-29.

Ezell, Kaine. "Uncle Silas in *Huck Finn*: 'A Mighty Nice Old Man.'" *Mark Twain Annual* 9 (2011): 98-110.

Fishkin, Shelley Fisher. *Lighting Out for the Territory: Reflections on Mark Twain and American Culture.* New York: Oxford UP, 1997.

_____. *Was Huck Black? Mark Twain and African-American Voices.* New York: Oxford UP, 1993.

Fishkin, Shelley Fisher, et al. "Looking over Mark Twain's Shoulder as He Writes: Stanford Students Read the *Huck Finn* Manuscript." *Mark Twain Annual* 2 (2004): 107-139.

Graff, Gerald & James Phelan, eds. *"Adventures of Huckleberry Finn": A Case Study in Critical Controversy.* Boston & New York: Bedford Books of St. Martin's P, 1995.

Green, Amy M. "Huck and Jim at the Bare Bodkin's Point: *Hamlet's* Mangled Soliloquy as Textual Commentary." *Mark Twain Annual* 5 (2007): 69-82.

Kassam, Hamada. "Huck Finn as the Fictive Son of George W. Harris's Sut Lovingood." *Mark Twain Journal* 54.1 (Spring 2016): 125-139.

---

Haupt, Clyde V. *"Huckleberry Finn" on Film: Film and Television Adaptations of Mark Twain's Novel, 1920–1993.* Jefferson, NC: MacFarland, 1994.

Hearn, Michael Patrick, ed. *The Annotated Huckleberry Finn.* New York: W. W. Norton, 2001.

Hill, Hamlin & Walter Blair, eds. *The Art of "Huckleberry Finn": Text, Sources, Criticisms.* San Francisco: Chandler Publishing, 1962.

Hentoff, Nat. *The Day They Came to Arrest the Book.* New York: Delacorte P, 1982.

Horn, Jason Gary. *Mark Twain: A Descriptive Guide to Biographical Sources.* Lanham, MD: Scarecrow P, 1999.

Howe, Lawrence. "Property and Dialect Narrative in *Huckleberry Finn*: The 'Jim Dilemma' Revisited." *Mark Twain Annual* 7 (2009): 5-21.

Hutchinson, Stuart, ed. *Mark Twain's "Tom Sawyer" and "Huckleberry Finn."* New York: Columbia UP, 1999.

Inge, M. Thomas, ed. *Huck Finn among the Critics: A Centennial Selection.* Frederick, MD: University Publications of America, 1985.

Kiskis, Michael J. *"Adventures of Huckleberry Finn* (Again!): Teaching for Social Justice or Sam Clemens' Children's Crusade." *Mark Twain Annual* 1 (2003): 63-78.

_____. "Critical Humbug: Samuel Clemens' *Adventures of Huckleberry Finn.*" *Mark Twain Annual* 3 (2005): 13-22.

LeMaster, J. R. & James D. Wilson, eds. *The Mark Twain Encyclopedia.* New York: Garland, 1993.

Leonard, James. S., ed. *Making Mark Twain Work in the Classroom.* Durham, NC: Duke UP, 1999.

_____, Thomas A. Tenney, & Thadious M. Davis. *Satire or Evasion? Black Perspectives on "Huckleberry Finn."* Durham, NC: Duke UP, 1992.

Levy, Andrew. *Huck Finn's America: Mark Twain and the Era That Shaped His Masterpiece.* New York: Simon & Schuster, 2015.

_____. *"Adventures of Huckleberry Finn." Mark Twain and Youth.* Ed. Kevin Mac Donnell & R. Kent Rasmussen. London: Bloomsbury Publishing, 2016. 176-184.

Luehr, Kristin. "'Just the way any other boy would a felt': Adventures, Violence, and the Reader in *Adventures of Huckleberry Finn. Mark Twain Annual* 5 (2007): 57-68.

McCoy, Sharon D. "No Evading the Jokes: Adventures of Huckleberry Finn, Mark Twain, and Male Friendship Across Racial and Class Lines." *Mark Twain Annual* 12 (2014): 46-69.

Mensh, Elaine & Harry Mensh. *Black, White and "Huckleberry Finn": Re-Imagining the American Dream.* Tuscaloosa: U of Alabama P, 2000.

Messent, Peter. *Mark Twain.* New York: St. Martin's P, 1997.

Morris, Linda A. *Gender Play in Mark Twain: Cross-Dressing and Transgression.* Columbia: U of Missouri P, 2007.

Morrison, Toni. Introduction. *Adventures of Huckleberry Finn.* By Mark Twain. New York: Oxford UP, 1996. xxxi-xli.

Niemeyer, Mark. "A Partial 'Reassurance of Fraticide': Redefining National Unity in *Adventures of Huckleberry Finn." Mark Twain Journal* 54.2 (Fall 2016): 54-59.

Norton, Charles. *Huckleberry Finn and Mark Twain: Death, Deceit, Dreams and Disguises.* Philadelphia: Xlibris Corporation, 2000.

Pitofsky, Alex. "Pap Finn's Overture: Fatherhood, Identity, and Southwestern Culture in *Adventures of Huckleberry Finn." Mark Twain Annual* 4 (2006): 55-70.

Purdon, Liam. "Early Predecessors of the King and the Duke in Mark Twain's *Adventures of Huckleberry Finn." Mark Twain Journal* 54.1 (Spring 2016): 116—124.

Quirk, Tom. *Coming to Grips with "Huckleberry Finn": Essays on a Book, a Boy and a Man.* Columbia: U of Missouri P, 1993.

_____, ed. *Mark Twain's "Adventures of Huckleberry Finn": A Documentary Volume.* New York: Gale Cengage Learning, 2009.

Railton, Stephen. *Mark Twain: A Short Introduction.* Malden, MA: Blackwell, 2004.

Rasmussen, R. Kent. *Critical Companion to Mark Twain: A Literary Reference to His Life and Work.* 2 vols. New York: Facts On File, 2007 (expanded edition of *Mark Twain A to Z,* first published in 1995).

_____. *Bloom's How to Write About Mark Twain*. New York: Bloom's Literary Criticism, 2008.

_____, ed. *Dear Mark Twain: Letters from His Readers*. Berkeley: U of California P, 2013.

Robinson, Forrest G. *In Bad Faith: The Dynamics of Deception in Mark Twain's America*. Cambridge, MA: Harvard UP, 1986.

Sattelmeyer, Robert & J. Donald Crowley, eds. *One Hundred Years of "Huckleberry Finn": The Boy, His Book and American Culture—Centennial Essays*. Columbia: U of Missouri P, 1985.

Seelye, John. *The True Adventures of Huckleberry Finn*. 2nd ed. Urbana: U of Illinois P, 1987.

Sloane, David E. E. "The N-Word in *Adventures of Huckleberry Finn* Reconsidered." *Mark Twain Annual* 12 (2014): 70-82.

_____. *Student Companion to Mark Twain*. Westport, CT: Greenwood P, 2001.

Smiley, Jane. "Say It Ain't So, Huck: Second Thoughts on Mark Twain's 'Masterpiece.'" *Harper's Magazine* (January 1996): 61ff.

Smith, David L. "Humor, Sentimentality, and Mark Twain's Black Characters." *Constructing Mark Twain: New Directions in Scholarship*. Ed. Laura E. Skandera Trombley & Michael J. Kiskis. Columbia: U of Missouri P, 2001. 151-168.

Tenney, Thomas Asa. *Mark Twain: A Reference Guide*. Boston: G. K. Hall, 1977.

Twain, Mark. *Adventures of Huckleberry Finn*. Ed. Shelley Fisher Fiskin; introduction Toni Morrison; afterword Victor Doyno. New York: Oxford UP, 1996.

_____. *Adventures of Huckleberry Finn*. Ed. Victor Fischer & Lin Salamo. Berkeley: U of California P, 2001 (supersedes UCP's 1985 edition).

_____. *Adventures of Huckleberry Finn: The NewSouth Edition*. Ed. Alan Gribben. Montgomery, AL: NewSouth Books, 2011 (also published in a combined volume with *Tom Sawyer*).

Wieck, Carl. *Refiguring "Huckleberry Finn."* Athens: U of Georgia P, 2000.

Wolfson, Nicholas. *Huckleberry Finn: Antidote to Hate*. Philadelphia: Xlibris, 2003.

Wonham, Henry B. *Mark Twain and the Art of the Tall Tale.* New York: Oxford UP, 1993.

Wuster, Tracy. *Mark Twain: American Humorist.* Columbia: U of Missiouri P, 2016.

# About the Editor

**R. Kent Rasmussen** is the recipient of numerous writing and editing awards and was honored as a Legacy Scholar in the *Mark Twain Journal* in 2015. He is a retired reference-book editor whose involvement in Mark Twain studies is actually his third career. After graduating from the University of California in Berkeley, he earned a doctorate in African history at UCLA, where he briefly taught. During the 1970s, he published four books on African history. He later became associate editor of the Marcus Garvey Papers at UCLA. While seeking the sources of two Mark Twain quotes in 1990, he read *Roughing It*, which he found so compelling he determined to read "all" of Mark Twain and compile a quote collection. He later achieved that goal with *The Quotable Mark Twain* (1997). Meanwhile, he wrote the book for which he is best known—the award-winning *Mark Twain A to Z* (1995; rev. as *Critical Companion to Mark Twain*, 2007).

As *A to Z* entered production, Rasmussen began his next career, editing reference books for Salem Press, then based in Pasadena, California. Over the next sixteen years, he worked on scores of multivolume reference works on literature, history, government, and other subjects. He also wrote dozens of reference articles and reviewed audiobooks for *Library Journal*. Through those years, he continued to write about Mark Twain and other subjects. The present volume is his twelfth Mark Twain book and his second in the Critical Insights series. Others include *Mark Twain's Book for Bad Boys and Girls* (1995), *Mark Twain for Kids* (2004), *Bloom's How to Write About Mark Twain* (2008), *Critical Insights: Mark Twain* (2011), *Dear Mark Twain: Letters from His Readers* (2013), *Mark Twain and Youth: Studies in His Life and Writings* (2016, coedited with Kevin Mac Donnell), and *Mark Twain for Dog Lovers* (2016). Rasmussen has also contributed introductions and notes to Penguin Classics editions of *Tom Sawyer* (2014), *Huckleberry Finn* (2014), and Mark Twain's *Autobiographical Writings* (2012). His next major projects include coauthoring a book on Mark Twain film adaptations with Mark Dawidziak.

# Contributors

**Philip Bader** received his bachelor of arts degree in English from the University of Nebraska in 1996. He is the author of *African-American Writers* in Facts On File's "A to Z of African Americans" series (2004; rev. 2011); several travel books for young readers; and numerous book reviews and literary essays for Salem Press, Marshall Cavendish, Greenwood Press, *Library Journal*, and other educational reference publishers. He contributed to Edward Quinn's *Critical Companion to George Orwell* (2009). For nearly a decade, he lived in Thailand and Cambodia, where he worked as a reporter and editor for regional print and online news agencies and traveled widely throughout Southeast Asia and surrounding regions. He currently resides in the state of Washington and works as a freelance writer and editor.

**John Bird** is Margaret M. Bryant Professor of English and director of the Teaching and Learning Center at Winthrop University in Rock Hill, South Carolina. The winner of the top teaching awards at two institutions where he has taught, he was also founding editor of *The Mark Twain Annual* through its first five issues. He is an associate editor of the University of Missouri Press's Mark Twain and His Circle series and a past president of the Mark Twain Circle of America. His many publications on Mark Twain include *Mark Twain and Metaphor* (2007) and articles in *American Literary Realism, The Mark Twain Annual, Texas Studies in Literature and Language*, and *Studies in American Fiction*, as well as chapters in five books. He also writes the annual roundup of new publications on Mark Twain for *American Literary Scholarship* and has published widely on American humor, Henry David Thoreau, and pedagogy.

**Jocelyn A. Chadwick**, the vice president of the National Council of Teachers of English, is an English teacher and scholar who lectures regularly and conducts seminars at the Harvard Graduate School of Education. She also works with teachers and students around the country and serves as a consultant for NBC News Education. She is the author of *The Jim Dilemma: Reading Race in "Huckleberry Finn"* (1998) and *Common Core: Paradigmatic Shifts* (2015), and she is coauthor of

*Teaching Literature in the Context of Literacy Instruction* (2015). Other recent publications include an article in *Mark Twain and Youth* (2016), edited by Kevin Mac Donnell and R. Kent Rasmussen. She is currently working on a book about using literature to teach writing. She has been honored with Harvard University's Honor a Teacher award, the Hugh M. Hefner First Amendment Award, and the Intellectual Freedom Award.

**Jon Clinch** is a native of upstate New York. After graduating from Syracuse University, he taught English and worked in a variety of occupations, ranging from metalworking and illustrating to copywriting and advertising. He made his entry into Mark Twain studies in 2007 with the publication of his first novel, *Finn*, about Huck's sadistic father. Since then, he has added more novels to his resume while living in Vermont. Just as Gregory Maguire's novel *Wicked* is a revealing backstory to L. Frank Baum's *The Wonderful Wizard of Oz*, Clinch's *Finn* is an eye-opening backstory to Mark Twain's most famous novel. The book won several major awards, attracted widespread praise, and made Clinch a welcome speaker at Mark Twain events, including the October 2016 symposium on Mark Twain and youth held at Quarry Farm in Elmira, New York, at which he was keynote speaker. Clinch's essay in the present volume about writing his novel offers a persuasive case for how an original work of fiction can provide unexpected insights into Mark Twain.

**Hugh H. Davis**, a former president of the Popular Culture Association in the South, teaches English at Winton, North Carolina's C. S. Brown High School, which named him its 2014–2015 Teacher of the Year. He frequently infuses his classes with aspects of popular culture to help bring texts to life for his students. The fall 2016 issue of the *Mark Twain Journal* contains an article in which he describes how he teaches *Huckleberry Finn* to his predominantly African American students. He has also published articles in *Studies in Popular Culture, Journal of American Culture, Edgar Allan Poe Review*, and *Literature/Film Quarterly* and has contributed chapters to *Shakespeare into Film* (2002), *Past Watchful Dragons* (2007), *Kermit Culture* (2009), *Undead in the West* (2012), *Dickens Adapted* (2012), and *Supernatural Youth* (2013).

**John H. Davis** is a professor of English at Chowan University and a member of the Mark Twain Circle and the Mark Twain Forum. His numerous essays about Mark Twain have appeared in *Mississippi Quarterly, The Mark Twain Annual, American Literary Realism, Mark Twain's Geographical Imagination,* and *The Mark Twain Encyclopedia.* He has presented papers about the author at the Mark Twain House, Lake Tahoe (ALA Meeting); the inaugural and most recent Clemens Conferences in Hannibal, Missouri; several times at the quadrennial Elmira College Mark Twain conferences; the Twain-Tolstoy Conference at Boston University; and at various other conferences. In addition to book reviews for the Mark Twain Forum, he contributed critical commentaries on nineteen works to R. Kent Rasmussen's *Critical Companion to Mark Twain* (2007).

**Robert C. Evans** is I. B. Young Professor of English at Auburn University at Montgomery, where he has been named both Distinguished Teaching Professor and Distinguished Research Professor. The recipient of many other honors and awards, he earned his doctoral degree at Princeton University. He has published several hundred articles and more than thirty books, including ten volumes in the Critical Insights series. His books have examined the writings of John Donne, William Shakespeare, Ben Jonson, Herman Melville, Willa Cather, Ken Kesey, Amy Tan, and many others.

**Victor Fischer** has been on the staff of the Mark Twain Papers and Project of the Bancroft Library at the University of California, Berkeley, since the late 1960s. He has served as editor of *The Prince and the Pauper* (1979, 1983), *Adventures of Huckleberry Finn* (1985, 1989, and again in 2001, 2003), volumes 3 and 4 of *Mark Twain's Letters* (1992, 1995), *Mark Twain's Helpful Hints for Good Living: A Handbook for the Damned Human Race* (2004), *Mark Twain's Letters, 1876–1880* (2007, web publication only), and—as a member of a team of editors—the three-volume *Autobiography of Mark Twain* (2010–2015), all published by the University of California Press. In 2016, he was honored for his scholarship by the Mark Twain Circle of the American Literature Association.

**Sarah Fredericks** earned her bachelor and master's degrees at Auburn University in Montgomery and is currently completing her doctorate at

---

the University of Arizona. Her dissertation will analyze anger, profanity, and rage in the works of Mark Twain and his contemporaries. Her published articles include "The Profane Twain: His Personal and Literary Cursing" in the *Mark Twain Journal* (2011); "Maya Angelou and Zora Neale Hurston as Authors of Autobiographies" in *Critical Insights: Maya Angelou* (2016), edited by Mildred R. Mickle; and "An Overview of Contemporary Guides to LGBTQ Literature" in *Critical Insights: Gay and Lesbian Literature* (2015), edited by Margaret Sonser Breen. She has also published on Herman Melville, Kate Chopin, and other authors and contributed to books on the American novel.

**Alan Gribben** is another Auburn University at Montgomery professor of English who has been honored with a Distinguished Research Professorship. His other teaching awards and honors have included two decades as head of his department and numerous honors from outside his university, particularly in the field of Mark Twain studies. He is one of the cofounders and a former president of the Mark Twain Circle of America and is presently editor of the *Mark Twain Journal* and a member of the editorial board of *American Literary Realism*. For fifteen years, he reviewed Mark Twain publications for the annual *American Literary Scholarship*. He may be best known as author of *Mark Twain's Library: A Reconstruction* (1980), which he is currently extensively revising. He is also coeditor (with Jeffrey Alan Melton) of *Mark Twain on the Move: A Travel Reader* (2009), biographer of the library founder Harry Ransom, and author of dozens of articles on Mark Twain's intellectual background. Since 2011, he has received national attention as editor of NewSouth Books' six-volume *Tom Sawyer* and *Huckleberry Finn* editions—the subject of his essay in the present volume.

**Kevin Mac Donnell** is an antiquarian book dealer whose important contributions to Mark Twain scholarship moved the *Mark Twain Journal* to honor him as a Legacy Scholar in 2016. Three years earlier, *The Chronicle of Higher Education* cited his discovery of a probable source of Mark Twain's famous pen name as "research of note" after his publication of that discovery had gone viral on the web. Since earning his MLS degree at the University of Texas, he has published on such diverse subjects as Louisa May Alcott, Richard Henry Dana, Charlotte Perkins Gilman, Nathaniel

Hawthorne, James Russell Lowell, Herman Melville, Henry David Thoreau, librarianship, and antiquarian bookselling. He is the coeditor (with Alan Gribben) of *Mark Twain's Rubáiyát* (1983) and (with R. Kent Rasmussen) *Mark Twain and Youth* (2016). In addition to contributing articles to *The Mark Twain Encyclopedia* (1993), he has reviewed dozens of books for the Mark Twain Forum and published numerous research articles on Mark Twain. He now serves on the editorial boards of the *Mark Twain Journal* and *Firsts Magazine*. His collection of more than 9,000 Mark Twain items—including first editions, archives, manuscripts, and artifacts—is the largest in private hands, and he is noted for generously sharing these materials with scholars and museums.

**Linda A. Morris** is a professor emerita at the University of California, Davis, where she served as director of writing, director of women's studies, and chair of the Department of English. Her honors include a Bancroft Library Fellowship, a University of California President's Fellowship, and the John Ben Snow Award from Syracuse University Press for her book *Women's Humor in the Age of Gentility: The Life and Works of Frances M. Whitcher* (1992). She is also the author of *Gender Play in Mark Twain: Cross-Dressing and Transgression* (2007) and editor of *American Women's Humor: Critical Essays* (1994) and *Women Vernacular Humorists in Nineteenth-Century America* (1988). Her many articles on Mark Twain and American humor have appeared in *Studies in American Fiction, Mark Twain Annual*, and *Studies in American Humor*, as well as such books as *A Companion to Mark Twain* (1999), *A Companion to Satire* (2007), and *Women and Comedy: History, Theory, Practice* (2013).

**Tracy Wuster** is the executive director of the American Humor Studies Association and director of the *Humor in America Project* at the University of Texas at Austin. He is also coeditor of the Humor in America book series from Penn State University Press, and he runs an online publication on humor studies. In 2016, he published *Mark Twain, American Humorist* in the University of Missouri Press' Mark Twain and His Circle series.

# Index

"True Story, A" (Twain) 79, 88, 89, 129, 130
typesetting machine 19
Twain, Mark. *See* Clemens, Samuel Langhorne

*Uncle Tom's Cabin* (Stowe) 9, 81-95
University of California Press 44, 131, 169, 254-256

Vonnegut, Kurt 58

Wallace, John H. 60
*Walter Scott* (fictional steamboat) 14, 31, 141, 144, 169, 190, 192-193, 200, 201
name of 138
Ward, Artemus 114
Warner, Charles Dudley 6, 115, 246
Washington, Booker T. 56, 58
Watson, Miss (character) 135, 146, 188, 189, 192, 197, 198, 212, 213, 215

death of 210
and Jim 125, 179, 203, 218
Webster, Charles L. 36, 37
*See also* Charles L. Webster & Co.
White, William Allen 56, 61
Whittier, John Greenleaf 140, 247
*Wicked: The Life and Times of the Wicked Witch of the West* (Maguire) 99
Wicks, Ulrich 11, 146-151, 155-162
Wilks family (characters) 135-136, 143-144, 172-175, 201, 221
Williams, Daniel 154, 155
Williams, Randall 70, 77, 78
Williams, True 227-229, 232
Wood, Grant 56
Wuster, Tracy 268